MIRANDA BEAUFORT & JANE NICHOLAS PHOTOGRAPHS BY JOHN GLOVER

EASY GARDENING
RECIPES FOR SUCCESSFUL PLANTING

The Daily Telegraph

MIRANDA BEAUFORT & JANE NICHOLAS PHOTOGRAPHS BY JOHN GLOVER

EASY GARDENING
RECIPES FOR SUCCESSFUL PLANTING

FRANCES LINCOLN

To those who inspired us:

Miranda Beaufort: to my mother, Primrose, and my husband, David
Jane Nicholas: to my parents, Laurence and Judy Nicholas

Frances Lincoln Limited
4 Torriano Mews
Torriano Avenue
London NW5 2RZ
www.franceslincoln.com

Easy Gardening
Copyright © Frances Lincoln Limited 2004
Text copyright © Miranda Beaufort and Jane Nicholas 2004
Plans copyright © Jane Nicholas 2004
Photographs copyright: see acknowledgments (page 183)

First Frances Lincoln edition: 2004
First paperback edition: 2006

British Library Cataloguing in Publication data
A catalogue record for this book is available from the
British Library

ISBN 0-7112-2385-8/978-0-7112-2385-1 (hardback)
ISBN 0-7112-2652-0/978-0-7112-2652-4 (paperback)

Printed in Singapore

CONTENTS

INTRODUCTION

Many people love the look of traditional English gardens with their soft, romantic planting, and long to recreate it in their own gardens, but have no idea how to set about doing so.

This book makes it easy.

You may have a hot sunny south-facing border and dream of a gentle, scented bed of lavenders and roses, or a difficult bed under trees which needs softening by careful planting. For such situations, and for many others, we will tell you exactly what to plant and how to look after it.

We have devised planting schemes for a variety of different garden locations and given a 'recipe' to show you how to reproduce them. For each recipe we show photographs of the plants we recommend. Opposite these we give a planting plan and a plant list. To work out how far each plant should be from its neighbours, look at the spread of the plant (under the heading 'Size and Position') and its position on the plan and plant accordingly. Where we recommend groups of the same plant we give details of how far apart to plant them. We also suggest additional planting to provide more colour for spring and summer and to fill in spaces in the early years, and we outline the general care the bed will need. To conclude each recipe we give a description of each plant 'ingredient' and how it needs to be treated.

On pages 9–11 you will find clear instructions on how to carry out the various tasks involved, as well as some simple advice on how to achieve the best from your garden.

All our plans are for a bed 12½ft/4m long and 6½ft/2m deep. If the bed you wish to plant is larger, you can repeat the plan as many times as necessary. If it is smaller, you can use fewer plants. In either case, you just need to do a quick calculation to work out the proportional number of plants required for your area. It is the combination of plants that is important: it does not matter if the plants are reduced or increased in number. In giving measurements we always indicate the height of the plant before the spread.

As you try the recipes that appeal to you, we hope you'll discover that, whatever you've heard to the contrary, gardening is really very straightforward!

WHAT YOU NEED TO KNOW

We have kept the care instructions simple, but there are a few things you need to know, and a few explanations that make gardening more interesting and understandable.

SOIL pH

The pH scale tells you whether your soil is acid or alkaline. You can buy a simple soil-testing kit using this scale from a garden centre. Neutral soil is pH 7; below this is acid and above is alkaline. Some plants have definite soil requirements – for example, rhododendrons like acid soil.

HOW TO WIRE A WALL FOR CLIMBERS

It really pays off to do this thoroughly before you start to plant. You will then be able to exert some control on the shape of your climbers.

First drill the wall at 18in/45cm intervals vertically as high as you are able and fix a vine eye in each hole. Repeat the process horizontally, placing vine eyes 18in/45cm apart at each level along a 6½ft/2m length, until the wall is studded with a grid of vine eyes. Fix the wire securely to the first vine eye in a horizontal run and thread it through the vine eyes, using a new length of wire for each level. It is important to keep the wire taut and not to let it sag. Repeat the process with the vertical vine eyes.

Tie the climbers to the wire with garden twine or, in the case of shrubby climbers, old tights, which are stronger and will stretch with fast-growing climbers without cutting into the plants' stems.

PLANTING

Before planting

The traditional, and the best, times for planting are October/November or March/April when the weather is not frosty. As most plants are now sold in pots it is possible to plant at almost any time of the year. The vital thing to remember is that new planting will need regular watering to help it settle in.

Mark out the bed and completely clear it of existing plants. If it is a different size from that of the plan (all the plans are 12½ft/4m long and 6½ft/2m deep), you will need to work out the exact number of plants needed for your bed (see page 6). Thoroughly dig it over, breaking up the soil so that it is ready for planting.

Stand the plants out on the bed in their pots in the positions given in the plan so that you can check that you have the right quantity and that they are in the right places.

How to plant

A good healthy start is important to successful growth and will give the plant the best resistance to pests and diseases.

If the plant is at all dry, put it into a bucket of water (in its pot) and press it down until all the bubbles disappear. Dig a hole slightly deeper and wider than the flowerpot. Leave the soil loose at the bottom and mix in a handful of fertilizer. For planting in autumn we normally use bonemeal, and for spring planting we use fish, blood and bone. These are good, organic, slow-acting fertilizers that are easily obtainable. Take the plant out of its pot and place it in the hole ½in/1cm below the existing soil level, fill in the sides with the soil you originally dug out and really firm the plant in. To finish, water the plant again.

Never plant in a straight line! Even a drift of plants are best planted in a staggered line. Having odd numbers of the plants is a deliberate ploy to stop the planting from becoming uniform.

Planting distances for the same plant may change in different beds: this is intentional.

Planting roses

If the rose is bare-rooted, soak the roots in water before planting to soften them. As you plant it, gradually spread the roots out like a spider. This will help the rose establish itself in a healthy way. Use the same approach with container roses, gently teasing out the roots at the edge of the pot. Make sure the rose is not planted too shallowly. Firm in the soil about ½in/1cm below the base of the branches, and water well until it is established. When planting a climbing rose, make sure that you plant it at least 12in/30cm away from the fence or wall.

WATERING

It is very important to remember that all plants need watering in dry weather, especially when they are newly planted.

HOW TO STAKE AND PROVIDE SUPPORT

Nothing looks worse than strangled plants, garrotted in line to rigid poles. Staking is an art that needs to be carefully carried out if the plants are to look natural. First have a good look at the plant, and respect the way it wants to grow. Do not force it; restrain it by staking, but do not pull it out of shape. Before staking you will need to think carefully about how you are helping the plant to perform its best. When you have staked, keep checking the results.

If a plant needs support because the flowers are likely to weigh down the stem (as a peony does, for instance), use one of the really good ready-made plastic or metal supports available from garden centres. You will need to put the support in place when the shoots are about 6in/15cm high so that they grow through the support as they mature.

Do not stake unless it is really necessary. Some of the more straggly perennials will gain more benefit from having twigs (hazel are best) pushed among them when the plants are still small to give them the support they need to keep shape.

Some of the more upright spires may need a bamboo cane (green if possible) to hold them straight, especially if they are liable to get blown about by the wind. Tie in the stems gently with garden twine – you may need to tie in each stem in several places rather than yank the flowering head back.

FEEDING THE SOIL

Many soils deteriorate over time as the humus level falls, and will benefit from the addition of bulky organic matter, which will gradually rot down, replace the lost humus and improve the soil quality. Adding decomposed organic material as a layer on top of the soil is known as mulching. Two kinds of bulky organic matter are manure and compost.

Manure

Manure can be bought either from a farm (it must be well rotted and at least a year old) or from a garden centre by the bag. It can be used as a mulch in late autumn, winter or early spring, but not when the ground is frozen, by covering the ground with a 2in/5cm layer. Make sure that it is not right up against the stems of the plants. It will help to improve the texture of the soil, and add nutrients. It is also useful in retaining moisture. Mushroom compost, which is often sold at garden centres, contains well-rotted manure and should be used in this way.

Compost

Compost is plant waste that has been rotted down in a heap, pit or purpose-made container (available from garden centres). The way we make compost is to build up layers of garden or kitchen waste about 6in/15cm in depth interspersed with 2in/5cm layers of damp straw or wet newspapers. It is a good idea to speed up the decomposition process by turning the heap every two months and forking the unrotted material to the centre of the heap. The composting process should be complete in 6–8 months when it can be spread around the plants at a rate of about a bucketful per 40in/1m.

Leaf mould

Leaf mould is a compost made from decayed leaves. If you have space, make a leaf heap and intersperse the layers with soil. The leaves will take about a year to decompose and become leaf mould, which you can then use by adding it to the soil or as a mulch. You can also make leaf mould by filling rubbish bags with leaves, punching holes in the plastic and simply leaving them to rot down.

FEEDING ESTABLISHED PLANTS

For feeding in spring we use a 'general fertilizer', by which we mean a good general compound fertilizer containing nitrogen, phosphate and potash. The pack will state the ratio of the ingredients. The best general compound is 7:7:7, which contains an equal percentage of each ingredient. This should be lightly hoed into the soil between the plants. Be very careful not to hoe off the tops of any plants or bulbs that are just beginning to emerge.

If you prefer to use an organic general fertilizer for feeding in spring, use fish, blood and bone (which has a balance of 5:7:5.) Organic fertilizers do not work so quickly, but they stay in the soil for longer.

When applying fertilizer do not be tempted to think 'more is better' – it is not! Stick to the quantities recommended and sprinkle it lightly, like salt.

Foliar feeding

A liquid fertilizer or powder dissolved in water and sprayed on to leaf surfaces from late spring to mid-summer is a useful way of giving a quick, albeit short-lived, boost to a plant, as the plant quickly absorbs the nutrients through its leaves. Again, do not be over generous: stick to the recommended dosage.

PESTS AND DISEASES

We will not go into too much detail here: the following is just a general guide on how to lessen the risk of those most likely to attack.

Slugs and snails

Surrounding plants most liable to attack (for example, hostas) with sharp grit can be effective, especially when used with a natural slug repellent powder available from garden centres. You can also water in a liquid slug killer, which is safe for birds, or use slug pellets, which are safe for animals. Don't forget that snails love crevices in walls and pots around the garden.

Insect attack

Do not panic. If the attack is not too severe, try pinching off, washing off or cutting out the affected area: you may be able to conquer the problem before it takes hold. Most insect attacks will sort themselves out over time without intervention: for example, ladybirds will eat greenfly (and if they don't you can order them by post), and blue tits will often keep a plant virtually clear of aphids. It may take a while for nature to get the predator balance right, but watching it evolve will be very satisfying. There are many insecticidal sprays available, but most harm beneficial bees and birds as well, so use these with caution. Gentler organic sprays are available and we recommend asking advice at your garden centre about which varieties they stock.

Mice, rabbits and squirrels

These may look sweet, but they can cause a great deal of damage. The best control is other animals; a cat or a dog will be a deterrent – they may not catch squirrels but their presence will limit the numbers. If you do not want a pet, put down traps for mice. Squirrels in particular can be a great pest: they are often numerous and curious destroyers of bulbs and flowers. A rabbit wire, at least 12in/30cm above and below the ground, though expensive, is an effective control for rabbits. We have successfully used mothballs against squirrels, planted round bulbs and in pots to protect new planting; netting can also be used. You will have to accept the challenge of outwitting them and keep varying your defences.

Deer

These are becoming a more common country problem. If you are troubled by deer, try to find out if there is a local gamekeeper you can talk to about controlling them. It may be necessary to wire the boundaries, and also to use tree guards.

Common diseases on roses

Over the twenty-five years we have gardened together we have concluded that spraying roses really makes little difference. There are some sensible precautions you can take to keep your roses as healthy as possible.

Mildew (where leaves are covered in white powder): this is caused by dryness at the roots. Keep the plants well watered and if you are really worried ask your local garden centre for the best and least toxic mildew treatment.

Rust (orange spots on the leaves) and black spot: pick off or prune out all affected growth and burn. Spray the plant with a fungicidal solution from your garden centre if you really need to. If the problem persists and worsens over a few years, so that the rose is a real eyesore, you may have to take it out.

To help a rose stay healthy it is important to pay attention to the planting (see page 9).

Clematis wilt

Another unpleasant experience you may encounter is the young shoots of a fast-growing clematis suddenly hanging limply down. If this happens, cut the plant right down to the ground, and young, healthy shoots should develop from the base.

PRUNING

We give details of how each plant needs to be pruned or shaped up in the plant details at the end of each recipe.

PLANTING ANNUALS AND BULBS

At the end of each recipe we suggest additional planting for spring and summer colour, using annuals for summer and bulbs or corms for spring. We usually buy annuals in pots so that they can start providing colour as soon as they are planted. However, sometimes we recommend sprinkling seeds of annuals over the bare soil to fill in any spaces. As with all planting, seeds need to be watered in when sown and the soil kept moist until seedlings appear. Whether grown from seed or container grown, all annuals need watering regularly throughout the growing season. They will die at the end of the season and need to be replaced the following year.

To plant single bulbs or corms, dig a hole to the depth specified on the packet (or roughly twice the depth of the bulb if you are buying them loose), plant the bulb and cover with soil. If you are planting a group of tulips or daffodils, dig out a hole, sprinkle the base with bonemeal and scatter the bulbs about 4–6in/10–15cm apart, then cover with soil. Always try to avoid planting in straight lines or groups that are exactly spaced, to help the bulbs look natural and informal when they flower.

At the end of their flowering season, we recommend sprinkling a handful of bonemeal around the group as you cut them down. This helps to enrich the soil they are growing in so that they come up each spring and should last for many years.

A SUNNY ISLAND BED:
YELLOW, WHITE AND BLUE

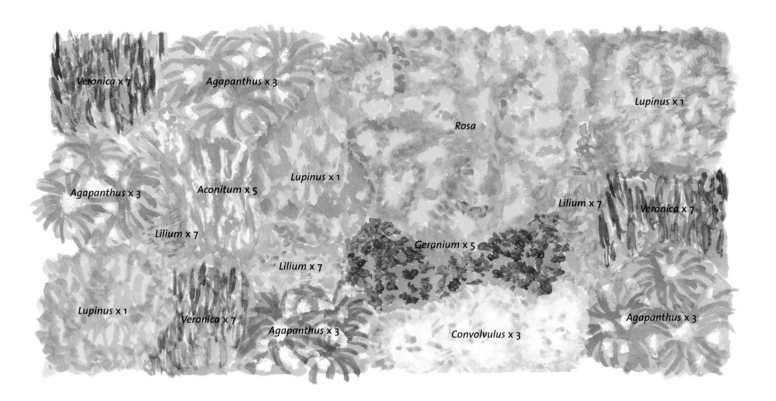

	THE PLANTS	QUANTITIES
1	*Lupinus arboreus*, any yellow variety	3
2	*Rosa xanthina* 'Canary Bird'	1
3	*Agapanthus* 'Alba' (or *A.* 'White Superior')	12
4	*Convolvulus cneorum*	3
5	*Aconitum* 'Ivorine'	5
6	*Geranium ibericum*	5
7	*Lilium* African Queen Group	21
8	*Veronica spicata*	21

SIZE AND POSITION

Aconitum 'Ivorine' grows to 30in x 9in/75cm x 23cm. Plant 8in/20cm apart.

Agapanthus 'Alba' grows to over 24in/60cm high. Plant 12in/30cm apart.

Convolvulus cneorum grows to 12in x 12in/30cm x 30cm. Plant 8in/20cm apart.

Geranium ibericum grows to 12in x 18in/30cm x 45cm. Plant 12in/30cm apart.

Lilium African Queen Group grows 36in–4ft/90cm–1.2m tall. Plant 6in/15cm apart.

Lupinus arboreus grows to 36in x 36in/90cm x 90cm.

Rosa xanthina 'Canary Bird' grows to 8ft x 5ft/2.5m x 1.5m.

Veronica spicata grows to 24in/60cm x 12in/30cm. Plant 8in/20cm apart.

ADDITIONAL PLANTING

SPRING COLOUR

In autumn:
Plant yellow and white tulip bulbs – e.g. 'West Point', 'White Triumphator', 'Candela', 'Purissima', 'Maureen', 'Bellona' – in groups of not less than 10. Plant different varieties separately.

In spring:
Plant pansies (*Viola* x *wittrockiana*) in yellow, blue and white in groups of the same colour among all the plants.

Plant *Myosotis* (forget-me-nots), buying as many as you need to fill the gaps.

SUMMER COLOUR

In late spring:
Plant antirrhinums in single colours of yellow or white and dot throughout the bed.

Sprinkle *Heliopsis* (ox-eye daisy) seeds in any gaps.

Plant white cosmos in any gaps at the back of the border.

GENERAL CARE

Keep new planting well watered.

In autumn pick up all dead leaves and debris, but do not cut anything back.

Add a good general-purpose fertilizer in spring.

Keep a lookout for slugs and snails and take action as soon as you spot any damage. Slug pellets and organic powders are both effective.

Stake the lilies if they start to flop too much.

Cut off dead stems and tidy through the border in spring.

PLANT DETAILS

Aconitum 'Ivorine'
SOIL: Moist.
CONDITIONS: Sun or part shade.
COLOUR: White.
FLOWERING: Late spring to mid-summer.
FEEDING: With a general fertilizer in spring.
PRUNING: Cut flower stems down to 9in/23cm after flowering.
GENERAL COMMENTS: A stately delphinium-like flower that has good strong stems and flowers early.

Agapanthus 'White Superior'
SOIL: Fertile, well drained.
CONDITIONS: Full sun.
COLOUR: White.
FLOWERING: Mid-summer to early autumn.
FEEDING: In spring, and again in mid-summer.
PRUNING: Cut off the old flower stems as near to the base as possible in autumn or after flowering.
GENERAL COMMENTS: A beautiful plant. It should need dividing every 3–4 years. Agapanthus also enjoys being grown in a pot, provided that it has a good layer of crocks for drainage.

Convolvulus cneorum
SOIL: Well drained, poor.
CONDITIONS: Full sun.
COLOUR: White with dark pink on the reverse of the flowers.

FLOWERING: Late spring to late summer.
FEEDING: Spring.
PRUNING: None.
GENERAL COMMENTS: A very pretty evergreen with narrow, silky, truly silver leaves.

Geranium ibericum
SOIL: Well drained.
CONDITIONS: Sun or part shade.
COLOUR: Violet blue.
FLOWERING: Early summer to mid-summer.
FEEDING: Spring, and again in mid-summer.
PRUNING: Cut back to half its height after flowering to encourage new flower growth.
GENERAL COMMENTS: A beautiful geranium, which makes a good companion for roses and herbaceous plants.

Lilium African Queen Group
SOIL: Well drained, fertile.
CONDITIONS: Sun.
COLOUR: White.
FLOWERING: Mid-summer to late summer.
FEEDING: Spring, and again in mid-summer.
PRUNING: Cut old flower stems down to 12in/30cm after flowering.

GENERAL COMMENTS: Plant with some grit to improve the drainage of the soil. Has a wonderful scent.

Lupinus arboreus, any yellow variety
SOIL: Well drained.
CONDITIONS: Full sun.
COLOUR: Pale yellow.
FLOWERING: Early spring to mid-summer.
FEEDING: Spring.
PRUNING: Cut to a neat shape after flowering.
GENERAL COMMENTS: Can be short-lived. You need to keep an eye on its shape, as it grows fast and can become an untidy sprawl.

Rosa xanthina 'Canary Bird'
SOIL: Good, well drained.
CONDITIONS: Sun.
COLOUR: Pale yellow.
FLOWERING: Late spring to early summer.
FEEDING: Spring, and again in mid-summer.
PRUNING: Cut back long stems to even up the shape after flowering.
GENERAL COMMENTS: One of the very best species roses. Has pretty, ferny foliage, and is slightly scented. The branches are covered with single flowers in late spring.

Veronica spicata
SOIL: Well drained.
CONDITIONS: Sun.
COLOUR: Blue.
FLOWERING: Early summer to early autumn.
FEEDING: Spring.
PRUNING: Cut back old flowering stems to their base after flowering.
GENERAL COMMENTS: A neat plant with spikes of bright blue flowers.

A SUNNY ISLAND BED:
PINK, BLUE AND WHITE

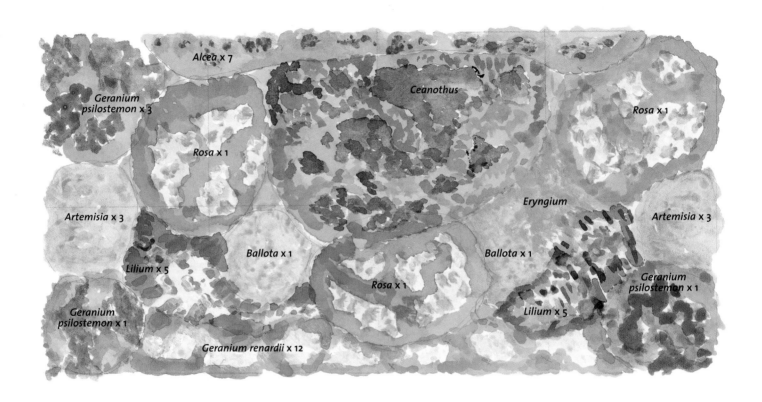

Alcea x 7

Geranium
psilostemon x 3

Ceanothus

Rosa x 1

Rosa x 1

Eryngium

Artemisia x 3

Artemisia x 3

Rosa x 1

Ballota x 1

Ballota x 1

Lilium x 5

Geranium
psilostemon x 1

Geranium
psilostemon x 1

Lilium x 5

Geranium renardii x 12

	THE PLANTS	QUANTITIES
1	*Ballota pseudodictamnus*	2
2	*Ceanothus thyrsiflorus* var. *repens*	1
3	*Rosa* 'Belle Isis'	3
4	*Alcea rosea*, any rose pink variety	7
5	*Geranium renardii*	12
6	*Eryngium giganteum*	1
7	*Geranium psilostemon*	5
8	*Artemisia* 'Powis Castle'	6
9	*Lilium speciosum* var. *rubrum*	10

SIZE AND POSITION

Alcea rosea grows to 5ft x 24in/1.5m x 60cm. Plant 24in/60cm apart.

Artemisia 'Powis Castle' makes a mound 24in x 24in/60cm x 60cm. Plant 24in/60cm apart.

Ballota pseudodictamnus grows to 18in x 24in/45cm x 60cm.

The ceanothus forms the backbone of this bed. It grows to 4–5ft x 5–6ft/1.2–1.5m x 1.5–1.8m but can be kept cut back as a mound of 36in x 5ft/90cm x 1.5m.

Eryngium giganteum grows to 36in–4ft x 24in/90cm–1.2m x 60cm. Plant 24in/60cm from its neighbour.

Geranium psilostemon grows to 30in x 24in/75cm x 60cm. Plant 18in/45cm apart.

Geranium renardii grows to 9in x 12in/23cm x 30cm. Plant in a staggered row at the front of the bed.

Lilium speciosum var. *rubrum* grows to 30in x 6in/75cm x 15cm. Plant 6in/15cm apart.

Rosa 'Belle Isis' grows to 31½ft x 30in/1.1m x 75cm.

ADDITIONAL PLANTING

SPRING COLOUR

In autumn:
Plant pink and white tulip bulbs – 20 of each of the following varieties: 'Clara Butt', 'China Pink', 'White Triumphator', 'White Swan' and 'Peach Blossom' – as singles all over the bed. It does not matter if the colours are mixed.

Plant *Anemone blanda* corms in mixed pink, white and blue all over the bed.

In spring:
Plant *Myosotis* (forget-me-nots) towards the front of the bed.

Add blue violas or pansies (*Viola* x *wittrockiana*) in any gaps.

SUMMER COLOUR

In spring:
Plant cosmos or cleomes in white or pink in any gaps, dotted throughout the bed.

GENERAL CARE

Feed in spring with a general fertilizer.

Keep an eye out for seedlings of eryngium and replant.

Cut off and feed tulips as the leaves turn yellow and die down.

Stake the lilies as they get to about 6in/15cm.

Tidy over the silver and grey planting in mid-spring.

Keep the roses deadheaded and spray against pests and diseases if required. Feed again with rose food in mid-summer.

Keep an eye on size of ceanothus and shape as required after flowering.

Cut off hollyhock flower heads after flowering.

PLANT DETAILS

Alcea rosea (hollyhock), any rose pink variety
SOIL: Heavy, rich.
CONDITIONS: Full sun.
COLOUR: Rose pink.
FLOWERING: Mid-summer to early autumn.
FEEDING: Give an annual mulch of well-rotted manure or compost. Feed in spring.
PRUNING: Cut back old flowers to base as it finishes flowering, unless you want it to re-seed.
GENERAL COMMENTS: Water freely during dry spells. We spray early in the year with unpasteurized milk and find it helps to keep rust at bay. It is a good idea to take old plants out from time to time and replace with seedlings, as they tend to get diseased.

Artemisia 'Powis Castle'
SOIL: Well drained.
CONDITIONS: Sun.
COLOUR: Grown for its silvery leaves.
FLOWERING: Do not let it flower.
FEEDING: Spring.
PRUNING: Trim back to new growth in spring, to keep the plant neat, and cut off any flower buds as soon as they form.
GENERAL COMMENTS: Has a beautiful, feathery silver leaf. It can be short-lived. It looks wonderful with roses or in any formal planting scheme.

Ballota pseudodictamnus
SOIL: Light, not too fertile. It does not like winter wet.
CONDITIONS: Full sun.
COLOUR: Grown mainly for its woolly silver-green foliage; has small pink flowers.
FLOWERING: Mid-summer.
FEEDING: Spring.
PRUNING: Cut back old stems to 12in/30cm in mid-spring.
GENERAL COMMENTS: A very pretty foliage plant.

Ceanothus thyrsiflorus var. repens
SOIL: Good, light.
CONDITIONS: Full sun.
COLOUR: Blue.
FLOWERING: Early spring to late spring.
FEEDING: Spring.
PRUNING: Cut back to a good shape after flowering.
GENERAL COMMENTS: A useful plant, which has attractive dark green leaves. It can be used effectively for covering a bank or hiding a drain cover. It is not too stiff, and makes a good neat mound.

Eryngium giganteum
SOIL: Well drained.
CONDITIONS: Sun.
COLOUR: Silver foliage, silver-blue flower heads.
FLOWERING: Early summer to mid-summer.

FEEDING: Spring.
PRUNING: None. The seedheads are attractive.
GENERAL COMMENTS: A handsome plant with strong silver foliage. It is a biennial, and so will need to be replaced after it flowers, but it is a rampant self-seeder, so keep an eye out for seedlings and replant them.

Geranium psilostemon
SOIL: Well drained.
CONDITIONS: Sun.
COLOUR: Magenta with a black eye.
FLOWERING: Early summer to mid-summer.
FEEDING: Spring.
PRUNING: Cut back whole plant to fresh young leaves after flowering to encourage a second flush of flowers.
GENERAL COMMENTS: An excellent, healthy plant.

Geranium renardii
SOIL: Any good, well drained.
CONDITIONS: Sun, part shade or shade.
COLOUR: White with purple veins.
FLOWERING: Late spring to mid-summer.
FEEDING: Spring.
PRUNING: Trim over after flowering. Take off any dead leaves.
GENERAL COMMENTS: Grey-green leaves in a compact mound. A very pretty plant which is easy to grow. Can be divided in early autumn and early spring.

Lilium speciosum var. rubrum
SOIL: Well drained, fertile.
CONDITIONS: Sun.
COLOUR: Deep pink.
FLOWERING: Late summer to early autumn.
FEEDING: Spring.
PRUNING: Cut flower stem down to 12in/30cm after flowering.
GENERAL COMMENTS: Provides a late and very pretty splash of flower with a delicious scent.

Rosa 'Belle Isis'
SOIL: Any except sand or chalk.
CONDITIONS: Sun.
COLOUR: Pale pink.
FLOWERING: Summer.
FEEDING: Spring and again in mid-summer.
PRUNING: Trim to a neat shape in winter, taking out any weak or dead wood, but do not prune hard.
GENERAL COMMENTS: A lovely, scented old-fashioned rose.

A SUNNY ISLAND BED:
PINK AND YELLOW

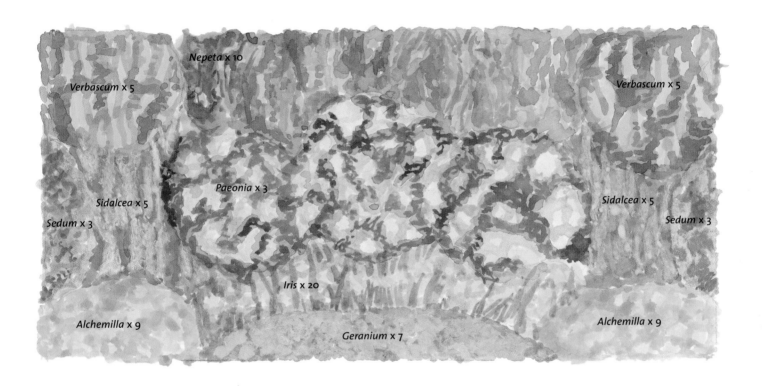

	THE PLANTS	QUANTITIES
1	*Iris*, any pale yellow variety (e.g. *I.* 'Jeanne Price' or *I.* 'Vinho Verde')	20
2	*Sidalcea* 'Elsie Heugh'	10
3	*Nepeta govaniana*	10
4	*Sedum* 'Herbstfreude' (Autumn Joy)	6
5	*Verbascum* (Cotswold Group) 'Gainsborough'	10
6	*Geranium sanguineum* var. *striatum*	7
7	*Alchemilla mollis*	18
8	*Paeonia*, any variety that is pink with a yellow centre (e.g. *P. lactiflora* 'Bowl of Beauty' or *P.* 'Golly')	3

SIZE AND POSITION

Alchemilla mollis spreads well. Plant 9in/23cm apart; it will grow into a clump 12in x 12in/30cm x 30cm.

Geranium sanguineum var. *striatum* grows to 6in x 9in/15cm x 23cm. Plant 9in/23cm apart.

The irises grow to 12in/30cm, with their flowers growing to 36in/90cm and a spread of 12in/30cm. Plant 6in/15cm apart in a half-moon shape.

Nepeta govaniana grows to 36in x 24in/90cm x 60cm. Plant 12in/30cm apart in a half-moon shape.

The peonies grow to 36in x 36in/90cm x 90cm. Plant 36in/90cm apart.

Sedum 'Herbstfreude' (Autumn Joy) grows to 18in x 9in/45cm x 23cm. Plant 12in/30cm apart.

Sidalcea 'Elsie Heugh' grows to 24in x 18in/60cm x 45cm. Plant 9in/23cm apart.

Verbascum (Cotswold Group) 'Gainsborough' grows to 36in x 18in/90cm x 45cm. Plant in a round group 12in/30cm apart.

ADDITIONAL PLANTING

When the bed is first planted we suggest that you add the following plants to bulk it out.

SPRING COLOUR

In autumn:
Plant tulip bulbs in black and pink – e.g. 'Queen of Night', 'Philippe de Comines', 'Black Parrot', 'China Pink', 'Angélique', 'Peach Blossom' – in groups of not less than 10 of the same variety.

Plant 100 *Narcissus* 'Hawera' bulbs towards the front.

Plant at least 50 *Anemone blanda* corms in mixed colours of pink, white

and blue all over the bed to give a lovely carpet of colour in early spring.

In autumn or spring:
Plant 10 *Viola cornuta*, a perennial that will spread among the plants.

SUMMER COLOUR

In spring:
Plant pink cosmos towards the back of the border.

Plant nicotiana (tobacco plants) in pink and lime green, filling in gaps with bold groups of 5 or 10 of the same colour.

GENERAL CARE

Put on a good general fertilizer in spring as new shoots start to appear.

The peonies will need staking early on as growth begins, with either green bamboos or ready-made supports.

When the tulips have finished flowering, cut the leaves to ground level and feed with fertilizer.

Don't cut the narcissus leaves until they turn brown.

As the flower heads fade cut them off. Many plants will flower again.

Sedum heads can be cut off before they go over to dry for flower arrangements.

Keep well watered.

PLANT DETAILS

Alchemilla mollis (lady's mantle)
SOIL: Any, but not boggy.
CONDITIONS: Sun or shade.
COLOUR: Greenish yellow.
FLOWERING: Early summer to early autumn.
FEEDING: Spring.
PRUNING: Tidy up when necessary, pulling off dead flowers and leaves.
GENERAL COMMENTS: A very versatile plant with sprays of tiny flowers held above pretty leaves, which look lovely when wet. It is very good for picking, and can be dried.

Geranium sanguineum var. *striatum*
SOIL: Good.
CONDITIONS: Sun or part shade.
COLOUR: Pale pink.
FLOWERING: Late spring to mid-summer.
FEEDING: Spring.
PRUNING: Cut back after flowering.
GENERAL COMMENTS: A pretty pale pink in colour, and makes very good ground cover.

Iris, pale yellow
SOIL: Well drained.
CONDITIONS: Full sun
COLOUR: Pale yellow.
FLOWERING: Late spring to early summer.
FEEDING: Bonemeal in mid-winter, and a general fertilizer in spring.
PRUNING: Cut off the old flower stem after flowering and cut the leaves back to 8in/20cm above the

ground in a fan shape.
GENERAL COMMENTS: Can
be divided and replanted in
mid-summer. To plant,
mound up the soil and place
the iris rhizome on top,
allowing only the roots to go
into the soil. The rhizome
likes to be out of the ground
so that it can be baked by
the sun.

Nepeta govaniana
SOIL: Well drained.
CONDITIONS: Full sun.
COLOUR: Pale yellow.
FLOWERING: Mid-summer
to early autumn.
FEEDING: Spring.
PRUNING: Cut to the
ground in autumn.
GENERAL COMMENTS: One
of the prettiest yellow
flowers. It likes to scramble
through other plants.

Paeonia, pink with a yellow centre
SOIL: Deep, rich.
CONDITIONS: Sun.
COLOUR: Pink and yellow.
FLOWERING: Late spring to
mid-summer.
FEEDING: Spring.
PRUNING: None.
GENERAL COMMENTS: Once
planted, a peony does not
like to be moved. It needs
staking because the flowers
are heavy.

Sedum 'Herbstfreude' (Autumn Joy)
SOIL: Well drained.

CONDITIONS: Full sun.
COLOUR: Pink.
FLOWERING: Late summer
to mid-autumn.
FEEDING: Spring.
PRUNING: None. Leave the
old stems on until spring,
then cut back to base.
GENERAL COMMENTS:
A very easy plant. It will
benefit from the support of
some twigs put around it in
early summer. The flowers
can be dried.

Sidalcea 'Elsie Heugh'
SOIL: Ordinary.
CONDITIONS: Sun.
COLOUR: Pink.
FLOWERING: Early summer
to early autumn.
FEEDING: Spring.
PRUNING: Cut back the old
stems as they die and they
should flower again later.
GENERAL COMMENTS:
Delicate, pale pink flowers
are held on strong flower
spikes.

Verbascum (Cotswold Group) 'Gainsborough'
SOIL: Well drained.
CONDITIONS: Sun.
COLOUR: Canary yellow.
FLOWERING: Late spring to
early summer.
FEEDING: Spring.
PRUNING: Cut back the
flower stems to the base as
they finish flowering, to
encourage new flowers.
GENERAL COMMENTS: This
majestic plant looks as good

in a wild garden as it does
when planted in a group in
borders.

A SUNNY ISLAND BED:
HOT COLOURS

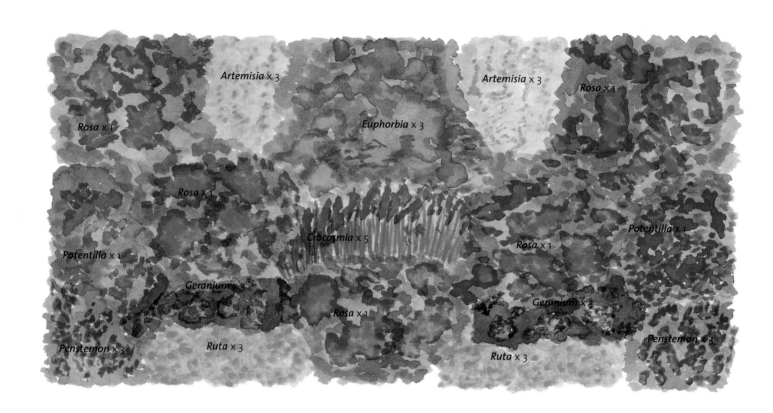

Artemisia x 3

Artemisia x 3

Rosa x 1

Rosa x 1

Euphorbia x 3

Rosa x 1

Potentilla x 1

Crocosmia x 5

Rosa x 1

Potentilla x 1

Geranium x 8

Geranium x 8

Rosa x 1

Penstemon x 3

Penstemon x 3

Ruta x 3

Ruta x 3

	THE PLANTS	QUANTITIES
1	*Potentilla fruticosa* 'Red Ace'	2
2	*Artemisia ludoviciana* 'Silver Queen'	6
3	*Euphorbia griffithii* 'Fireglow'	3
4	*Rosa* 'Frensham'	5
5	*Penstemon* 'Firebird'	6
6	*Ruta graveolens* 'Jackman's Blue'	6
7	*Crocosmia* × *crocosmiiflora* 'Emily McKenzie'	5
8	*Geranium* × *magnificum*	6

SIZE AND POSITION

Artemisia ludoviciana 'Silver Queen' grows to 36in x 24in/90cm x 60cm.

Crocosmia x *crocosmiiflora* 'Emily McKenzie' grows to 30in x 30in/75cm x 75cm and will spread sideways. Plant 12in/30cm apart.

Euphorbia griffithii 'Fireglow' grows to 36in x 24in/90cm x 60cm. Plant 18in/45cm apart.

Geranium x *magnificum* grows to 24in x 18in/60cm x 45cm. Plant 12in/30cm apart.

Penstemon 'Firebird' grows to 24in x 24in/60cm x 60cm. Plant 12in/30cm apart.

Potentilla fruticosa 'Red Ace' grows to 4ft x 3½ft/1.2m x 1.1m.

Rosa 'Frensham' grows to 4ft x 36in/1.2m x 90cm. Plant 36in/90cm apart.

Ruta graveolens 'Jackman's Blue' grows to 12in x 12in/30cm x 30cm. Plant 12in/30cm apart.

ADDITIONAL PLANTING

SPRING COLOUR

In autumn:
Plant bright tulip bulbs in groups of 10: e.g. 'Generaal de Wet', 'Red Shine', 'Estella Rijnveld' in any gaps.

Plant 50 *Crocus korolkowii* 'Kiss of Spring' corms at the front of the bed.

Plant *Fritillaria imperialis* 'Lutea' bulbs in two groups of 5 where there are spaces.

Plant 15 mixed-colour *Erysimum cheiri* (wallflowers) throughout the bed.

SUMMER COLOUR

In mid-autumn or mid-spring:
Scatter *Papaver rhoeas* (corn poppy) seeds throughout the bed.

In spring:
Plant 5 *Tropaeolum majus* 'Empress of India' (nasturtium, bright red) in gaps towards the front of the border.

In late spring:
Plant 10 dark red dahlias as single plants in gaps at the back of the border.

GENERAL CARE

Spring feed the whole bed.

Do not let the artemisia or the rue flower: cut off the flower buds as they form. Wear gloves when handling the rue and the euphorbia as they both have irritant sap and can cause bad skin reactions.

Cut off the tulip leaves and feed as they turn yellow.

Keep the roses well deadheaded and feed again in mid-summer with rose food. Spray against pests and diseases if required.

Pull out spent nasturtiums and poppies in late autumn and compost.

Lift the dahlias in late autumn and store the tubers over the winter for replanting next year.

PLANT DETAILS

Artemisia ludoviciana **'Silver Queen'**
SOIL: Well drained.
CONDITIONS: Sun.
COLOUR: Grown for its silver leaves.
FLOWERING: Do not let it flower.
FEEDING: Spring.
PRUNING: In spring cut off the old stems to fresh new growth to maintain the shape. In early spring cut off the flowers before they form.
GENERAL COMMENTS: One of the very best silver plants, grown for its lovely feathery leaves. It looks very pretty planted with old roses.

Crocosmia x *crocosmiiflora* **'Emily McKenzie'**
SOIL: Any well drained.
CONDITIONS: Sun.
COLOUR: Deep orange, with a rich brown throat.
FLOWERING: Late summer to early autumn.
FEEDING: Spring.
PRUNING: None. Pull out excess growth in spring.
GENERAL COMMENTS: A good compact crocosmia. Its erect sword-shaped leaves give useful structure to the border.

Euphorbia griffithii **'Fireglow'**
SOIL: Any well drained.
CONDITIONS: Sun.
COLOUR: Deep orange red.
FLOWERING: Late spring to mid-summer.
FEEDING: Spring.

PRUNING: None. Cut old flower heads back to the ground if they start to look untidy.

GENERAL COMMENTS: Be careful when handling, as the sap is a skin irritant.

Geranium x magnificum

SOIL: Well drained.

CONDITIONS: Sun.

COLOUR: Purple blue.

FLOWERING: Late spring to early summer.

FEEDING: Spring.

PRUNING: Cut back to the leaf clump after first flowering to encourage fresh growth.

GENERAL COMMENTS: A geranium with good rich colour and strong growth. Makes good ground cover.

Penstemon 'Firebird'

SOIL: Fertile, well drained.

CONDITIONS: Sun.

COLOUR: Rich, bright red.

FLOWERING: Mid-summer to early autumn.

FEEDING: Spring.

PRUNING: Leave old flower spikes on the plant until spring, when the danger of frost has passed, then cut back by about one third to clean new growth.

GENERAL COMMENTS: A reliable and tough penstemon with lovely bright red flower spikes.

Potentilla fruticosa 'Red Ace'

SOIL: Any light.

CONDITIONS: Sun to part shade.

COLOUR: Vermilion red.

FLOWERING: Late spring to early autumn.

FEEDING: Spring.

PRUNING: Prune lightly, cutting to a mounded shape in early spring.

GENERAL COMMENTS: The flowers are tinged with yellow on the reverse. They are freely borne over a long period, and although the individual flowers are short-lived they are quickly replaced.

Rosa 'Frensham'

SOIL: Any, except pure chalk or sand.

CONDITIONS: Sun.

COLOUR: Pure red.

FLOWERING: Early summer to early autumn.

FEEDING: Spring and again in mid-summer.

PRUNING: Cut back by about half in late winter.

GENERAL COMMENTS: This rose used to be planted widely, and is recommended because of its good clear red.

Ruta graveolens 'Jackman's Blue' (rue)

SOIL: Any well drained.

CONDITIONS: Sun or part shade.

COLOUR: Grown for its silvery leaves.

FLOWERING: Do not let it flower.

FEEDING: Spring.

PRUNING: Cut back in mid-spring to keep a good neat mound. Cut off flowers as they form in early summer.

GENERAL COMMENTS: Take care! Do not touch the leaves as they can cause bad skin allergies, especially if it is sunny. It has very pretty foliage, and is lovely planted with roses or used as an edging.

A SUNNY ISLAND BED:
MAROON, PALE YELLOW AND CREAM

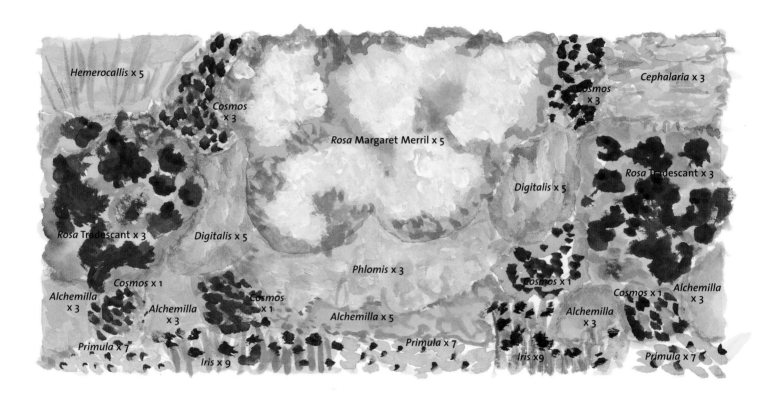

Hemerocallis x 5

Cosmos x 3

Cosmos x 3

Cephalaria x 3

Rosa Margaret Merril x 5

Rosa Tradescant x 3

Digitalis x 5

Rosa Tradescant x 3

Digitalis x 5

Phlomis x 3

Cosmos x 1

Cosmos x 1

Alchemilla x 3

Alchemilla x 3

Cosmos x 1

Cosmos x 1

Alchemilla x 3

Alchemilla x 5

Alchemilla x 3

Primula x 7

Primula x 7

Primula x 7

Iris x 9

Iris x9

	THE PLANTS	QUANTITIES
1	*Alchemilla mollis*	17
2	*Phlomis russeliana*	3
3	*Primula auricula,* any greenish maroon variety	21
4	*Digitalis grandiflora*	10
5	*Hemerocallis* 'Green Flutter'	5
6	*Iris,* any dark maroon variety (e.g. 'Rosette Wine' or 'Fort Apache')	18
7	*Cosmos atrosanguineus*	10
8	*Rosa* Margaret Merril	5
9	*Cephalaria gigantea*	3
10	*Rosa* Tradescant	6

SIZE AND POSITION

Alchemilla mollis grows to 12in x 12in/30cm x 30cm. Plant 6in/15cm apart.

Cephalaria gigantea grows to 6ft x 24in/1.8m x 60cm.

Cosmos atrosanguineus grows to 24in x 18in/60cm x 45cm. Plant 12in/30cm apart.

Digitalis grandiflora grows to 36in x 12in/90cm x 30cm. Plant 8in/20cm apart.

Hemerocallis 'Green Flutter' grows to 36in x 24in/90cm x 60cm. Plant 18in/45cm apart.

Iris leaves grow to 12in/30cm high and the flowers to 24in x 12in/60cm x 30cm.

Phlomis russeliana grows to 36in/90cm with a spread of 24in/60cm. Plant 15in/38cm apart.

Primula auricula grows to 6in x 6in/15cm x 15cm. Plant 8in/20cm apart.

Rosa Margaret Merril grows to 36in x 36in/90cm x 90cm. Plant 24in/60cm apart.

Rosa Tradescant grows to 24in x 30in/60cm x 75cm. Plant 24in/60cm apart.

ADDITIONAL PLANTING

SPRING COLOUR

In autumn:
Plant tulip bulbs in deep reds, pale yellows and cream, – e.g. plant two drifts of 20 each of 'Havran' and 'Burgundy Lace' (dark red); 20 'Maja' (soft yellow); 20 'Purissima' (creamy white).

In autumn or spring:
Plant *Primula vulgaris* (primrose) in any gaps.

SUMMER COLOUR

In spring:
Plant some *Lilium* 'Roma' bulbs in groups of 5, planting at least four groups in any gaps.

Plant pale yellow *Viola* 'Moonlight' in the front of the bed.

GENERAL CARE

Feed in spring with a general fertilizer.

Feed and mulch the roses in spring.

Keep well watered.

Deadhead roses and feed again in July with rose food.

Support the cephalaria with twigs if it starts to flop.

Make sure that the cosmos is protected from frost with a good layer of compost.

Tidy through the bed in autumn.

In spring pull off and cut back dead foliage and flowers.

PLANT DETAILS

***Alchemilla mollis* (lady's mantle)**
SOIL: Any, but not boggy.
CONDITIONS: Sun or shade.
COLOUR: Greenish yellow.
FLOWERING: Early summer to early autumn.
FEEDING: Spring.
PRUNING: Cut back to clean leaves after flowering.
GENERAL COMMENTS: A very versatile plant with its sprays of tiny flowers held above pretty leaves that look lovely when wet. It is very good for picking (especially with red roses) and can be dried.

Cephalaria gigantea
SOIL: Well drained.
CONDITIONS: Sunny.
COLOUR: Pale yellow.
FLOWERING: Early summer to late summer.
FEEDING: Spring, sparingly.
PRUNING: Cut down flowering stems to 12in/30cm in autumn.
GENERAL COMMENTS: A tough plant with tall branches of scabious-type flowers in a soft pale yellow. Can be unruly, but it is well worth growing for its impressive display and stature.

Cosmos atrosanguineus
SOIL: Well drained, which does not dry out.
CONDITIONS: Sun.
COLOUR: Deep maroon/black.
FLOWERING: Mid-summer to early autumn.
FEEDING: Spring.
PRUNING: None.
GENERAL COMMENTS: Often known as chocolate cosmos

because of the smell of its flowers. It needs some winter protection: a good mulch over the top of its tubers in winter should protect it from frost. It can be slow to emerge in spring, so remember where it is and leave enough space for it to come through its neighbours.

Digitalis grandiflora (yellow foxglove)

SOIL: Ordinary garden soil that does not dry out.
CONDITIONS: Sun or partial shade.
COLOUR: Soft yellow.
FLOWERING: Early summer to late summer.
FEEDING: Spring.
PRUNING: Cut to the ground after first flowering, and cut back again to 12in/30cm in mid-autumn.
GENERAL COMMENTS: The leaves are evergreen. Not so showy as the common foxglove, but valuable for the colour of its flowers.

Hemerocallis 'Green Flutter'

SOIL: Any.
CONDITIONS: Tolerant of sun or shade.
COLOUR: Pale greenish yellow.
FLOWERING: Mid-summer to early autumn.
FEEDING: Spring.
PRUNING: None.
GENERAL COMMENTS: A truly adaptable plant that needs little attention. The flowers, which are held over a good clump of green strappy leaves, are fragrant; each lasts for only one or two days, but there are many of them.

Iris, any dark maroon variety

SOIL: Well drained, rich but not acid.
CONDITIONS: Open sunny position.
COLOUR: Maroon.
FLOWERING: Late spring to early summer.
FEEDING: Sparingly, in spring.
PRUNING: Cut leaves back into a fan shape after flowering to stop wind rock and to allow the sun to bake the rhizome.
GENERAL COMMENTS: Adds good structure to the border and requires little attention. Keep leaves and debris away from the base of the plant, and make sure that they are planted with the rhizome sitting on top and only the roots penetrating the soil. Divide every three years; in this way one plant will make many more.

Phlomis russeliana

SOIL: Any.
CONDITIONS: Sun.
COLOUR: Yellow.
FLOWERING: Early summer to early autumn.
FEEDING: Spring.
PRUNING: Cut off old flower stalks to the base in autumn. Pull off old leaves in spring unless you want to leave them for winter effect.
GENERAL COMMENTS: An impressive, good ground-cover plant with whorls of hooded yellow flowers held well above the leaf clump.

Primula auricula, any greenish maroon variety

SOIL: Rich, gritty, well-drained, containing humus.
CONDITIONS: Sun or part shade.
COLOUR: Maroon and greeny yellow (auriculas come in many mixtures of colours).
FLOWERING: Early spring to late spring.
FEEDING: Spring.
PRUNING: Remove old flower stems.
GENERAL COMMENTS: A lovely, old-fashioned plant, unusual and eyecatching. It is often thought of as difficult but we have always found it very reliable if given free-draining rich soil.

Rosa Margaret Merril

SOIL: Any with good drainage, except sand or pure chalk.
CONDITIONS: An open sunny position, lots of water.
COLOUR: White.
FLOWERING: Early summer to mid-summer, and again in early autumn to mid-autumn.
FEEDING: Spring and again in mid-summer with rose fertilizer. Add bonemeal in late autumn and some well-rotted manure in winter.
PRUNING: Deadhead as the flowers die. In winter cut back hard all over to about 28in/45cm above outward-facing buds.
GENERAL COMMENTS: A lovely rose, especially as a cut flower, which has a good scent.

Rosa Tradescant

SOIL: Any enriched, but not sand or pure chalk.
CONDITIONS: Sun or partial shade.
COLOUR: Deep dark crimson.
FLOWERING: Repeats throughout the summer.
FEEDING: Spring and again in mid-summer.
PRUNING: Prune in winter, removing any weak, crossing or dead wood, but do not cut too hard.
GENERAL COMMENTS: Grown for the richness of its colour and continuous flowering.

A SUNNY ISLAND BED:
BLUE AND WHITE

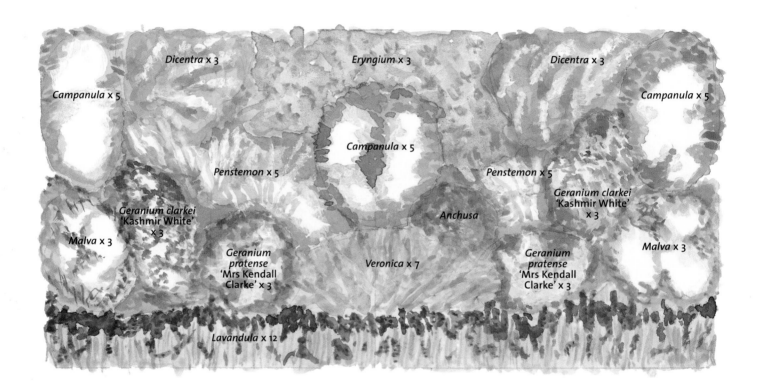

Dicentra x 3

Eryngium x 3

Dicentra x 3

Campanula x 5

Campanula x 5

Campanula x 5

Penstemon x 5

Penstemon x 5

Geranium clarkei
'Kashmir White'
x 3

Geranium clarkei
'Kashmir White'
x 3

Anchusa

Malva x 3

Malva x 3

Geranium
pratense
'Mrs Kendall
Clarke' x 3

Veronica x 7

Geranium
pratense
'Mrs Kendall
Clarke' x 3

Lavandula x 12

	THE PLANTS	QUANTITIES
1	*Anchusa azurea* 'Opal'	1
2	*Campanula lactiflora* 'Alba'	15
3	*Geranium pratense* 'Mrs Kendall Clark'	6
4	*Geranium clarkei* 'Kashmir White'	6
5	*Lavandula angustifolia* 'Hidcote'	12
6	*Veronica gentianoides*	7
7	*Malva moschata* f. *alba*	6
8	*Dicentra spectabilis* 'Alba'	6
9	*Penstemon* 'White Bedder'	10
10	*Eryngium giganteum* 'Silver Ghost'	3

SIZE AND POSITION

Anchusa azurea 'Opal' grows to 3½ft x 24in/1.1m x 60cm.

Campanula lactiflora 'Alba' grows to 4ft x 24in/1.2m x 60cm. Plant 12in/30cm apart.

Dicentra spectabilis 'Alba' grows to 18in x 18in/45cm x 45cm. Plant 12in/30cm apart.

Eryngium giganteum 'Silver Ghost' grows to 36in–4ft x 24in/90cm–1.2m x 60cm. Plant 18in/45cm apart.

Geranium clarkei 'Kashmir White' grows to 18in x 12in/45cm x 30cm. Plant 12in/30cm apart.

Geranium pratense 'Mrs Kendall Clark' grows to 24in x 18in/60cm x 45cm. Plant 12in/30cm apart.

Lavandula angustifolia 'Hidcote' grows to 15in x 15in/38cm x 38cm. Plant 12in/30cm apart.

Malva moschata f. *alba* grows to 30in x 18in/75cm x 45cm. Plant 12in/30cm apart.

Penstemon 'White Bedder' grows to 18in x 12in/45cm x 30cm. Plant 12in/30cm apart.

Veronica gentianoides grows to 18in x 18in/45cm x 45cm. Plant 12in/30cm apart.

ADDITIONAL PLANTING

SPRING COLOUR

In autumn:
Plant 100 *Muscari armeniacum* 'Blue Spike' bulbs (grape hyacinths) in drifts all over the bed.

Plant 100 white *Anemone blanda* corms in groups of not less than 10 all over the bed.

Plant 60 'White Triumphator' tulips in groups of 10.

SUMMER COLOUR

In spring:
Plant 30 white antirrhinums where there are gaps.

Plant 20 *Salvia farinacea* 'Strata' in groups of 10.

In mid-spring:
Sprinkle seeds of *Nigella damascena* 'Miss Jekyll' (love-in-a-mist) in any spaces.

GENERAL CARE

Clear the bed of any debris in spring, and feed with a general fertilizer.

Cut the lavender into shape in mid-spring, and trim over again after it has finished flowering.

When the geraniums finish their first flowering, cut back to encourage a second flush of flowers.

Stake the campanulas if necessary.

PLANT DETAILS

***Anchusa azurea* 'Opal'**
SOIL: Well drained.
CONDITIONS: Sun.
COLOUR: Bright blue.
FLOWERING: Early summer to mid-summer.
FEEDING: Spring.
PRUNING: None.
GENERAL COMMENTS: A beautiful plant, but it is short-lived.

***Campanula lactiflora* 'Alba'**
SOIL: Any.
CONDITIONS: Sun or partial shade.
COLOUR: White.
FLOWERING: Early summer to mid-summer, with a few later spikes.
FEEDING: Spring.
PRUNING: Cut back after first flowering. Cut back old flower spikes again as the flowers fade.
GENERAL COMMENTS: It may need staking in late spring. A good, upright plant which is extremely reliable.

***Dicentra spectabilis* 'Alba'** (white bleeding heart)
SOIL: Moist, rich and fertile.
CONDITIONS: Sun, partial shade or shade.
COLOUR: White.
FLOWERING: Mid-spring to early summer.
FEEDING: Spring.
PRUNING: None. It disappears in winter.
GENERAL COMMENTS: A lovely plant, with very pretty locket-shaped flowers that dangle over green ferny foliage.

Eryngium giganteum
'Silver Ghost'
SOIL: Well drained.
CONDITIONS: Sun.
COLOUR: Silver foliage with blue flowers.
FLOWERING: Late summer to early autumn.
FEEDING: Spring.
PRUNING: Deadhead.
GENERAL COMMENTS: A handsome plant. It is biennial but a rampant self-seeder, so if you keep an eye out you should be able to transplant seedlings as you need them.

Geranium clarkei
'Kashmir White'
SOIL: Any ordinary.
CONDITIONS: Sun or partial shade.
COLOUR: White.
FLOWERING: Early summer to early autumn.
FEEDING: Spring.
PRUNING: Cut back after flowering, to encourage a later flush of flowers.
GENERAL COMMENTS: A reliable white geranium with pretty, finely divided leaves. It flowers profusely. Once established it is inclined to spread fast, so you will need to watch the size of the clump.

Geranium pratense
'Mrs Kendall Clark'
SOIL: Good.

CONDITIONS: Sun or partial shade.
COLOUR: Pale greyish blue with white flushing.
FLOWERING: Early summer, and again later.
FEEDING: Spring.
PRUNING: Cut back after first flowering. This will encourage a second flush of flowers.
GENERAL COMMENTS: A happy companion to most plants, and also looks good grown in wild gardens in grass.

Lavandula angustifolia
'Hidcote'
SOIL: Light, well drained.
CONDITIONS: Sun.
COLOUR: Deep purple blue.
FLOWERING: Early summer to early autumn.
FEEDING: Spring.
PRUNING: Cut old flower heads off after flowering. Trim the whole plant in spring to help maintain a neat shape, making sure you do not cut into old wood.
GENERAL COMMENTS: A wonderful plant, but it hates the wet, so if you have any doubts about your soil mix in some grit when planting. The flower is a really vibrant blue, well worth picking. If you want to dry the flower heads, pick them just as they come into flower and tie in bunches to

dry upside down in a cool dry place.

Malva moschata f. *alba*
SOIL: Fertile, well drained.
CONDITIONS: Sun.
COLOUR: White.
FLOWERING: Late spring to late summer.
FEEDING: Spring, and with a liquid tomato food in summer.
PRUNING: Cut back to new growth in spring.
GENERAL COMMENTS: Bushy, and a mass of white saucer-shaped flowers on spikes. Can be short-lived but is easy to grow and reliable.

Penstemon **'White Bedder'**
SOIL: Fertile, well drained.
CONDITIONS: Sun or part shade.
COLOUR: White.
FLOWERING: Mid-summer to mid-autumn.
FEEDING: Spring.
PRUNING: Leave old flower stems on the plant over winter as protection from frost and cut the plant down to at least half in spring to encourage new growth.
GENERAL COMMENTS: One of the nicest penstemons, with profuse bell-shaped flowers over a long season.

Veronica gentianoides
SOIL: Moist, but well drained.

CONDITIONS: Sun or part shade.
COLOUR: Pale blue.
FLOWERING: Late spring to mid-summer.
FEEDING: Spring.
PRUNING: Cut off flower spikes as they go over.
GENERAL COMMENTS: A lovely pale blue flower held over neat leaves. Tough and reliable.

A SUNNY ISLAND BED: PINK AND RED

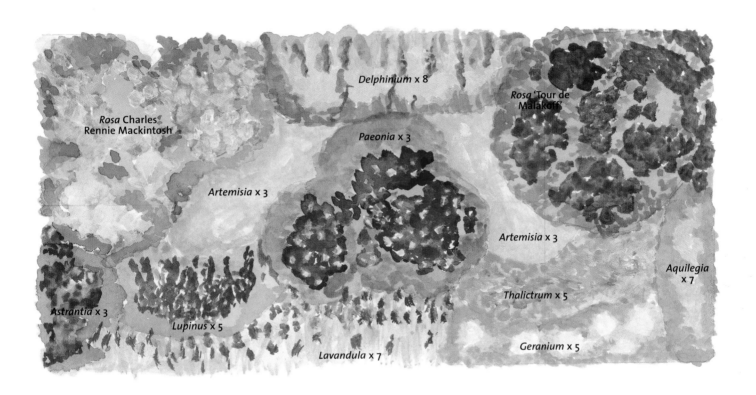

Delphinium x 8

Rosa 'Tour de Malakoff'

Rosa Charles Rennie Mackintosh

Paeonia x 3

Artemisia x 3

Artemisia x 3

Aquilegia x 7

Thalictrum x 5

Astrantia x 3

Lupinus x 5

Geranium x 5

Lavandula x 7

THE PLANTS	QUANTITIES
1 *Delphinium* 'Langdon's Royal Flush'	8
2 *Astrantia* 'Hadspen Blood'	3
3 *Paeonia*, any single red with a yellow centre	
(e.g. *P.* 'America' or *P. peregrina*)	3
4 *Artemisia ludoviciana* 'Silver Queen'	6
5 *Aquilegia vulgaris*	7
6 *Rosa* Charles Rennie Mackintosh	1
7 *Lupinus*, any red variety	
(e.g. 'My Castle' or 'Judith Chalmers')	5
8 *Lavandula stoechas* 'Kew Red'	7
9 *Thalictrum aquilegiifolium*	5
10 *Geranium sanguineum* var. *striatum*	5
11 *Rosa* 'Tour de Malakoff'	1

SIZE AND POSITION

Aquilegia vulgaris grows to 30in x 12in/75cm x 30cm. Plant 8in/20cm apart.

Artemisia ludoviciana 'Silver Queen' grows to 36in x 24in/90cm x 60cm. Plant 15in/38cm apart.

Astrantia 'Hadspen Blood' grows to 24in x 15in/60cm x 38cm. Plant 12in/30cm apart.

Delphinium 'Langdon's Royal Flush' grows to 4–5ft x 18in/1.2–1.5m x 45cm. Plant 12in/30cm apart.

Geranium sanguineum var. *striatum* 6in x 9in/15cm x 23cm. Plant 8in/20cm apart.

Lavandula stoechas 'Kew Red' grows to 15in x 12in/38cm x 30cm. Plant 12in/30cm apart.

The lupins grow to 36in x 18in/90cm x 45cm. Plant 12in/30cm apart.

The peonies grow to 36in x 36in/90cm x 90cm. Plant 18in/45cm apart.

Rosa Charles Rennie Mackintosh grows to 3½ft x 36in/1.1m x 90cm. Plant 24in/60cm apart.

Rosa 'Tour de Malakoff' grows to 6ft x 5ft/1.8m x 1.5m.

Thalictrum aquilegiifolium grows to 36in–4ft x 18in/90cm–1.2m x 45cm. Plant 12in/30cm apart.

ADDITIONAL PLANTING

SPRING COLOUR

In autumn:
Plant the following tulip bulbs: 'Marilyn', 'Angélique', 'Red Wing', 'Carnaval de Nice' – 20 of each variety, in groups of 5 of each type – in any spaces.

Plant 50 *Muscari armeniacum* 'Blue Spike' at the edges of the bed.

Plant 25 *Narcissus* 'Thalia' bulbs in a clump at the back of the bed where the delphiniums will be.

SUMMER COLOUR

In spring:
Plant *Dianthus barbatus* (sweet Williams) in pink and red, in groups of 5 towards the front of the bed.

Plant pink cosmos singly where there are spaces towards the back.

Plant scented-leaved geraniums in any spaces around the roses and at the edges of the bed.

GENERAL CARE

Thoroughly clear through the bed in spring, removing debris and dead leaves. Mulch around the roses and peonies with well-rotted manure or leaf mould.

Feed the whole bed with a general fertilizer in spring.

Scatter slug pellets as the delphiniums start to come through in early spring.

Trim over the lavenders in mid-spring and again after flowering.

Stake the delphiniums and the peonies.

Spray the roses if necessary.

Do not let the artemisia flower. Cut off flowers as soon as buds appear.

Keep the roses deadheaded as the flowers fade.

Feed the roses again in mid-summer with rose food.

Cut back the lupins, geraniums, delphiniums, thalictrum and aquilegias after they have finished flowering to encourage a second show.

Leave the leaves on the peonies until autumn and then cut to ground level.

PLANT DETAILS

Aquilegia vulgaris
(granny's bonnet or columbine)
SOIL: Any.
CONDITIONS: Sun or part shade.
COLOURS: White, pink, purple or red.
FLOWERING: Late spring to mid-summer.
FEEDING: Spring.
PRUNING: Cut off old flower stems as they die.
GENERAL COMMENTS: A really worthwhile old-fashioned plant, with beautiful, nodding, graceful flowers held above a clump of pretty, ferny leaves. Looks at its best planted in a group. Has a great tendency to self-seed.

Artemisia ludoviciana **'Silver Queen'**
SOIL: Well drained.
CONDITIONS: Sun.
COLOUR: Grown for its silver leaves.
FLOWERING: Do not let it flower.
FEEDING: Spring.
PRUNING: Cut off the flowers before they form in early summer. In spring cut off the old stems to fresh new growth to maintain the shape.
GENERAL COMMENTS: One of the very best silver plants, grown for its lovely feathery leaves. It looks very pretty planted with old roses.

Astrantia **'Hadspen Blood'**
SOIL: Any well drained.
CONDITIONS: Light shade or sun, provided that the soil does not dry out.
COLOUR: Dark red.
FLOWERING: Early summer to late summer.
FEEDING: Spring.
PRUNING: Cut down the old flowering stems to base in late summer.

GENERAL COMMENTS: Makes a dense leafy clump with the flowers held well above the leaves on thin, strong stems. It may need supporting with twiggy sticks in exposed areas. It does well when cut.

Delphinium 'Langdon's Royal Flush'
SOIL: Well drained, deeply dug, rich, with plenty of added manure or compost.
CONDITIONS: Full sun, but out of the wind.
COLOUR: Pink.
FLOWERING: Mid-summer to late summer.
FEEDING: Spring, and again in summer.
PRUNING: Cut back the stems to the base as they finish flowering to encourage a second flush. In established clumps, cut off any weak stems in early spring.
GENERAL COMMENTS: It will need protection from slugs and snails: put down slug pellets as soon as they start to appear in early spring. The plant will also need staking, which is best done when it is about 12in/30cm high.

Geranium sanguineum var. striatum
SOIL: Any well drained.
CONDITIONS: Sun.
COLOUR: Pale pink flowers with darker veins.
FLOWERING: Early summer to autumn.
FEEDING: Spring.
PRUNING: Cut back to a neat clump after flowering.

GENERAL COMMENTS: A neat and easy plant for the edge of the border, with lovely soft pink flowers.

Lavandula stoechas 'Kew Red'
SOIL: Light, well drained.
CONDITIONS: Full sun.
COLOUR: Dark red base with pink ears.
FLOWERING: Mid-summer to early autumn.
FEEDING: Spring.
PRUNING: Cut off the old flower stems as the flowers fade. In spring trim over the plant to maintain a neat shape, making sure not to cut into old wood. If this is done every year it will encourage new growth and stop the plant from becoming untidy and woody.
GENERAL COMMENTS: Lavenders are easy plants, but they hate wet soil, so if you are in any doubt about your soil, mix in some grit when planting. They are quite short-lived, but root very easily from cuttings. 'Kew Red' is a wonderful colour combination, and makes an eyecatching addition to the border.

Lupinus, any red variety
SOIL: Light, well drained.
CONDITIONS: Sun or part shade.
COLOUR: Good strong red.
FLOWERING: Early summer to mid-summer, with a second flush in late summer to early autumn.
FEEDING: In spring, and again after first flowering.

PRUNING: Cut back to a neat clump after first flowering to encourage a second show. Cut old flower spikes to 12in/30cm in autumn.
GENERAL COMMENTS: Cutting the flowers off after flowering also helps to stop the plant's rampant self-seeding, which is necessary because it does not come true from seed. You can dry off the old seedheads and sow them elsewhere in the autumn, or grow them on in pots until you can see what colour they are. They will need protection from slugs and snails, and do not like manure.

Paeonia, any single red variety with a yellow centre
SOIL: Deep, rich.
CONDITIONS: Sun.
COLOUR: Dark red single flowers with a yellow centre.
FLOWERING: Late spring to mid-summer.
FEEDING: In spring.
PRUNING: None.
GENERAL COMMENTS: A deep opulent red.

Rosa Charles Rennie Mackintosh
SOIL: Any, except sand or chalk.
CONDITIONS: Sun.
COLOUR: Pink, flushed lilac pink.
FLOWERING: Early summer, and repeats.
FEEDING: Spring, and again in mid-summer.
PRUNING: After its second year prune to 24in/60cm and cut out any weak, spindly growth.
GENERAL COMMENTS: A lovely

rose planted with others or on its own. It needs to be kept well deadheaded.

Rosa 'Tour de Malakoff'
SOIL: Any, except sand or chalk.
CONDITIONS: Sun.
COLOUR: Large double flowers of magenta violet, fading to purple grey.
FLOWERING: Strongly scented flowers in early and mid-summer.
FEEDING: Spring and again in mid-summer.
PRUNING: Reduce any very long new growth in early autumn to stop wind rock and cut out any weak or crossing stems in late winter.
GENERAL COMMENTS: The richness of colour and scent make this rose a valuable addition to the border. It is best to give it some support.

Thalictrum aquilegiifolium
SOIL: Any, but prefers rich.
CONDITIONS: Sun or light shade.
COLOUR: Fluffy deep lilac-pink flowers.
FLOWERING: Early summer.
FEEDING: Spring. Top dress in early spring with well-rotted manure.
PRUNING: Cut down in late autumn to 12in/30cm.
GENERAL COMMENTS: A fluffy mass of flowers held over delicate, blue-grey ferny foliage makes this a very pretty plant, which looks good planted anywhere.

A SUNNY ISLAND BED: MIXED SOFT COLOURS

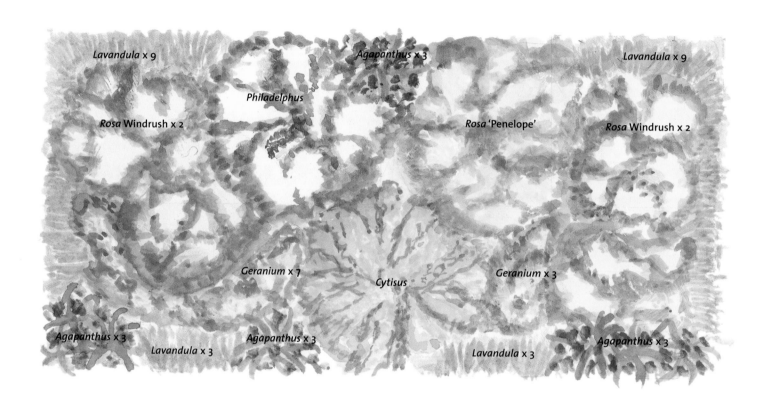

Lavandula x 9

Agapanthus x 3

Lavandula x 9

Philadelphus

Rosa Windrush x 2

Rosa 'Penelope'

Rosa Windrush x 2

Geranium x 7

Cytisus

Geranium x 3

Agapanthus x 3

Agapanthus x 3

Lavandula x 3

Lavandula x 3

Agapanthus x 3

	THE PLANTS	QUANTITIES
1	*Lavandula angustifolia* 'Hidcote Pink'	24
2	*Agapanthus* Headbourne hybrid	12
3	*Rosa* 'Penelope'	1
4	*Philadelphus* 'Belle Etoile'	1
5	*Cytisus* x *praecox*	1
6	*Geranium pratense* 'Mrs Kendall Clark'	10
7	*Rosa* Windrush	4

SIZE AND POSITION

Agapanthus Headbourne hybrid grows to 30in x 18in/75cm x 45cm. Plant 12in/30cm apart.

Cytisus x *praecox* grows to 36in x 5ft/90cm x 1.5m.

Geranium pratense 'Mrs Kendall Clark' grows to 24in x 18in/60cm x 45cm. Plant 12in/30cm apart.

Lavandula angustifolia 'Hidcote Pink' grows to 15in x 15in/38cm x 38cm. Plant 12in/30cm apart.

Philadelphus 'Belle Etoile' grows to 6ft x 5ft/1.8m x 1.5m.

Rosa 'Penelope' grows to 5ft x 5ft/1.5m x 1.5m.

Rosa Windrush grows to 4ft x 4ft/1.2m x 1.2m. Plant 36in/90cm apart.

ADDITIONAL PLANTING

SPRING COLOUR

In autumn:
Plant 35 black *Tulipa* 'Queen of Night' as single bulbs throughout the bed.

Plant white *Tulipa* 'Purissima' and 'White Triumphator' – 20 of each – as single bulbs throughout the bed.

SUMMER COLOUR

In autumn:
Plant 10 *Allium cristophii* and 20 *A. atropurpureum* bulbs in front of the roses in the middle of the bed and around the cytisus.

In spring:
Plant white antirrhinums and white cosmos to fill in gaps, remembering that the cosmos will grow tall.

GENERAL CARE

Tidy through the bed in early spring and feed with a general fertilizer.

Trim over the lavenders after they have finished flowering and cut them back in mid-spring.

Cut off the tulip leaves as they yellow and feed the tulips with a general fertilizer.

Cut back geraniums after flowering to encourage a second flush.

Deadhead the roses regularly throughout the flowering season. Feed them with a rose fertilizer in mid-summer. Spray against pests and diseases if required.

Trim the philadelphus after flowering.

Compost bedding plants after the first frost.

Mulch the roses, philadelphus and cytisus in winter with well-rotted manure.

PLANT DETAILS

Agapanthus **Headbourne hybrid**
SOIL: Fertile, well drained.
CONDITIONS: Full sun.
COLOUR: Blue.
FLOWERING: Mid-summer to early autumn.
FEEDING: Spring, and again in mid-summer.
PRUNING: Cut off old flower stems as near to the bottom as possible.
GENERAL COMMENTS: A beautiful plant with drumstick flowers on a long stem. It should be divided every 3–4 years.

Cytisus **x praecox**
SOIL: Well drained, poor rather than heavily fertilized.
CONDITIONS: Full sun.
COLOUR: Creamy white.
FLOWERING: Mid-spring to late spring.
FEEDING: Spring.
PRUNING: As much as necessary, after flowering, to shape up untidy growth.
GENERAL COMMENTS: A useful shrub, which fits in with all types of planting. Looks good on a bank, and its low arching habit is useful for covering a drain cover.

Geranium pratense
'Mrs Kendall Clark'
SOIL: Good.
CONDITIONS: Sun or part shade.
COLOUR: Pale greyish blue flushed white.
FLOWERING: Early summer and again later.
FEEDING: Spring.

PRUNING: Cut back after first flowering to encourage a second show.

GENERAL COMMENTS: A good foil and a happy companion to most plants.

Lavandula angustifolia 'Hidcote Pink'

SOIL: Well drained.

CONDITIONS: Sun.

COLOUR: Pale pink.

FLOWERING: Mid-summer to early autumn.

FEEDING: Spring.

PRUNING: Trim off old flower heads as they finish flowering and neaten up the bush. Cut back any straggly growth in mid-spring to keep the plant to a neat mound.

GENERAL COMMENTS: If you want to dry the flower heads, pick them just as they show colour, when the oils they contain are at their strongest. If you have heavy soil, you will need to add plenty of grit to the planting area before planting, as lavenders really hate being waterlogged.

Philadelphus 'Belle Etoile'

SOIL: Well drained.

CONDITIONS: Sun or part shade.

COLOUR: White.

FLOWERING: Early summer to mid-summer.

FEEDING: Spring, and again after flowering.

PRUNING: Thin out the old wood as necessary after flowering by cutting some shoots back to the base. Leave the young branches, which will carry flowers the following year.

GENERAL COMMENTS: Has a wonderful scent. Short-lived when picked, but if you take off the leaves it will last a little longer.

Rosa 'Penelope'

SOIL: Any, except pure sand or chalk.

CONDITIONS: Sun.

COLOUR: Creamy pink.

FLOWERING: Early summer, and again later.

FEEDING: Spring, and again in mid-summer.

PRUNING: Trim the whole plant lightly in winter when the weather is not frosty. Cut out any dead, diseased or crossing stems and take a few of the oldest stems back to the base.

GENERAL COMMENTS: A lovely shrub rose with a strong scent.

Rosa Windrush

SOIL: Any, except sand or chalk.

CONDITIONS: Sun.

COLOUR: Pale lemon yellow.

FLOWERING: Early summer to mid-autumn, if kept well deadheaded.

FEEDING: Spring, and again in mid-summer.

PRUNING: In winter cut out any weak, diseased or crossing stems and cut back to maintain a good shape.

GENERAL COMMENTS: A beautiful rose, which can be grown as a climber. Very disease-free. Needs to be kept really well deadheaded if it is to repeat well. It has a delicate scent.

A SHADY ISLAND BED: DAMP SHADE

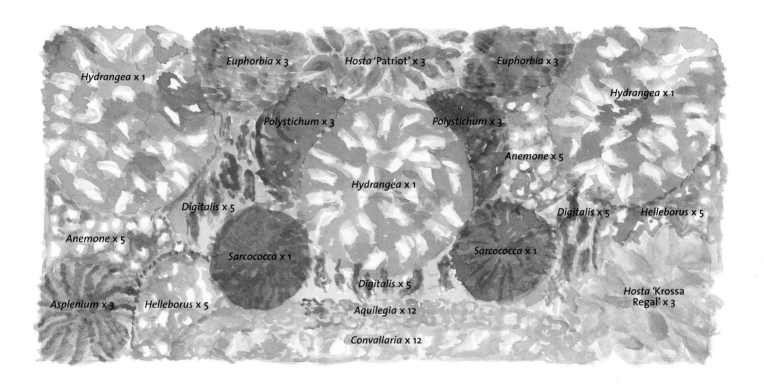

Hydrangea x 1

Euphorbia x 3

Hosta 'Patriot' x 3

Euphorbia x 3

Hydrangea x 1

Polystichum x 3

Polystichum x 3

Anemone x 5

Hydrangea x 1

Digitalis x 5

Digitalis x 5

Helleborus x 5

Anemone x 5

Sarcococca x 1

Sarcococca x 1

Digitalis x 5

Hosta 'Krossa Regal' x 3

Asplenium x 3

Helleborus x 5

Aquilegia x 12

Convallaria x 12

	THE PLANTS	QUANTITIES
1	*Aquilegia*, any pale yellow variety (e.g. *A. longissima* or *A.* 'Origami Yellow')	12
2	*Euphorbia amygdaloides* var. *robbiae*	6
3	*Hosta* 'Patriot'	3
4	*Polystichum setiferum* Divisilobum Group	6
5	*Digitalis purpurea*	15
6	*Hydrangea arborescens* 'Annabelle'	3
7	*Convallaria majalis*	12
8	*Hosta* 'Krossa Regal'	3
9	*Sarcococca confusa*	2
10	*Helleborus niger*	10
11	*Asplenium scolopendrium* (syn. *Phyllitis scolopendrium*)	3
12	*Anemone* x *hybrida* 'Honorine Jobert'	10

SIZE AND POSITION

Anemone x *hybrida* 'Honorine Jobert' grows to 36in x 24in/90cm x 60cm and should be planted 12in/30cm apart.

Aquilegias grow to 36in x 12in/90cm x 30cm. Plant 8in/20cm apart.

Asplenium scolopendrium grows to 18in x 15in/45cm x 38cm. Plant 12in/30cm apart.

Convallaria majalis grows to 8in x 12in/20cm x 30cm. Plant 6in/15cm apart.

Digitalis purpurea grows to 5ft x 8in/1.5m x 20cm. Plant 8in/20cm apart.

Euphorbia amygdaloides var. *robbiae* grows to 12in x 12in/30cm x 30cm. Plant 12in/30cm apart.

Helleborus niger grows to 8in x 8in/20cm x 20cm. Plant 8in/20cm apart.

Hosta 'Krossa Regal' grows to 36in x 18in/90cm x 45cm. Plant 12in/30cm apart.

Hosta 'Patriot' grows to 30in x 14in/75cm x 35cm. Plant 18in/45cm apart.

Hydrangea arborescens 'Annabelle' grows to 36in x 36in/90cm x 90cm.

Polystichum setiferum Divisilobum Group grows to 24in x 18in/60cm x 45cm. Plant 15in/38cm apart.

Sarcococca confusa grows to 36in x 24in/90cm x 60cm.

ADDITIONAL PLANTING

SPRING COLOUR

In autumn:
Plant 10 *Trillium cuneatum* (toad lilies) all over the bed.

Plant 10 *Fritillaria meleagris* and 25 *F. meleagris* subvar. *alba* bulbs all over the bed.

Plant 30 *Tulipa* 'West Point' bulbs in groups of 10.

SUMMER COLOUR

In spring:
Plant white *Impatiens* (busy Lizzies) in any spaces.

Plant white pansies (*Viola* x *wittrockiana*) towards the front of the bed.

GENERAL CARE

Beware of slugs, especially in late winter and early spring if there is a warm wet spell of weather. The hostas need special care: use a slug killer as soon as the shoots start to appear and keep at slug prevention all season.

Cut off any brown or dead leaves in early spring.

Apply a general fertilizer in spring.

PLANT DETAILS

Anemone x hybrida 'Honorine Jobert'
SOIL: Fertile, which does not dry out.
CONDITIONS: Part shade.
COLOUR: White with a yellow eye.
FLOWERING: Late summer to mid-autumn.
FEEDING: Spring.
PRUNING: Cut down the flower stem to the base after flowering.
GENERAL COMMENTS: It does not like to be moved once planted. If it is happy it will spread. A wonderful plant for late summer: it looks very good against shrubs that have finished flowering, and lightens up the border late in the season.

Aquilegia, any pale yellow variety (granny's bonnet or columbine)
SOIL: Any.
CONDITIONS: Sun or shade.
COLOUR: Yellow.
FLOWERING: Mid-spring to early summer.
FEEDING: Spring.
PRUNING: Cut back old flower stems when they get too untidy.
GENERAL COMMENTS: Has beautiful nodding flowers held above a clump of pretty divided ferny leaves. A really hardy and versatile plant, which looks best when planted in groups. It is a rampant self-seeder.

Asplenium scolopendrium (hart's tongue fern)
SOIL: Moist, rich and well drained.
CONDITIONS: Part shade.
COLOUR: Green leaves.
FLOWERING: None.
FEEDING: Spring.
PRUNING: Tidy up the dead leaves as necessary.
GENERAL COMMENTS: Evergreen, with long bright green feathery fronds.

Convallaria majalis
(lily of the valley)
SOIL: Ordinary, containing plenty of leaf mould or compost, but well drained.
CONDITIONS: An open site in partial shade.
COLOUR: White.
FLOWERING: Mid- to late spring.
FEEDING: Spring.
PRUNING: None.
GENERAL COMMENTS: Has a fantastic scent. It can be difficult to establish, but will suddenly take off in the most unlikely places; if it does not succeed at first it is worth persevering with it and it will let you know where it is happy.

Digitalis purpurea **(foxglove)**
SOIL: Ordinary, which does not dry out.
CONDITIONS: Part shade.
COLOUR: Pink, red and purple.
FLOWERING: Early summer to late summer.
FEEDING: Spring.
PRUNING: Cut old flower heads back to the ground after flowering unless you want them to self-seed. They will produce some later flowers. Cut the plant back again in mid-autumn.
GENERAL COMMENTS: A biennial, which grows very easily from seed. If you save the old flower spikes and dry them in the sun you can sow the seeds where you want them in late spring and they will flower the following year.

Euphorbia amygdaloides **var. robbiae**
SOIL: Any.
CONDITIONS: Part shade or shade.
COLOUR: Yellow/green.
FLOWERING: Early spring to late spring.
FEEDING: Spring.
PRUNING: Cut back the dead flowers when they start to look ugly. Take back to first leaves.
GENERAL COMMENTS: A handsome evergreen ground-cover plant, which spreads; very useful in shade. Wear gloves when handling as the sap is a powerful skin irritant.

Helleborus niger
(Christmas rose)
SOIL: Moisture-retentive, well drained and fertile.
CONDITIONS: Shade.
COLOUR: White.
FLOWERING: Mid-winter to mid-spring.
PRUNING: Pull off the dead leaves and flowers.
FEEDING: With bonemeal in November and general fertilizer after flowering.
PRUNING: Pull off the dead leaves and flowers.
GENERAL COMMENTS: An especially valuable plant, as it flowers in the middle of winter. Most of the leaves disappear, but they start to return in a good dark green as the flowers begin to appear.

Hosta **'Krossa Regal'**
SOIL: Well drained but moisture-retentive, enriched with leaf mould or manure.

CONDITIONS: Sun or part shade.
COLOUR: Lovely blue-grey foliage with stems of lilac flowers.
FLOWERING: Mid-summer to late summer.
FEEDING: Spring. Sometimes benefits from an extra foliar feed in early summer.
PRUNING: None. Cut off old flower spikes as they fade.
GENERAL COMMENTS: A fantastically showy hosta. Beware of slugs and snails. Wonderful ground cover, it can be left undisturbed for years.

Hosta **'Patriot'**
SOIL: Any well drained and moisture-retentive.
CONDITIONS: Sun or part shade. Variegated-leaved hostas are best in shade where they will not lose their colour.
COLOUR: Good mid-green leaves edged in white. Tall lavender-purple trumpet flowers are carried well above on strong stems.
FLOWERING: Spring.
FEEDING: Spring.
PRUNING: Cut off old flower spikes.
GENERAL COMMENTS: This is an eyecatching hosta with a neat and tidy habit. Beware of slugs and snails and take action before the leaves appear.

Hydrangea arborescens **'Annabelle'**
SOIL: Moist, fertile and well drained.
CONDITIONS: Partial shade.

COLOUR: Greenish white in bud opening to creamy white.
FLOWERING: Mid-summer to early autumn.
FEEDING: Spring.
PRUNING: Remove weak and old wood, but prune as little as possible to shape up the plant after flowering. Leave old flower heads on over the winter, to protect the stems from frost, and remove in early spring, cutting back to a strong pair of sprouting buds.
GENERAL COMMENTS: This hydrangea is a very attractive addition to the border.

Polystichum setiferum **Divisilobum Group**
SOIL: Moist, well drained and fertile.
CONDITIONS: Part shade.
COLOUR: Green leaves.
FLOWERING: None.
FEEDING: Spring.
PRUNING: Tidy up in spring; pull leaves off as they fade.
GENERAL COMMENTS: A handsome evergreen, or semi-evergreen, fern.

Sarcococca confusa **(sweet box or winter box)**
SOIL: Moist, fertile.
CONDITIONS: Sun or shade.
COLOUR: Glossy evergreen with small white flowers.
FLOWERING: Early winter to mid-winter.
FEEDING: Spring.
PRUNING: Tidy up in summer if necessary to neaten the shape.
GENERAL COMMENTS: Grown for its foliage and tiny sweet-smelling flowers in winter.

A SHADY ISLAND BED: DAMP SHADE

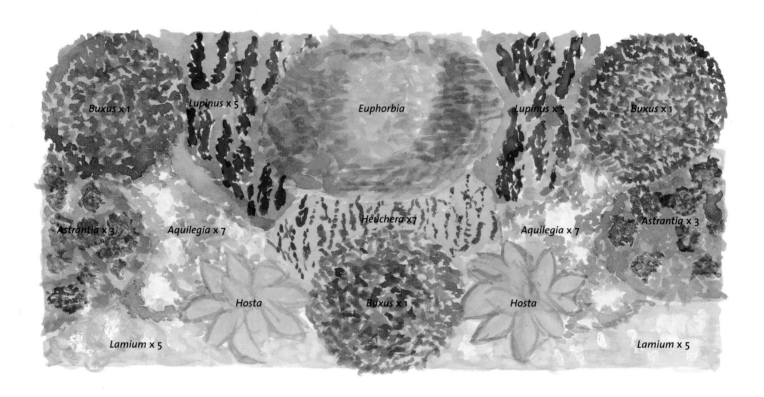

Buxus x 1

Lupinus x 5

Euphorbia

Lupinus x 5

Buxus x 1

Astrantia x 3

Aquilegia x 7

Heuchera x 7

Aquilegia x 7

Astrantia x 3

Hosta

Buxus x 1

Hosta

Lamium x 5

Lamium x 5

	THE PLANTS	QUANTITIES
1	*Euphorbia characias* subsp. *wulfenii*	1
2	*Astrantia major* 'Ruby Wedding'	6
3	*Lupinus*, any red variety (e.g. 'My Castle' or 'Judith Chalmers')	10
4	*Heuchera* 'Strawberry Swirl'	7
5	*Aquilegia*, any white variety (e.g. *A. vulgaris* 'Nivea')	14
6	*Buxus sempervirens*	3 balls
7	*Hosta fortunei* var. *albopicta*	2
8	*Lamium maculatum* 'White Nancy'	10

SIZE AND POSITION

Aquilegias grow to 36in x 12in/90cm x 30cm. Plant 8in/20cm apart.

Astrantia major 'Ruby Wedding' grows to 24in x 15in/60cm x 38cm. Plant 12in/30cm apart.

The box balls can be kept cut to size. We suggest an eventual height of 30in x 30in/75cm x 75cm.

Euphorbia characias subsp. *wulfenii* grows to 4ft x 4ft/1.2m x 1.2m.

Heuchera 'Strawberry Swirl' grows to 18in x 12in/45cm x 30cm. Plant 8in/20cm apart.

Hosta fortunei var. *albopicta* grows to 24in x 24in/60cm x 60cm.

Lamium maculatum 'White Nancy' grows to 6in/15cm high and spreads. Plant 18in/45cm apart.

Lupins grow to 36in x 18in/90cm x 45cm. Plant 12in/30cm apart.

ADDITIONAL PLANTING

SPRING COLOUR

In autumn:
Plant 100 double *Narcissus* 'Yellow Cheerfulness' bulbs throughout the bed .

Plant 50 dwarf *Narcissus* 'Hawera' bulbs in groups of 10 towards the sides of the bed.

SUMMER COLOUR

In spring:
Plant dark red nicotianas (tobacco plants) in spaces towards the front.

Plant white *Impatiens* (busy Lizzies) in any spaces, remembering that they will grow large.

GENERAL CARE

You will need to watch for slugs as soon as the first spike of the hostas appears. They and the lupins will need protection.

Feed herbaceous plants with general fertilizer in spring.

To tidy up the bed, cut the old flowers of the euphorbia down towards the base of the stem when they finish flowering.

Trim the box in early summer.

Feed with bonemeal in the autumn.

PLANT DETAILS

Aquilegia, **any white variety (granny's bonnet or columbine)**
SOIL: Any.
CONDITIONS: Sun or part shade.
COLOUR: White.
FLOWERING: Late spring to mid-summer.
FEEDING: Spring.
PRUNING: Cut off old flower stems.
GENERAL COMMENTS: Has pretty nodding flowers held singly above a clump of ferny green-grey leaves. A tough and trouble-free plant that lightens up the border. It loves to self-seed.

Astrantia major **'Ruby Wedding'**
SOIL: Any well drained.
CONDITIONS: Light shade.
COLOUR: Dark red flowers with dark red stems.
FLOWERING: Early summer to late summer.
FEEDING: Spring.
PRUNING: Cut down flowering stems in late summer.
GENERAL COMMENTS: Makes a dense leafy clump with the flowers held above on thin strong stems. The flowers do well when cut. The plant may need support with twigs if it is in an exposed and windy spot, but in the main it is tough and reliable.

Buxus sempervirens **(box)**
SOIL: Any, except one that stays waterlogged.

CONDITIONS: Sun or part shade.
COLOUR: Evergreen foliage; may have small yellowish flowers.
FLOWERING: Is not important.
FEEDING: Autumn with bonemeal.
PRUNING: Early summer. Cutting back promotes fresh new growth.
GENERAL COMMENTS: Grown for its dark evergreen foliage and shape, this is a very good plant for giving structure to a bed. Buy ready-shaped at a decent size so that you only have to worry about maintenance.

Euphorbia characias subsp. *wulfenii*
SOIL: Ordinary, well drained.
CONDITIONS: Sun or part shade.
COLOUR: Yellowish green flower bracts.
FLOWERING: Mid-spring to mid-summer.
FEEDING: Spring.
PRUNING: Cut the faded flower heads back to ground level.
GENERAL COMMENTS: A very impressive plant. The stems produce distinctive grey-green leaves in the first year and greeny yellow

flowers follow in early summer. Be careful when cutting it back as the milky sap is highly irritating to the skin and eyes.

Heuchera 'Strawberry Swirl'
SOIL: Dry or damp, but not waterlogged.
CONDITIONS: Sun or part shade.
COLOUR: Red flowers, with bright green leaves mottled with silver.
FLOWERING: Late spring to mid-summer.
FEEDING: Spring.
PRUNING: Cut back dead flower stems.
GENERAL COMMENTS: A valuable and easy plant with many attributes. Has graceful bell-like flowers held in feathery sprays above a neat mound of leaves that remain evergreen. It can be divided in the autumn or spring by slicing through with a spade.

Hosta fortunei var. *albopicta*
SOIL: Any well drained but moisture-retentive, enriched with manure or leaf mould.
CONDITIONS: Shade or partial shade is best for the variegated leaves.
COLOUR: Pale leaves edged with darker green; lilac

flowers.
FLOWERING: Mid-summer.
FEEDING: Spring.
PRUNING: Cut off old flower spikes.
GENERAL COMMENTS: The beauty of this variety is in its spring foliage: pale yellow leaves edged with dark green. As the year goes on the leaves turn mid-green all over. Beware of slugs and snails and give the plant protection as soon as you notice the leaves beginning to emerge in spring.

Lamium maculatum 'White Nancy'
SOIL: Prefers moist.
CONDITIONS: Full or partial shade.
COLOUR: Silver leaves and white flowers.
FLOWERING: Late spring to mid-summer.
FEEDING: Spring.
PRUNING: Cut back to the main clump in mid-summer to promote new leaves and restrict spread.
GENERAL COMMENTS: A wonderful semi-evergreen ground-cover plant, which thrives in damp shade under other, bigger plants. Do not let it become too invasive.

Lupinus, any red variety
SOIL: Any well drained. Does not like manure.
CONDITIONS: Sun or partial shade.
COLOUR: Red.
FLOWERING: Early summer with a second flush in late summer.
FEEDING: Spring, and again after first flowering.
PRUNING: Cut down after first flowers fade and they will flower again later.
GENERAL COMMENTS: Lupins self-seed rapidly, but the seedlings may be a different colour. If you want to save seed, put the cut stems in a hot place until the seed ripens, save in a labelled envelope and plant elsewhere in the garden next year.

A SHADY ISLAND BED: DAPPLED SHADE

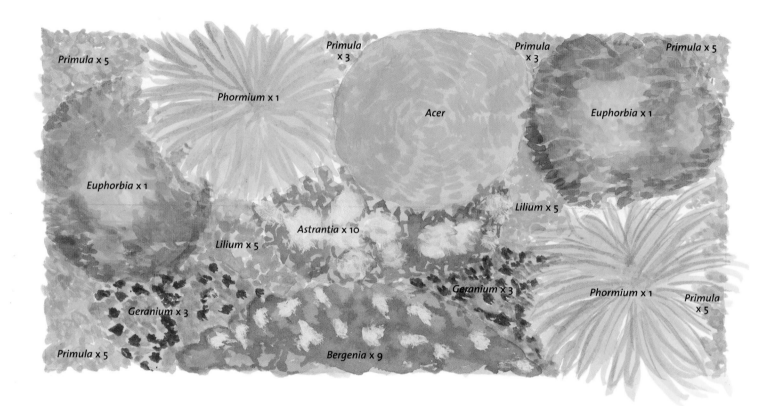

Primula x 5

Primula x 3

Phormium x 1

Primula x 3

Acer

Primula x 5

Euphorbia x 1

Euphorbia x 1

Lilium x 5

Astrantia x 10

Lilium x 5

Geranium x 3

Geranium x 3

Phormium x 1

Primula x 5

Primula x 5

Bergenia x 9

	THE PLANTS	QUANTITIES
1	*Acer palmatum* var. *dissectum* Dissectum Viride Group	1
2	*Euphorbia characias* subsp. *wulfenii*	2
3	*Geranium phaeum*	6
4	*Lilium* African Queen Group	10
5	*Bergenia* 'Silberlicht'	9
6	*Primula auricula* 'Greenpeace' (or any yellow variety)	26
7	*Phormium* 'Yellow Wave'	2
8	*Astrantia major* subsp. *involucrata* 'Shaggy'	10

SIZE AND POSITION

The acer goes at the back of the bed. Although it is a slow grower it will eventually make a large mound of 4ft x 4ft/1.2m x 1.2m.

Astrantia major subsp. *involucrata* 'Shaggy' grows to 24in x 12in/60cm x 30cm. Plant in a circle about 6in/15cm apart.

Bergenia 'Silberlicht' grows to 12in x 12in/30cm x 30cm. Plant 12in/30cm apart.

Euphorbia characias subsp. *wulfenii* grows to 4ft x 4ft/1.2m x 1.2m.

Geranium phaeum grows to 24in x 24in/60cm x 60cm. Plant 12in/30cm apart in a triangle.

Lilium African Queen Group grows to 36in x 6in/90cm x 15cm. Plant 6in/15cm apart.

Phormium 'Yellow Wave' grows to 36in x 24in/90cm x 60cm.

Primula auricula 'Greenpeace' grows to 6in x 6in/15cm x 15cm. Plant 8in/20cm apart.

ADDITIONAL PLANTING

SPRING COLOUR

In autumn:
Plant 50 *Narcissus* 'Thalia' bulbs in clusters of 5 throughout the bed.

Plant 25 *Erythronium dens-canis* bulbs in groups of 5 towards the front.

Plant 25 *Cyclamen coum* corms all over the bed.

Plant 50 *Puschkinia scilloides* var. *libanotica* bulbs throughout the bed in any gaps.

SUMMER COLOUR

In spring:
Plant 25 low nicotianas (F1 hybrid) (tobacco plants) in white all over the bed in spaces.

Plant 30 *Digitalis purpurea* f. *albiflora* (white foxgloves) all over the bed.

Plant 12 white *Lunaria annua* (honesty) in groups of 3 in any gaps.

GENERAL CARE

Put down slug pellets in spring, especially around the bergenias and primulas.

Feed the whole bed with a general fertilizer in spring.

The lilies will need staking.

Make sure that the plants do not dry out.

Cut off any dead leaves from plants, and pick up fallen leaves in autumn.

When the honesty has finished flowering, leave two or three of the best plants and pull out the rest – otherwise you will have too many seedlings.

PLANT DETAILS

Acer palmatum var. *dissectum* **Dissectum Viride Group**
SOIL: Moist.
CONDITIONS: Part shade with shelter from direct sun and drying winds.
COLOUR: Soft yellowish green.
FLOWERING: None.
FEEDING: Spring.
PRUNING: None.
GENERAL COMMENTS: Slowly grows into a delicate arching mound of finely divided foliage.

Astrantia major subsp. *involucrata* **'Shaggy'**
SOIL: Any well drained.
CONDITIONS: Light shade. It does not like to dry out.
COLOUR: White tinged with green.
FLOWERING: Early summer to late summer.
FEEDING: Early spring.
PRUNING: Cut down stems in early autumn.
GENERAL COMMENTS: A tolerant and rewarding plant, which always looks fresh.

Bergenia **'Silberlicht'**
SOIL: Any well drained.
CONDITIONS: Sun or light shade.
COLOUR: White with a pinkish tinge.
FLOWERING: Late winter to late spring.
FEEDING: Spring
PRUNING: Cut off leaves and flowers as they go brown to keep plant neat.

GENERAL COMMENTS: Wonderful ground-cover plant, with tough, rounded partly evergreen leaves. The flowers are carried on stout, straight stems and last for weeks. It produces babies that can be pulled off the main plant for use elsewhere. It is a really useful plant, and deserves protection from slugs and snails, which sometimes attack them.

Euphorbia characias **subsp. wulfenii**

SOIL: Ordinary, well drained.
CONDITIONS: Sun or light shade or shade.
COLOUR: Greenish yellow bracts on glaucous green foliage.
FLOWERING: Mid-spring to mid-summer.
FEEDING: Spring.
PRUNING: Cut the faded flower heads to ground level.
GENERAL COMMENTS: A stately and impressive plant. The stems produce grey-green leaves in the first year, which are followed in spring by yellow-green flower bracts. Wear gloves when touching it, as the milky sap is a well-known skin irritant.

Geranium phaeum

SOIL: Any.
CONDITIONS: Happy in shade but will grow well in some sun.
COLOUR: Blackish purple.
FLOWERING: Mid-spring to mid-summer.
FEEDING: In spring, and again in mid-summer.
PRUNING: Cut back the old flower stems almost to the ground once they have finished, and you will encourage new growth and a second flush of flowers.
GENERAL COMMENTS: A marvellous ground-cover plant for shade – it even grows well in deep shade – and a very easy plant. It has a tendency to spread once it is established, but is very easy to divide into new plants between early autumn and early spring.

Lilium **African Queen Group**

SOIL: Free draining, with added bonemeal and grit.
CONDITIONS: Sun or light shade.
COLOUR: Strong golden yellow.
FLOWERING: Early summer and mid-summer.
FEEDING: Feed with bonemeal when planting and again in late spring with general fertilizer.
PRUNING: Cut off flower heads before they go to seed. Cut flower stems back to 4in/10cm in autumn.
GENERAL COMMENTS: Add grit to the hole when planting.

Phormium **'Yellow Wave'**

SOIL: Any well drained.
CONDITIONS: Although this is known as a sun-loving plant, we have found that it will grow well in dappled shade.
COLOUR: Grown for the yellow leaves with green margins.
FLOWERING: Yellowish flowers in summer, but these are not really the point.
FEEDING: Spring.
PRUNING: None.
GENERAL COMMENTS: A very architectural plant with bright yellow and green, drooping and sword-shaped leaves. It can be divided in spring.

Primula auricula **'Greenpeace'**

SOIL: Gritty, well drained.
CONDITIONS: Tolerates sun, but prefers partial shade.
COLOUR: Yellowish green to pale yellow, often with a white centre.
FLOWERING: Fragrant flowers in early spring and late spring.
FEEDING: Early spring.
PRUNING: None.
GENERAL COMMENTS: Primulas are delightful clump-forming plants with lovely oval soft grey to pale green leaves, and unusual greenish flowers which invite attention. They were especially loved by the Victorians, and have lost none of their appeal.

A SHADY ISLAND BED:
DAPPLED SHADE

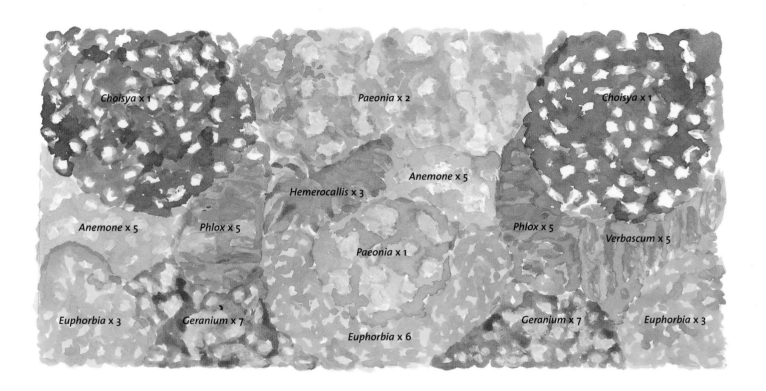

Choisya x 1

Paeonia x 2

Choisya x 1

Anemone x 5

Hemerocallis x 3

Anemone x 5

Phlox x 5

Phlox x 5

Verbascum x 5

Paeonia x 1

Euphorbia x 3

Geranium x 7

Geranium x 7

Euphorbia x 3

Euphorbia x 6

	THE PLANTS	QUANTITIES
1	*Phlox paniculata*, any lavender blue variety (e.g. 'Franz Schubert')	10
2	*Geranium maculatum*	14
3	*Paeonia lactiflora* 'Sarah Bernhardt'	3
4	*Euphorbia polychroma*	12
5	*Choisya ternata*	2
6	*Anemone hupehensis* 'Hadspen Abundance'	10
7	*Verbascum* 'Pink Domino'	5
8	*Hemerocallis*, any pink variety, but not salmon pink (e.g. 'Catherine Woodbery')	3

SIZE AND POSITION

Anemone hupehensis 'Hadspen Abundance' grows to 30in x 18in/75cm x 45cm. Plant 15in/38cm apart.

Choisya ternata grows to 5ft x 5ft/1.5m x 1.5m.

Euphorbia polychroma grows to 18in x 8in/45cm x 20cm. Plant 8in/20cm apart.

Geranium maculatum grows to 12in x 12in/30cm x 30cm. Plant 12in/30cm apart.

Hemerocallis grows to 30in x 24in/75cm x 60cm. Plant 18in/45cm apart.

Paeonia lactiflora 'Sarah Bernhardt' grows to 30in x 24in/75cm x 60cm. Plant 18in/45cm apart.

Phlox paniculata grows to 3½ft x 24in/1.1m x 60cm. Plant 18in/45cm apart.

Verbascum 'Pink Domino' grows to 3½ft x 12in/1.1m x 30cm. Plant 18in/45cm apart.

ADDITIONAL PLANTING

SPRING COLOUR

In autumn:
Plant 30 *Anemone coronaria* corms dotted throughout the bed.

Plant 25 *Fritillaria meleagris* bulbs mixed in groups of 5 where there are gaps near the front.

Plant 50 *Muscari armeniacum* 'Blue Spike' (grape hyacinths) bulbs in drifts of 10.

Plant 20 parrot *Tulipa* 'Estella Rijnveld' bulbs in groups of 5 where there are spaces.

Plant 30 *Tulipa* 'Maywonder' bulbs in groups of 10 in any gaps.

SUMMER COLOUR

In late spring:
Plant 10 purple heliotropes among the euphorbia. These have a delicious scent.

In spring:
Plant 20 pink or white nicotianas (tobacco plants) in any spaces.

Plant scented-leaved geraniums in any spaces around the peonies.

In autumn:
Plant 20 blue camassia bulbs to flower in early summer in any gaps towards the back of the bed.

GENERAL CARE

Mulch the bed with leaf mould or manure in early winter or spring.

Feed the whole bed with a general fertilizer in spring.

Cut off the old tulip leaves as they turn yellow and sprinkle fertilizer over the ground.

Stake the peonies as they begin to put on growth. This is best done when they are about 6in/15cm high.

Tidy through the bed in autumn and take out the summer annuals.

PLANT DETAILS

Anemone hupehensis **'Hadspen Abundance'**
SOIL: Good.
CONDITIONS: Sun or shade.
COLOUR: Deep purple pink.
FLOWERING: Late summer to mid-autumn.
FEEDING: Spring.
PRUNING: Just pull out excess growth from time to time.
GENERAL COMMENTS: It likes to spread, so you will have to watch it and pull out any that you do not need.

Choisya ternata
SOIL: Any.
CONDITIONS: Sun, partial shade or shade.
COLOUR: White.
FLOWERING: Mid-spring to early summer and a little in mid-autumn.
FEEDING: Spring.
PRUNING: Cut as hard as necessary to shape up after flowering in summer.
GENERAL COMMENTS: One of the very best shrubs. It goes with anything; it has lovely shining leaves, which are aromatic when touched; it is very healthy and good for picking – in fact, a must for every garden.

Euphorbia polychroma
SOIL: Any.
CONDITIONS: Sun or shade.
COLOUR: Acid greeny yellow.
FLOWERING: Early spring to early summer.
FEEDING: Spring.

PRUNING: Tidy up when needed.
GENERAL COMMENTS: A very useful plant which gives a good strong colour, much needed in the early spring. Remember that euphorbia sap is highly irritating to the skin.

Geranium maculatum
SOIL: Good, fertile.
CONDITIONS: Sun or part shade.
COLOUR: Pink.
FLOWERING: Early summer to mid-summer.
FEEDING: Spring.
PRUNING: Cut off the dead leaves and flowers as they fade.
GENERAL COMMENTS: A very pretty flower with a good leaf clump.

Hemerocallis, **any pale pink variety**
SOIL: Rich, moist.
CONDITIONS: Sun or part shade.
COLOUR: Pale pink.
FLOWERING: Mid-summer to late summer.
FEEDING: Spring.
PRUNING: None.
GENERAL COMMENTS: The grassy leaves always look fresh and although the scented individual flowers do not last long there are many of them borne over a long period. A trouble-free plant.

Paeonia lactiflora
'Sarah Bernhardt'
SOIL: Deep, rich.
CONDITIONS: Sun or partial shade.
COLOUR: Pale pink.
FLOWERING: Late spring to early summer.
FEEDING: Spring.
PRUNING: Cut off the old leaves in autumn.
GENERAL COMMENTS: The individual flower heads can be heavy and the plant benefits from careful staking.

Phlox paniculata,
any lavender blue variety
SOIL: Well drained, fertile and moisture-retentive.
CONDITIONS: Sun or part shade.
COLOUR: Blue with a darker eye.
FLOWERING: Mid-summer to early autumn.
FEEDING: Spring.
PRUNING: Cut back old flowers in autumn.
GENERAL COMMENTS: Has a lovely scent. Clumps may need dividing in late autumn or spring if they get too large.

Verbascum **'Pink Domino'**
SOIL: Good.
CONDITIONS: Sun or partial shade.
COLOUR: Lilac pink.
FLOWERING: Early summer to mid-summer.

FEEDING: Spring.
GENERAL COMMENTS: Makes a good stately spike for the border.

A SHADY ISLAND BED: DEEP SHADE

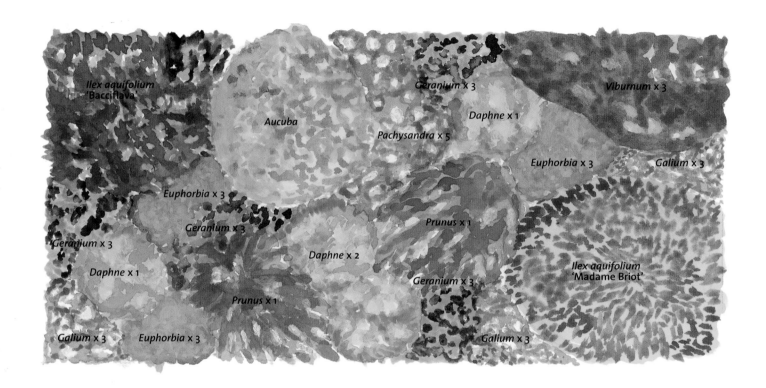

Ilex aquifolium 'Bacciflava'

Aucuba

Geranium x 3

Daphne x 1

Pachysandra x 5

Viburnum x 3

Euphorbia x 3

Galium x 3

Euphorbia x 3

Geranium x 3

Prunus x 1

Geranium x 3

Daphne x 2

Daphne x 1

Geranium x 3

Ilex aquifolium 'Madame Briot'

Prunus x 1

Galium x 3

Euphorbia x 3

Galium x 3

	THE PLANTS	QUANTITIES
1	*Ilex aquifolium* 'Bacciflava'	1
2	*Galium odoratum* (syn. *Asperula odorata*)	9
3	*Prunus laurocerasus* 'Otto Luyken' (or 'Zabeliana')	2
4	*Ilex aquifolium* 'Madame Briot'	1
5	*Viburnum davidii*	3
6	*Pachysandra terminalis*	5
7	*Euphorbia amygdaloides* var. *robbiae*	9
8	*Aucuba japonica* 'Crotonifolia'	1
9	*Geranium phaeum* 'Lily Lovell'	12
10	*Daphne pontica*	4

SIZE AND POSITION

Aucuba japonica 'Crotonifolia' grows to 6ft x 5ft/1.8m x 1.5m, and can be kept to size.

Daphne pontica grows to 36in x 18in/90cm x 45cm.

Euphorbia amygdaloides var. *robbiae* grows to 12in x 12in/30cm x 30cm and spreads.

Galium odoratum makes a neat carpet 6in x 12in/15cm x 30cm and spreads rapidly. Plant 12in/30cm apart.

Geranium phaeum 'Lily Lovell' grows to a clump 18in x 18in/45cm x 45cm. Plant 12in/30cm apart.

Ilex aquifolium 'Bacciflava' grows tall, but can be kept in check.

Ilex aquifolium 'Madame Briot' grows large, but can be kept in check.

Pachysandra terminalis is a neat ground-cover plant about 6in/15cm high and spreads. Plant 12in/30cm apart.

Prunus laurocerasus 'Otto Luyken' grows to 36in x 4½ft/90cm x 1.4m.

Viburnum davidii grows to 36in x 36in/90cm x 90cm. Plant 24in/60cm apart.

ADDITIONAL PLANTING

SPRING COLOUR

In autumn:
Plant 10 each of *Erythronium* 'Pagoda' (yellow) and *E. revolutum* 'White Beauty' (smaller) in groups of 5 towards the front.

In spring: plant 20 snowdrops *Galanthus nivalis* f. *pleniflorus* 'Flore Pleno' (double snowdrops) after flowering in groups of 5 in any spaces.

Plant 30 corms of *Eranthis hyemalis* (winter aconite) all over the bed.

SUMMER COLOUR

In autumn or spring:
Plant *Digitalis purpurea* f. *albiflora* (white foxgloves) to fill in any gaps.

In late spring:
Plant white *Impatiens* (busy Lizzies) in gaps where there is most light.

GENERAL CARE

Mulch with well-rotted manure in spring.

Make sure that the bed does not dry out.

Keep the hollies in shape by cutting hard back in mid-summer.

Keep an eye on the ground-cover plants to make sure that the different varieties do not swamp each other and thin out if necessary.

Feed the bed in autumn with bonemeal.

PLANT DETAILS

Aucuba japonica **'Crotonifolia'**
SOIL: Any.
CONDITIONS: Good in shade, but will tolerate sun.
COLOUR: Grown for its large leaves speckled with gold.
FLOWERING: Insignificant flowers in spring.
FEEDING: Spring.
PRUNING: Keep to desired size by cutting back in spring.
GENERAL COMMENTS: A very tolerant plant which withstands deep shade and tolerates pollution well. If you want berries you must grow both male and female in the same garden. 'Crotonifolia' is a good male, 'Gold Dust' a good female.

Daphne pontica
SOIL: Good, loamy.
CONDITIONS: Shade.
COLOUR: Greenish yellow.
FLOWERING: Spring.
FEEDING: Spring.
PRUNING: None, unless the shape needs neatening up.
GENERAL COMMENTS: A good tough, glossy-leaved plant for deep shade.

Euphorbia amygdaloides var. *robbiae*
SOIL: Any.
CONDITIONS: Shade, but will also tolerate sun.
COLOUR: Greenish yellow.
FLOWERING: Early spring to late spring.
FEEDING: Spring.

PRUNING: Cut off the old flower sprays when they become too drab, cutting back to first leaves or right down to the ground if it will keep the plant neater.
GENERAL COMMENTS: A handsome plant that is easy and trouble-free. Beware of the irritant sap, which can hurt both skin and eyes.

Galium odoratum (sweet woodruff)
SOIL: Any, but should not dry out.
CONDITIONS: Shade or part shade.
COLOUR: White.
FLOWERING: Late spring to mid-summer.
FEEDING: Spring.
PRUNING: No need, except to curb its exuberant growth by digging out.
GENERAL COMMENTS: A wonderful plant with a delightful scent. The flowers can be picked and put into a pillow to help sleep. Once the flowers have faded the leaves turn hay-like and can be picked off as new ones soon appear. Keep an eye on this plant, as it likes to travel.

Geranium phaeum 'Lily Lovell'
SOIL: Any.
CONDITIONS: Shade.

COLOUR: Dark purple.
FLOWERING: Late spring to mid-summer.
FEEDING: Spring.
PRUNING: Cut back old flower stems after they have finished.
GENERAL COMMENTS: A lovely plant for a difficult shady place.

Ilex aquifolium 'Bacciflava'
SOIL: Any, even dry and root-filled.
CONDITIONS: Tolerant of extreme situations, sun, wind and shade.
COLOUR: Grown for its yellow fruits and green leaves.
FLOWERING: Spring.
FEEDING: Early spring.
PRUNING: Can be cut back hard in mid-summer or late summer.
GENERAL COMMENTS: The yellow berries stay on the plant for a long while, as birds do not seem to like them.

Ilex aquifolium 'Madame Briot'
SOIL: Any neutral.
CONDITIONS: Tolerant of shade and partial shade.
COLOUR: Grown for its pretty yellow and green leaf colour.
FLOWERING: Late spring to early summer.
FEEDING: Spring.

PRUNING: Can be cut back hard to maintain its required shape in mid-summer and late summer.
GENERAL COMMENTS: Has attractive purple stems in spring, and spiny green leaves with strong yellow margins.

Pachysandra terminalis
SOIL: Fertile.
CONDITIONS: Shade or partial shade.
COLOUR: White, but the flowers are unimportant.
FLOWERING: Mid-spring.
FEEDING: Spring.
PRUNING: None.
GENERAL COMMENTS: A wonderful spreading ground-cover plant which will grow in difficult places where very little else will survive. It can be lifted and divided in early spring.

Prunus laurocerasus 'Otto Luyken'
SOIL: Any.
CONDITIONS: Extremely tolerant.
COLOUR: White flowers, then red fruits, which turn black.
FLOWERING: Mid-spring to late spring.
FEEDING: Spring.
PRUNING: Cut back in early spring or mid-spring to keep in shape.
GENERAL COMMENTS:

A handsome evergreen with glossy dark green leaves. It is tough and reliable, with attractive horizontal growth.

Viburnum davidii
SOIL: Good, moist.
CONDITIONS: Tolerant of sun or shade but needs some shelter from cold winds.
COLOUR: White flowers, which are sometimes followed by blue-black berries.
FLOWERING: Late spring to early summer.
FEEDING: Spring.
PRUNING: Cut out any dead or damaged wood in mid-spring to late spring.
GENERAL COMMENTS: A good evergreen plant for deep shade, with large, leathery, deeply veined leaves.

A DRY SHADY BED UNDER TREES

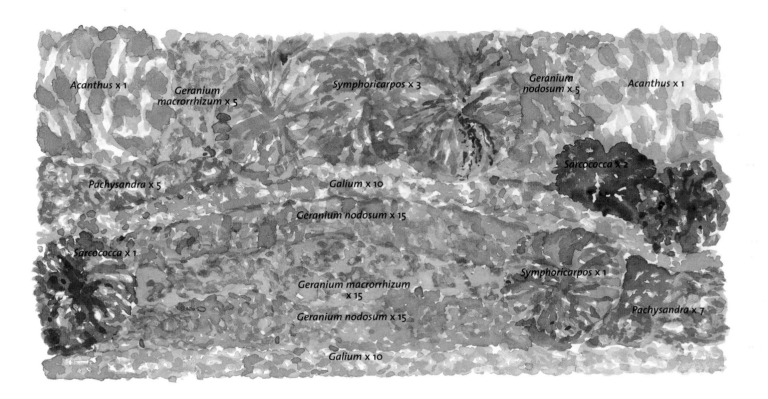

Acanthus x 1

Geranium macrorrhizum x 5

Symphoricarpos x 3

Geranium nodosum x 5

Acanthus x 1

Pachysandra x 5

Galium x 10

Sarcococca x 2

Geranium nodosum x 15

Sarcococca x 1

Symphoricarpos x 1

Geranium macrorrhizum x 15

Geranium nodosum x 15

Pachysandra x 7

Galium x 10

	THE PLANTS	QUANTITIES
1	*Geranium macrorrhizum*	20
2	*Geranium nodosum*	35
3	*Acanthus mollis*	2
4	*Pachysandra terminalis*	12
5	*Symphoricarpos* x *doorenbosii* 'Mother of Pearl'	4
6	*Galium odoratum* (syn. *Asperula odorata*)	20
7	*Sarcococca confusa*	3

SIZE AND POSITION

Acanthus mollis grows to 3½ft x 36in/1.1m x 90cm.

Galium odoratum grows to 6in/15cm high and spreads rapidly. Plant 12in/30cm apart.

Geranium macrorrhizum grows to 8in x 8in/20cm x 20cm. Plant 8in/20cm apart.

Geranium nodosum grows to 8in x 8in/20cm x 20cm. Plant 8in/20cm apart.

Pachysandra terminalis grows to 36in/90cm high, and spreads. Plant 12in/30cm apart.

Sarcococca confusa grows to 24in/60cm. Plant 18in/45cm apart.

Symphoricarpos x *doorenbosii* 'Mother of Pearl' grows to 24in x 18in/60cm x 45cm. Plant 18in/45cm apart.

ADDITIONAL PLANTING

SPRING COLOUR

In autumn:
Plant 150 *Anemone blanda* corms all over the bed.

Plant 25 *Cyclamen coum* corms singly all over the bed.

Plant 20 *Erythronium* 'Citronella' in groups of 5.

In spring:
Plant 50 *Hyacinthoides non-scripta* (bluebells) and 50 *Galanthus nivalis* f. *pleniflorus* 'Flore Pleno' (double snowdrops) after flowering, in drifts through the bed.

SUMMER COLOUR

We do not recommend the addition of annual plants for the summer, as they are liable to dry out too quickly.

In spring:
Plant 50 *Cyclamen cilicium* corms in groups of 25 around the base of any trees. These will flower in the autumn.

GENERAL CARE

Feed the bed with a general fertilizer in spring, and check that the plants are well mulched.

Cut back the dead flowers as they fade on the perennial plants and they should flower again later.

As the galium loses its leaves in late summer, trim off the old leaves and new ones should appear towards the autumn.

Tidy through the bed in winter, cutting off any dead leaves, and mulch the plants well with leaf mould or well-rotted manure to try to retain as much moisture as possible.

Even though these plants are tough, don't forget to water, especially the acanthus.

PLANT DETAILS

Acanthus mollis
SOIL: Well drained.
CONDITIONS: Sun or shade.
COLOUR: Purple and white flowers.
FLOWERING: Mid-summer to late summer.
FEEDING: Spring.
PRUNING: Cut stems down to ground level after flowering.
GENERAL COMMENTS: Good leaf shape and handsome flowers make this a good architectural addition to the border.

Galium odoratum (sweet woodruff)
SOIL: Well drained.
CONDITIONS: Sun or shade.
COLOUR: White.
FLOWERING: Late spring to mid-summer.
FEEDING: Spring.
PRUNING: Neaten clump as required.
GENERAL COMMENTS: A creeping ground-cover plant with small white star-shaped scented flowers. The leaves are aromatic. Once established it is a rampant spreader that is likely to crop up all over the garden.

Geranium macrorrhizum
SOIL: Good.
CONDITIONS: Sun or partial shade.
COLOUR: Pink.
FLOWERING: Mid-spring to early summer.
FEEDING: Spring.
PRUNING: Pull off old leaves as

they get tired. Reduce size of clump as necessary.

GENERAL COMMENTS: A useful early-flowering geranium with an attractive aromatic leaf, which often reddens in autumn.

Geranium nodosum

SOIL: Any good.

CONDITIONS: Sun or shade.

COLOUR: Pink.

FLOWERING: Spring to summer.

FEEDING: Spring.

PRUNING: None.

GENERAL COMMENTS: A useful plant that is tolerant of difficult conditions and has a very pretty bright green leaf.

Pachysandra terminalis

SOIL: Fertile.

CONDITIONS: Shade or partial shade.

COLOUR: White, but its flowers are not the point.

FLOWERING: Mid-spring.

FEEDING: Spring.

PRUNING: No need, but pull out if it gets too vigorous.

GENERAL COMMENTS: A wonderful spreading ground-cover plant under trees where little else will grow. It can be lifted and divided in early spring.

Sarcococca confusa

(sweet box or winter box)

SOIL: Moist, fertile.

CONDITIONS: Sun or shade.

COLOUR: A glossy evergreen with small white flowers.

FLOWERING: Early winter to mid-winter.

FEEDING: Spring.

PRUNING: Tidy up in summer if necessary.

GENERAL COMMENTS: Also known as sweet box or winter box because of its tiny sweet-smelling flowers in winter. It has handsome glossy foliage.

Symphoricarpos x doorenbosii

'Mother of Pearl'

SOIL: Any.

CONDITIONS: Shade to deep shade, even among tree roots and dripping trees.

COLOUR: White berries with a pink flush.

FLOWERING: Greeny white flowers in mid-summer to late summer.

FEEDING: Spring.

PRUNING: If needed, prune hard in early spring.

GENERAL COMMENTS: Not many plants will grow so happily in dark and dreary conditions.

A SUNNY BED AGAINST A WALL: WHITE

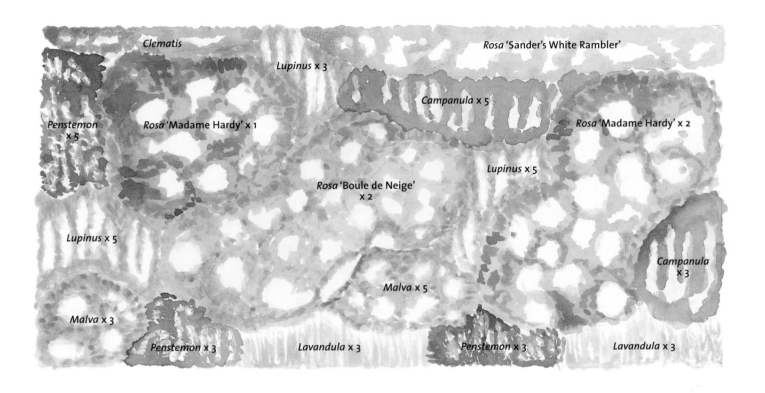

Clematis

Rosa 'Sander's White Rambler'

Lupinus x 3

Campanula x 5

Penstemon x 5

Rosa 'Madame Hardy' x 1

Rosa 'Madame Hardy' x 2

Lupinus x 5

Rosa 'Boule de Neige' x 2

Lupinus x 5

Campanula x 3

Malva x 5

Malva x 3

Penstemon x 3

Lavandula x 3

Penstemon x 3

Lavandula x 3

	THE PLANTS	QUANTITIES
1	*Malva moschata* f. 'Alba'	8
2	*Campanula pyramidalis* 'Alba'	8
3	*Clematis* 'Huldine'	1
4	*Rosa* 'Sander's White Rambler'	1
5	*Lupinus* 'Noble Maiden'	13
6	*Lavandula angustifolia* 'Alba'	6
7	*Penstemon* 'White Bedder'	11
8	*Rosa* 'Madame Hardy'	3
9	*Rosa* 'Boule de Neige'	2

SIZE AND POSITION

Campanula pyramidalis 'Alba' grows to 6ft x 24in/1.8m x 60cm. Plant 12in/30cm apart.

Clematis 'Huldine' grows to 12ft x 5ft/3.7m x 1.5m.

Lavandula angustifolia 'Alba' grows to 18in x 15in/45cm x 38cm. Plant 12in/30cm apart.

Lupinus 'Noble Maiden' grows to 36in x 14in/90cm x 35cm. Plant 12in/30cm apart.

Malva moschata f. *alba* grows to 30in x 18in/75cm x 45cm. Plant 9in/23cm apart.

Penstemon 'White Bedder' grows to 18in x 12in/45cm x 30cm. Plant 12in/30cm apart.

Rosa 'Boule de Neige' grows to 4ft x 4ft/1.2m x 1.2m.

Rosa 'Madame Hardy' grows to 4ft x 36in/1.2m x 90cm.

Rosa 'Sander's White Rambler' grows to 18ft x 8ft/5.5m x 2.5m.

ADDITIONAL PLANTING

SPRING COLOUR

In autumn:
Plant 25 *Ornithogalum balansae* bulbs and 30 *Anemone blanda* 'White Splendour' corms towards the front of the bed.

Plant as many tulip bulbs as you need to fill any spaces: white tulips in groups of 10 at the back of the bed – e.g. 'White Triumphator' or 'Maureen' – and *Tulipa* 'Diana', a shorter white, towards the middle of the bed in groups of 5.

SUMMER COLOUR

In late spring:
Plant *Nicotiana affinis* (the large, scented tobacco plant) singly in spaces to come through the edges of the roses.

GENERAL CARE

Watch out for slugs near the lupins and put down slug pellets.

Feed the bed with a general fertilizer in early spring.

Mulch the roses with manure or compost in spring.

Cut off tulip leaves as they yellow, and feed.

Spray the roses against pests and diseases if required.

Stake the lupins.

Deadhead roses as the flowers fade.

Feed the roses again with rose food in mid-summer.

Add bonemeal in autumn.

Pull out old bedding in autumn.

PLANT DETAILS

Campanula pyramidalis **'Alba'**
SOIL: Well drained but moist.
CONDITIONS: Sun or part shade.
COLOUR: White.
FLOWERING: Early summer to late summer.
FEEDING: Spring.
PRUNING: Cut off dead flower stems as they die.
GENERAL COMMENTS: The tall impressive racemes of star-shaped flowers are carried over heart-shaped leaves. It is biennial, so it will need to be replaced every year, but it is well worth growing for its performance. It will need protection from slugs and staking.

Clematis **'Huldine'**
SOIL: Rich, well fed.
CONDITIONS: Sun.
COLOUR: White.
FLOWERING: Mid-summer to early autumn.
FEEDING: With bonemeal in autumn. General fertilizer in spring. Tomato fertilizer every two weeks from late spring until flowering starts.
PRUNING: In late winter, prune hard to 12in/30cm from the base, cutting each stem above a leaf joint.
GENERAL COMMENTS: A lovely white variety. When planting, dig a good deep hole at last 12in/30cm from the wall and sprinkle in a little bonemeal. Plant deeply, so that the soil goes at least 2in/5cm up the stem. Place some crocks around the base of

the plant to shade the roots from sun. Keep well watered.

Lavandula angustifolia 'Alba'

SOIL: Ordinary, well drained.
CONDITIONS: Full sun.
COLOUR: White.
FLOWERING: Mid-summer to late summer.
FEEDING: Spring.
PRUNING: Cut off the old flower heads at the end of summer and lightly shape up any straggly growth. In spring trim over the whole plant to encourage a good shape, but do not cut back into old wood.
GENERAL COMMENTS: As lavenders hate the wet, if you are in any doubt about your soil being free-draining it is a good idea to add some grit when planting. If you want to dry the flower heads to make lavender bags etc., it is important to cut the flowers just before they open fully, when the oil is at its strongest.

Lupinus 'Noble Maiden'

SOIL: Any, but does best in well drained.
CONDITIONS: Sun or partial shade.
COLOUR: White.
FLOWERING: Early summer to late summer.
FEEDING: Spring.

PRUNING: Cut back the flower stems after first flowering and the flowers will come again.
GENERAL COMMENTS: Lupins are quite short-lived, but it is worth replacing them with new plants of the same variety when they are past their prime, as their seeds do not come true to colour. If you save the seeds, you can scatter them in a different part of the garden the following spring and wait to see what colours appear.

Malva moschata f. alba

SOIL: Fertile, well drained.
CONDITIONS: Sun.
COLOUR: White.
FLOWERING: Late spring to late summer.
FEEDING: Spring, and again with a liquid tomato feed in summer.
PRUNING: Cut back to new growth in spring.
GENERAL COMMENTS: This is an extremely worthwhile plant which produces a mass of white saucer-shaped flowers on spikes above bushy foliage. It can be quite short-lived, but it is very easy and reliable.

Penstemon 'White Bedder'

SOIL: Fertile, well drained.
CONDITIONS: Sun or partial shade.
COLOUR: White.

FLOWERING: Mid-summer to mid-autumn.
FEEDING: Spring.
PRUNING: Leave old flower stems on the plant over winter as a protection from frost, and cut the plant down by at least half in spring, to encourage good new growth.
GENERAL COMMENTS: A very useful plant, with profuse spikes of bell-shaped flowers over a long season.

Rosa 'Boule de Neige'

SOIL: Any, except sand or chalk.
CONDITIONS: Sun.
COLOUR: Creamy white.
FLOWERING: Early summer and mid-summer, and again later.
FEEDING: Spring, and again in mid-summer.
PRUNING: Cut out weak and diseased wood in winter, when the weather is not frosty, and lightly shape up the plant.
GENERAL COMMENTS: A lovely rose, with good glossy leaves and well-shaped clusters of soft, double strongly scented flowers in small clusters.

Rosa 'Madame Hardy'

SOIL: Any, except sand or chalk.
CONDITIONS: Sun.
COLOUR: White.

FLOWERING: Mid-summer to late summer.
FEEDING: Spring, and again with rose fertilizer in mid-summer.
PRUNING: In winter when it is not frosty prune out any diseased, crossing or dead branches. Reduce any spindly growth.
GENERAL COMMENTS: A true old rose with a delicious strong fragrance. Pure white, deliciously fragrant full flowers and clean light green foliage make it a wonderful rose.

Rosa 'Sander's White Rambler'

SOIL: Any, except pure sand or chalk.
CONDITIONS: Sun.
COLOUR: White.
FLOWERING: Mid-summer and late summer.
FEEDING: Spring with general fertilizer, and again in mid-summer with rose food.
PRUNING: After flowering in early autumn, trim to the size you want. Train in some of the stems horizontally, by tying to the wire, to give the plant a good structure against the wall.
GENERAL COMMENTS: Long graceful growth with sprays of dainty white flowers and a lovely scent make this a very useful rambling rose.

A SUNNY BED AGAINST A WALL:
ROSES WITH UNDERPLANTING

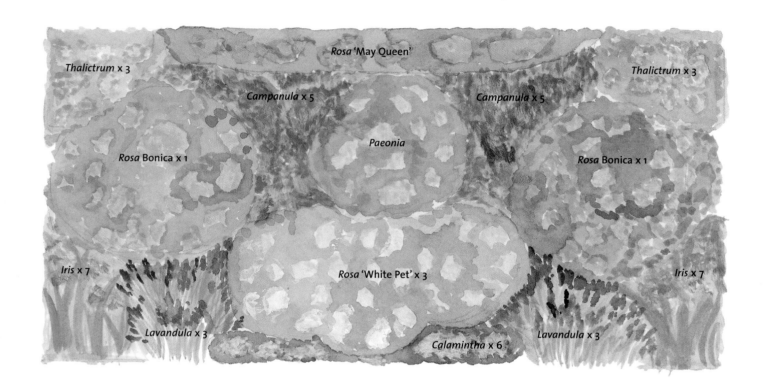

	THE PLANTS	QUANTITIES
1	*Thalictrum aquilegiifolium*	6
2	*Iris* 'Jane Phillips'	14
3	*Lavandula angustifolia* 'Twickel Purple'	6
4	*Calamintha nepeta* subsp. *nepeta*	6
5	*Campanula lactiflora* 'Prichard's Variety'	10
6	*Rosa* Bonica	2
7	*Paeonia suffruticosa* 'Yoshinogawa' (or any pale silver pink variety, e.g. *P. lactiflora* 'Clare Dubois')	1
8	*Rosa* 'May Queen'	1
9	*Rosa* 'White Pet'	3

SIZE AND POSITION

Calamintha nepeta subsp. *nepeta* grows to 8in x 8in/20cm x 20cm. Plant 8in/20cm apart.

Campanula lactiflora 'Prichard's Variety' grows to 4ft x 12in/1.2m x 30cm. Plant 12in/30cm apart.

Iris 'Jane Phillips' grows to 4ft x 12in/1.2m x 30cm. Stagger planting 12in/30cm apart.

Lavandula angustifolia 'Twickel Purple' grows to 24in x 30in/60cm x 75cm. Plant 18in/45cm apart.

Paeonia 'Yoshinogawa' grows to 36in x 36in/90cm x 90cm.

Rosa Bonica grows to 36in x 4ft/90cm x 1.2m.

Rosa 'White Pet' grows to 24in x 30in/60cm x 75cm spread. Plant 18in/45cm apart.

Rosa 'May Queen' grows to 25ft x 8ft/7.5m x 2.5m.

Thalictrum aquilegiifolium grows to 4ft x 24in/1.2m x 60cm. Plant 12in/30cm apart.

ADDITIONAL PLANTING

SPRING COLOUR

In autumn:
Plant 60 tulip bulbs towards the back in 15 of each variety, e.g. 'White Triumphator', 'Maureen', 'Bellflower', 'Picture' and 'China Pink'.

Plant 50 *Anemone blanda* corms in mixed colours all over the bed.

In spring:
Plant 15 pink *Primula* Pink Posy Series in clumps of 5 towards the front of the bed.

SUMMER COLOUR

In mid-spring:
Sprinkle seeds of *Nigella damascena* Persian Jewels Series (love-in-a-mist) in white, pink and blue all over the bed.

GENERAL CARE

Feed with a general fertilizer in spring.

Stake the thalictrums if necessary.

Cut back and feed the tulips as they yellow.

Watch the roses for pests and diseases and spray if required.

Deadhead the roses.

Feed the roses again in mid-summer with rose food.

Cut off lavender spikes after flowering.

Pull out the nigella as it finishes flowering and compost.

PLANT DETAILS

Calamintha nepeta **subsp.** *nepeta*
SOIL: Any.
CONDITIONS: Sun or part shade.
COLOUR: Pale blue.
FLOWERING: Early summer to early autumn.
FEEDING: Spring.
PRUNING: Cut old flowering stems back to base in autumn.
GENERAL COMMENTS: Has neat clumps of very aromatic leaves with sprays of blue mint-like flowers which are borne over a long flowering season. This is not a show-stopping plant, but it quietly sustains a reliable performance throughout the summer. Bees love it.

Campanula lactiflora **'Prichard's Variety'**
SOIL: Moist, rich.
CONDITIONS: Sun or partial shade.
COLOUR: Purple blue.
FLOWERING: Mid-summer to mid-autumn.
FEEDING: Spring.
PRUNING: Cut back the old flowering stems as they finish.
GENERAL COMMENTS: A very good plant with roses.

Iris **'Jane Phillips'**
SOIL: Well drained, with really sharp drainage.
CONDITIONS: Full sun.
COLOUR: Soft blue.
FLOWERING: Late spring to mid-summer.
FEEDING: Feed with bonemeal in mid-winter, and with a general fertilizer in spring.

PRUNING: Cut the leaves into a fan shape about 9in/23cm above ground in late summer.
GENERAL COMMENTS: A lovely gentle blue and good strong leaves make this an invaluable plant.

Lavandula angustifolia **'Twickel Purple'**
SOIL: Any well drained.
CONDITIONS: Full sun.
COLOUR: Deep purple blue.
FLOWERING: Early summer to late summer.
FEEDING: Spring.
PRUNING: Clip off the old flower heads after flowering. In spring clip over the whole plant to shape it up, but do not cut right back into old wood.
GENERAL COMMENTS: A beautiful strong-coloured lavender.

Paeonia, **any pale silver pink variety**
SOIL: Deep, enriched with manure or leaf mould.
CONDITIONS: Sun.
COLOUR: Pale silver pink.
FLOWERING: Late spring to mid-summer.
FEEDING: Spring.
PRUNING: Cut off the old leaves in autumn.
GENERAL COMMENTS: Once planted, peonies do not like to be moved. The heads are heavy, and so you will need to stake the plant.

Rosa **Bonica**
SOIL: Any except pure sand or chalk.
CONDITIONS: Sun.
COLOUR: Rose pink.
FLOWERING: Early summer to mid-autumn.
FEEDING: Spring with general fertilizer and mid-summer with rose food.
PRUNING: In winter, prune as hard as necessary to keep to a good shape and healthy growth.
GENERAL COMMENTS: There is nothing spectacular about this rose, but it is robust and tidy with many sprays of small pink flowers over a long season. It is tough, reliable and disease-free.

Rosa **'White Pet'**
SOIL: Any except pure chalk or sand.
CONDITIONS: Sun.
COLOUR: White flowers from pink buds.
FLOWERING: Summer, and again later.
FEEDING: Spring with a general fertilizer and again in mid-summer with rose food.
PRUNING: In winter, when the weather is not frosty, prune lightly all over.
GENERAL COMMENTS: A beautiful rose that flowers really well. Its only flaw is that the old flowers make a mass of brown heads on the plant and need to be clipped off. If you can, wait until the whole bush is brown and go over it all with garden shears. It will soon start flowering again.

Rosa **'May Queen'**
SOIL: Any, except sand or chalk.
CONDITIONS: Sun.
COLOUR: Rose pink.
FLOWERING: Late spring to early summer.
FEEDING: In spring with a general fertilizer, and in mid-summer with rose food.
PRUNING: In early autumn cut out dead wood and growth that is too dense.
GENERAL COMMENTS: A very pretty Rambler with large rose-pink blooms on good strong growth. It flowers early but is well worth growing for its beautiful display and delicate scent. Make sure it is planted at least 12in/30cm away from the base of the wall.

Thalictrum aquilegiifolium
SOIL: Any, but prefers moist, rich.
CONDITIONS: Sun or light shade.
COLOUR: Pinkish mauve.
FLOWERING: Late spring to early summer.
FEEDING: In spring with a general fertilizer; also likes to have a dressing of manure in early spring.
PRUNING: In late autumn cut the stalks down to 12in/30cm.
GENERAL COMMENTS: Lovely grey-green leaves like a maidenhair fern. It is a very pretty plant, which looks good planted anywhere.

A SUNNY BED AGAINST A WALL: ROSES WITH UNDERPLANTING

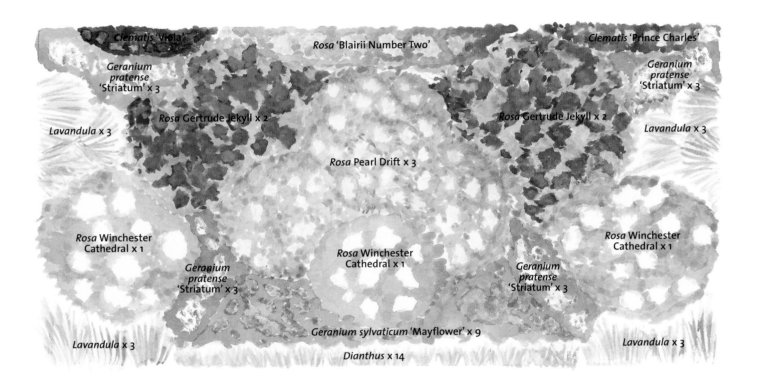

Clematis 'Viola'

Rosa 'Blairii Number Two'

Clematis 'Prince Charles'

Geranium pratense 'Striatum' x 3

Geranium pratense 'Striatum' x 3

Rosa Gertrude Jekyll x 2

Rosa Gertrude Jekyll x 2

Lavandula x 3

Lavandula x 3

Rosa Pearl Drift x 3

Rosa Winchester Cathedral x 1

Rosa Winchester Cathedral x 1

Rosa Winchester Cathedral x 1

Geranium pratense 'Striatum' x 3

Geranium pratense 'Striatum' x 3

Geranium sylvaticum 'Mayflower' x 9

Lavandula x 3

Lavandula x 3

Dianthus x 14

	THE PLANTS	QUANTITIES
1	*Clematis* 'Prince Charles'	1
2	*Clematis* 'Viola'	1
3	*Geranium sylvaticum* 'Mayflower'	9
4	*Rosa* 'Blairii Number Two'	1
5	*Geranium pratense* 'Striatum'	12
6	*Rosa* Winchester Cathedral	3
7	*Rosa* Gertrude Jekyll	4
8	*Dianthus* 'Mrs Sinkins'	14
9	*Rosa* Pearl Drift	3
10	*Lavandula angustifolia* 'Alba'	12

SIZE AND POSITION

Clematis 'Viola' grows to 8ft x 4ft/2.5m x 1.2m.

Clematis 'Prince Charles' grows to 12ft x 36in/3.7m x 90cm.

Dianthus 'Mrs Sinkins' grows to 8in x 8in/20cm x 20cm. Plant 6in/15cm apart.

Geranium pratense 'Striatum' grows to 36in x 12in/90cm x 30cm. Plant 12in/30cm apart.

Geranium sylvaticum 'Mayflower' grows to 24in x 18in/60cm x 45cm. Plant 12in/30cm apart.

Lavandula angustifolia 'Alba' grows to 18in x 15in/45cm x 38cm. Plant 12in/30cm apart.

Rosa 'Blairii Number Two' grows to 12ft x 8ft/3.7m x 2.5m.

Rosa Gertrude Jekyll grows to 4ft x 3½ft/1.2m x 1.1m. Plant 24in/60cm apart.

Rosa Pearl Drift grows to 3½ x 3½ft/1.1m x 1.1m. Plant 30in/75cm apart.

Rosa Winchester Cathedral grows to 4ft x 4ft/1.2m x 1.2m.

ADDITIONAL PLANTING

SPRING COLOUR

In autumn:
Plant 100 scilla bulbs all over the bed.

Plant 50 *Fritillaria meleagris* bulbs in mixed colours in groups of 5 in any gaps.

Plant the following tulips: 10 *T.* Bakeri Group 'Lilac Wonder' at the front of the bed, and 10 'Lilac Time', 10 'Swan Wings', 10 'Burgundy Lace', 10 'Eros' and 10 'Angélique', in groups of 5 of each type, throughout the bed.

SUMMER COLOUR

In spring:
Plant 20 white *Dianthus barbatus* (sweet Williams) in groups of 5.

Plant pansies (*Viola* x *wittrockiana*) and violas in pale blue and pale pink – 15 of each type – to fill in any gaps towards the front of the bed.

Sprinkle seeds of *Nigella damascena* 'Miss Jeykll' (love-in-a-mist) in any gaps.

In late spring:
Plant 5 *Senecio cineraria* (silver leaf) in any gaps.

GENERAL CARE

Wire the wall with vine eyes.

Feed the whole bed in spring with a general fertilizer.

Put crocks on the soil around the base of the clematis, to help keep it cool.

Keep the rose and the clematis carefully tied in.

Trim over lavender after flowering and again in mid-spring to shape it up.

Keep deadheading the roses and the dianthus throughout the summer to encourage more flowers.

Feed the roses again in mid-summer with rose food.

Feed the clematis with tomato fertilizer every three weeks while they are flowering.

Cut back the geraniums after flowering.

Tidy through the bed in winter and mulch the roses and the clematis with manure or leaf mould.

PLANT DETAILS

Clematis 'Prince Charles'
SOIL: Good, deep, enriched with manure or leaf mould.
CONDITIONS: Sun or part shade.
COLOUR: Pale blue.
FLOWERING: From early summer to early autumn.
FEEDING: Spring, with a general fertilizer, and every two weeks with a liquid plant food.
PRUNING: Prune each stem down to 12in/30cm in late winter, cutting above a pair of healthy buds.
GENERAL COMMENTS: The flowers start as bells and open out as they age. It looks lovely with roses.

Clematis 'Viola'
SOIL: Good, rich.
CONDITIONS: Sun or part shade.
COLOUR: Deep purple with golden stamens.
FLOWERING: Mid-summer to early autumn.
FEEDING: Spring, with a general fertilizer, and every two weeks with a liquid fertilizer.
PRUNING: Prune down to 12in/30cm in late winter, cutting above a pair of healthy buds.
GENERAL COMMENTS: A colour that goes with everything, and a very profuse flowerer.

Dianthus 'Mrs Sinkins'
SOIL: Any well drained.
CONDITIONS: Full sun.
COLOUR: White.
FLOWERING: Early summer to mid-summer with a wonderful scent.
FEEDING: Bonemeal in late autumn. In spring a fertilizer high

in potash, and again in early summer/mid-summer.

PRUNING: Cut off the old flower heads and stalks as they go over and tidy up the clump in spring.

GENERAL COMMENTS: Make sure that you keep the plant free from winter leaves and debris, as it really hates being covered up. When planting, do not plant too deep, as it hates the stems being buried. It looks tired until the last moment, but will suddenly sprout in April. The plants are quite short-lived and will need replacing from time to time.

Geranium pratense 'Striatum'

SOIL: Any well drained.
CONDITIONS: Sun or part shade.
COLOUR: White flowers, streaked and spotted with blue.
FLOWERING: Late spring to mid-summer.
FEEDING: Spring.
PRUNING: Cut back after flowering.
GENERAL COMMENTS: This geranium is lovely and fresh-looking, especially when grown with roses.

Geranium sylvaticum 'Mayflower'

SOIL: Any well drained.
CONDITIONS: Full sun or part shade.

COLOUR: Blue with a white eye.
FLOWERING: Late spring to early summer.
FEEDING: Spring.
PRUNING: Cut back after flowering, to encourage more flowers later in the year.
GENERAL COMMENTS: An early-flowering geranium with a good leaf shape.

Lavandula angustifolia 'Alba'

SOIL: Ordinary, well drained.
CONDITIONS: Full sun.
COLOUR: White.
FLOWERING: Mid-summer to early autumn.
FEEDING: Spring.
PRUNING: Cut off the old flower heads as soon as flowering is over. Trim over the whole bush in spring, removing straggly growth and shaping it into a neat mound, but do not cut back into old wood.
GENERAL COMMENTS: If you wish to dry flowers to make lavender bags etc., cut off the flowers before they fully open when the oil is at its freshest. Lavenders really hate the wet, so if there is any danger of the soil being too heavy mix in some grit with the soil when planting.

Rosa 'Blairii Number Two'

SOIL: Good, rich.
CONDITIONS: Sun.
COLOUR: Pale pink.

FLOWERING: Late spring to early summer.
FEEDING: Spring with a general fertilizer, and in mid-summer with rose food.
PRUNING: In autumn cut out any diseased or dead wood, and any badly placed branches. It does not like much pruning, but if the old flower stems look too long the job is best done after flowering.
GENERAL COMMENTS: It has a short flowering season, but is a beautiful rose with a wonderful smell.

Rosa Gertrude Jekyll

SOIL: Good.
CONDITIONS: Full sun.
COLOUR: Deep pink.
FLOWERING: Early summer and repeats well.
FEEDING: Spring and again in mid-summer with rose food.
PRUNING: In winter, when the weather is not frosty, remove weak or diseased wood and prune down to 24in/60cm.
GENERAL COMMENTS: A beautiful rose with the very best scent. It is well worth growing, although it does not naturally grow into a neat shape.

Rosa Pearl Drift

SOIL: Good, rich.
CONDITIONS: Full sun.
COLOUR: White-pink.

FLOWERING: Early summer to mid-autumn.
FEEDING: Spring with a general fertilizer, and in mid-summer with rose food.
PRUNING: In winter when it is not frosty, prune to shape up and to remove any weak, crossing, dead or diseased wood. It can be pruned hard.
GENERAL COMMENTS: A reliable rose with a semi-double flower. It has little disease, and is in flower for many months.

Rosa Winchester Cathedral

SOIL: Good, rich.
CONDITIONS: Full sun.
COLOUR: White.
FLOWERING: Starts in early summer and repeats well throughout the summer.
FEEDING: Spring with a general fertilizer, and in mid-summer with a rose food.
PRUNING: In winter, when the weather is not frosty, cut out any badly placed, spindly, dead or diseased wood. Cut back the shrub to a good strong framework; it does not mind being pruned hard.
GENERAL COMMENTS: This is a good white rose with a strong scent which looks lovely planted alone or with many others.

A SUNNY BED AGAINST A WALL: ROSES WITH UNDERPLANTING

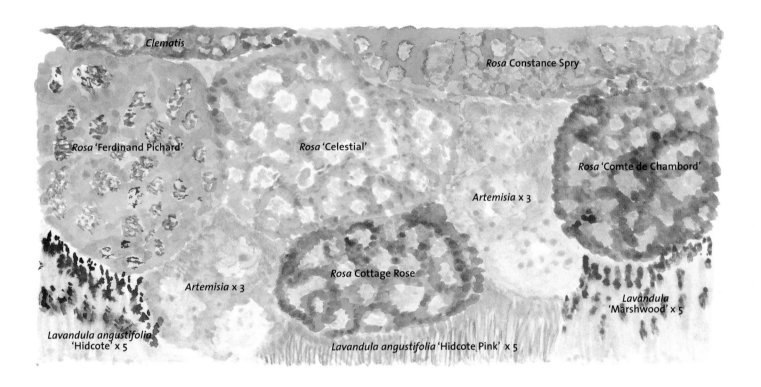

Clematis

Rosa Constance Spry

Rosa 'Ferdinand Pichard'

Rosa 'Celestial'

Rosa 'Comte de Chambord'

Artemisia x 3

Rosa Cottage Rose

Artemisia x 3

Lavandula 'Marshwood' x 5

Lavandula angustifolia 'Hidcote' x 5

Lavandula angustifolia 'Hidcote Pink' x 5

	THE PLANTS	QUANTITIES
1	*Lavandula* 'Marshwood'	5
2	*Rosa* Constance Spry	1
3	*Rosa* 'Celestial' (also named 'Céleste')	1
4	*Rosa* 'Comte de Chambord' (syn. *Rosa* 'Madame Knorr')	1
5	*Artemisia ludoviciana* 'Silver Queen'	6
6	*Lavandula angustifolia* 'Hidcote'	5
7	*Rosa* Cottage Rose	1
8	*Rosa* 'Ferdinand Pichard'	1
9	*Lavandula angustifolia* 'Hidcote Pink'	5
10	*Clematis* 'Margot Koster'	1

SIZE AND POSITION

Artemisia ludoviciana 'Silver Queen' grows to 36in x 24in/90cm x 60cm. Plant 15in/38cm apart.

Clematis 'Margot Koster' grows to 10ft x 5ft/3m x 1.5m.

Lavandula angustifolia 'Hidcote' grows to 18in x 15in/45cm x 38cm. Plant 12in/30cm apart.

Lavandula angustifolia 'Hidcote Pink' grows to 15in x 15in/38cm x 38cm. Plant 12in/30cm apart.

Lavandula 'Marshwood' grows to 15in x 15in/38cm x 38cm. Plant 12in/30cm apart.

Rosa 'Celestial' grows to 5ft x 36in/1.5m x 90cm.

Rosa 'Comte de Chambord' grows to 4ft x 36in/1.2m x 90cm.

Rosa Constance Spry grown as a climber grows to 12ft x 8ft/3.7m x 2.5m.

Rosa Cottage Rose grows to 3½ft x 30in/1.1m x 75cm.

Rosa 'Ferdinand Pichard' grows to 4ft x 4ft/1.2m x 1.2m.

ADDITIONAL PLANTING

SPRING COLOUR

In autumn:
Plant the following tulip bulbs in groups of 10 all over the bed: 20 'Ballade', 20 'Fancy Frills', 20 'Blue Parrot' and 20 'Purissima'.

Plant 100 *Chionodoxa luciliae* 'Alba' bulbs throughout the bed.

SUMMER COLOUR

In autumn:
Plant 10 *Camassia leichtlinii* 'Alba' bulbs in two groups of 5.

In autumn or spring:
Plant 15 *Lilium speciosum* var. *rubrum* bulbs in groups of 5 among the artemisia and in front of the Cottage Rose.

In spring:
Plant blue, white and pink violas in any gaps in the bed.

In mid-spring:
Sprinkle seeds of *Nigella damascena* Persian Jewels Series (love-in-a-mist) around the base of the roses.

In late spring:
Plant 20 white cleomes in spaces throughout the bed.

GENERAL CARE

Wire the wall with vine eyes.

Mulch the roses and clematis at any time between early winter and early spring, and feed the bed with a general fertilizer in spring.

Keep the Constance Spry rose and the clematis well tied in.

Cut the artemisia back by about 12in/30cm when you notice it is going to flower, to keep the leaves silver.

Cut the tulip leaves back as they yellow, and feed.

In late autumn pick up dead leaves.

Keep the roses well deadheaded, and feed again with rose food in mid-summer.

Cut off the lavender flower stalks as they finish flowering.

PLANT DETAILS

Artemisia ludoviciana **'Silver Queen'**
SOIL: Well drained.
CONDITIONS: Sun.
COLOUR: Grown for its lovely silver leaves.
FLOWERING: Do not let it flower.
FEEDING: Spring.
PRUNING: Cut back to new strong buds in mid-spring. When you notice flower buds appearing, cut the foliage back by about 12in/30cm and keep cutting back throughout the season whenever you notice flower buds, as this will encourage new growth, which is the most silvery.
GENERAL COMMENTS: The bright silver foliage acts as a very good foil for other plants, especially roses.

Clematis **'Margot Koster'**
SOIL: Good, rich.
CONDITIONS: Sun or part shade.
COLOUR: Strong rose pink.
FLOWERING: Mid-summer to early autumn.
FEEDING: In spring with a general fertilizer and in summer every two to three weeks with a liquid feed.
PRUNING: In late winter, cut back each stem to 12in/30cm, cutting above a pair of strong buds.
GENERAL COMMENTS: A lovely climber with plenty of flowers over a long period.

Lavandula angustifolia '**Hidcote' and** *L.a.* '**Hidcote Pink'**

SOIL: Light, well drained.
CONDITIONS: Sun.
COLOUR: Deep purple blue and soft pale pink.
FLOWERING: Early summer to early autumn.
FEEDING: Spring.
PRUNING: Cut off flower stems as they die. Trim the whole plant in mid-spring, making sure that you do not cut back into old wood.
GENERAL COMMENTS: These lavenders are compact and neat and perform well throughout the summer. They hate the wet, so if you are in any doubt about the suitability of your soil mix in a handful of grit when planting.

Lavandula '**Marshwood'**

SOIL: Any well drained.
CONDITIONS: Sun.
COLOUR: Deep purple with paler ears.
FLOWERING: Mid-summer to late summer.
FEEDING: General fertilizer in spring.
PRUNING: Take off old flower stalks as they finish flowering. Shape up in spring by trimming lightly over the whole plant.
GENERAL COMMENTS: Best planted in groups.

Rosa **Constance Spry**

SOIL: Any good, which is not pure chalk or sand.
CONDITIONS: Sun.
COLOUR: Warm true pink.
FLOWERING: A good flush in early summer.
FEEDING: Spring with a general fertilizer, and in mid-summer with a rose food.
PRUNING: This is a shrub rose which is often grown as a climber. It has rather lax, untidy growth and you need to take a firm hand to establish a good shape from the beginning. It can be pruned as hard as necessary in autumn.
GENERAL COMMENTS: As well as almost luminous pink flowers it has a wonderful fragrance.

Rosa **Cottage Rose**

SOIL: Any except chalk.
CONDITIONS: Sun.
COLOUR: Warm pink.
FLOWERING: Early summer to early autumn.
FEEDING: General fertilizer in spring and a rose food in mid-summer.
PRUNING: In winter, cut out any dead, crossing, damaged or diseased wood and create a good framework of strong branches. You can cut it back quite hard if necessary.

GENERAL COMMENTS: A really good rose with many merits. It flowers continuously, it smells delicious and it is tough. We love it.

Rosa '**Comte de Chambord'**

SOIL: Any good, except chalk.
CONDITIONS: Sun.
COLOUR: Warm pink.
FLOWERING: Early summer to mid-summer, repeating in early autumn to mid-autumn.
FEEDING: General fertilizer in spring and a rose food in mid-summer.
PRUNING: In winter, cut out weak, diseased or badly placed wood, and reduce the growth a little to establish a good shape.
GENERAL COMMENTS: One of our real favourites, a repeat-flowering old rose with wonderful scent and colour. It is easy to grow and very reliable.

Rosa '**Celestial'**

SOIL: Any good, which is not chalk or sand.
CONDITIONS: Sun.
COLOUR: Pale pink.
FLOWERING: Early summer and mid-summermer.
FEEDING: General fertilizer in spring and a rose food in mid-summer.

PRUNING: In late winter, when the weather is not frosty, remove any dead, diseased or badly placed stems, and lightly shape.
GENERAL COMMENTS: Makes a beautifully shaped bush with healthy flowers followed by hips.

Rosa '**Ferdinand Pichard'**

SOIL: Any that is not sand or chalk.
CONDITIONS: Sun or partial shade.
COLOUR: Pink flowers striped with crimson and purple.
FLOWERING: Early summer to mid-summer and early autumn to mid-autumn.
FEEDING: General fertilizer in spring and a rose food in mid-summer.
PRUNING: A light prune in winter is all this rose will need. It does not like hard pruning.
GENERAL COMMENTS: A good-shaped plant with a rich scent. The flowers are the best of the striped varieties.

A SUNNY BED AGAINST A WALL:
BLUE, WHITE AND PALE PINK

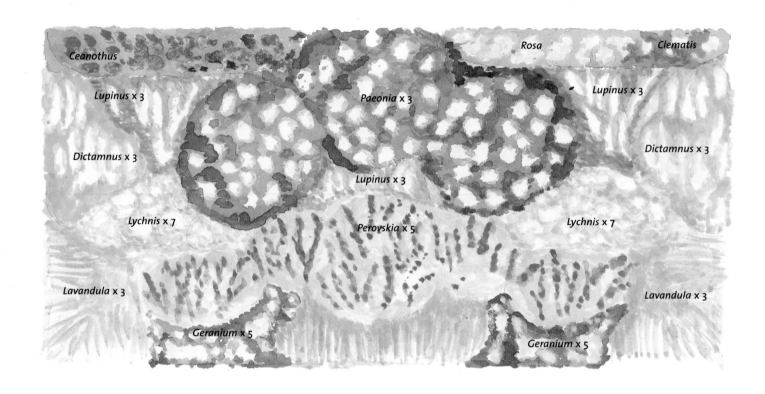

Ceanothus

Rosa

Clematis

Lupinus x 3

Paeonia x 3

Lupinus x 3

Dictamnus x 3

Dictamnus x 3

Lupinus x 3

Lychnis x 7

Perovskia x 5

Lychnis x 7

Lavandula x 3

Lavandula x 3

Geranium x 5

Geranium x 5

	THE PLANTS	QUANTITIES
1	*Clematis* 'Betty Corning'	1
2	*Perovskia* 'Blue Spire'	5
3	*Ceanothus* 'Puget Blue'	1
4	*Geranium renardii*	10
5	*Paeonia lactiflora* 'Duchesse de Nemours' (or any double white variety)	3
6	*Lavandula angustifolia* 'Hidcote Pink'	9
7	*Rosa* 'Blush Noisette' (also known as *Rosa* 'Noisette Carnée')	1
8	*Lychnis coronaria* 'Alba'	14
9	*Lupinus* 'Noble Maiden'	9
10	*Dictamnus albus*	6

SIZE AND POSITION

Ceanothus 'Puget Blue' grows to 5ft x 4ft/1.5m x 1.2m.

Clematis 'Betty Corning' grows to 10ft x 36in/3m x 90cm.

Dictamnus albus grows to 15in x 15in/38cm x 38cm. Plant 12in/30cm apart.

Geranium renardii grows to 9in x 12in/23cm x 30cm. Plant 6in/15cm apart.

Lavandula angustifolia 'Hidcote Pink' grows to 15 x 15in/38cm x 38cm. Plant 12in/30cm apart.

Lupinus 'Noble Maiden' grows to 36in x 24in/90cm x 60cm. Plant 12in/30cm apart.

Lychnis coronaria 'Alba' grows to 24in x 12in/60cm x 30cm. Plant 6in/15cm apart.

Paeonia lactiflora 'Duchesse de Nemours' grows to 36in x 36in/90cm x 90cm. Plant 24in/60cm apart.

Perovskia 'Blue Spire' grows to 36in x 18in/90cm x 45cm. Plant 18in/45cm apart.

Rosa 'Blush Noisette' grows to 8ft x 5ft/2.5m x 1.5m.

ADDITIONAL PLANTING

SPRING COLOUR

In autumn or spring:
Plant 10 *Myosotis* (forget-me-nots) throughout the bed.

In autumn:
Plant tulip bulbs in groups of 5 – e.g. 'Shirley', 'China Pink' and 'Queen of Night' – in any spaces.

Plant 50 *Chionodoxa gigantea* bulbs throughout the bed.

Plant 50 *Narcissus* 'Hawera' bulbs throughout the bed.

SUMMER COLOUR

In autumn:
Plant 10 *Allium hollandicum* 'Purple Sensation' bulbs all around the perovskia.

In spring:
Sprinkle seeds of *Nigella damascena* 'Miss Jekyll' (blue love-in-a-mist) in spaces in the bed.

Plant verbena in very pale pink (e.g. 'Silver Anne') in groups of 5 behind the *Geranium renardii*.

GENERAL CARE

Wire the walls with vine eyes.

Clean the bed up in spring and mulch around the rose, ceanothus and peonies.

Keep the rose and clematis tied in with string. Use old tights to tie in the ceanothus as the stems are heavy and string will break.

Feed with a general fertilizer in spring, and feed the rose again in mid-summer.

Stake the peonies.

PLANT DETAILS

Ceanothus 'Puget Blue'
SOIL: Any.
CONDITIONS: Sun.
COLOUR: Blue.
FLOWERING: Mid-spring to late spring, and a few flowers in autumn.
FEEDING: Spring, and again after flowering.
PRUNING: In spring, after flowering, train against the wall by cutting off the stems that grow out into the bed, and reduce height and width to keep the plant tidy.
GENERAL COMMENTS: This ceanothus has a mass of flowers in spring, and small dark leaves. It is a tough and compact variety.

Clematis 'Betty Corning'
SOIL: Good, enriched with manure or leaf mould.
CONDITIONS: Sun or part shade, with crocks at the roots to keep them cool.
COLOUR: Pale violet fading to white.
FLOWERING: Early summer until autumn.
FEEDING: Spring.
PRUNING: In late winter, cut each stem down to 12in/30cm above a pair of buds.
GENERAL COMMENTS: A lovely scented clematis with nodding bell-shaped flowers.

Dictamnus albus
SOIL: Well drained but not acid.
CONDITIONS: Sun.
COLOUR: White.

FLOWERING: Early summer to mid-summer.
FEEDING: Feed in spring with a general fertilizer and mulch with leaf mould in spring and autumn.
PRUNING: Cut to the ground in mid-autumn.
GENERAL COMMENTS: Does not like to be disturbed once established. It is not the easiest of plants, but is well worth trying as it is so pretty.

Geranium renardii
SOIL: Good, well drained.
CONDITIONS: Sun, part shade or shade.
COLOUR: White with purple veining.
FLOWERING: Late spring to early summer.
FEEDING: Spring.
PRUNING: Trim after flowering. Take off any dead leaves.
GENERAL COMMENTS: A very pretty geranium with a compact clump of dark green lobed leaves.

Lavandula angustifolia 'Hidcote Pink'
SOIL: Light, well drained.
CONDITIONS: Sun.
COLOUR: Pale pink.
FLOWERING: Early summer to early autumn.
FEEDING: Spring.
PRUNING: Cut off the dead flowers as soon as they fade, and trim over the whole bush again in mid-spring, but do not cut back into old wood.
GENERAL COMMENTS: A pretty soft pink lavender.

Lupinus 'Noble Maiden'
SOIL: Well drained.
CONDITIONS: Sun or part shade.
COLOUR: White
FLOWERING: Early summer to late summer.
FEEDING: Spring.
PRUNING: Cut back after first flowering and you will encourage a second flush of flowers.
GENERAL COMMENTS: You can save the seed pods and scatter them elsewhere in the garden. Lupins do not come true from seed, so you are likely to get a variety of colours.

Lychnis coronaria 'Alba'
SOIL: Well drained.
CONDITIONS: Sun or light shade.
COLOUR: White.
FLOWERING: Mid-summer to early autumn.
FEEDING: Spring.
PRUNING: Deadhead. Cut off stems and pull out any messy old plants in autumn.
GENERAL COMMENTS: Rather a short-lived plant, but it self-seeds so you are likely to find it cropping up near by, in which case you can transplant it.

Paeonia lactiflora 'Duchesse de Nemours'
SOIL: Deep, rich.
CONDITIONS: Sun.
COLOUR: White.
FLOWERING: Late spring to early summer.
FEEDING: Autumn with bonemeal. Mulch in early spring with well-rotted manure.
PRUNING: Deadhead. Cut to the ground in autumn.
GENERAL COMMENTS: A long-lasting double-flowered peony which is reliable and fragrant.

Perovskia 'Blue Spire'
SOIL: Well drained, light, including chalk.
CONDITIONS: Sun.
COLOUR: Violet blue.
FLOWERING: Late summer to early autumn.
FEEDING: Spring.
PRUNING: Leave the old flower stems on over the winter and cut back to 12in/30cm in spring.
GENERAL COMMENTS: Has good grey-white foliage which looks good with roses. Although it is a shrub it has a lovely light look, with finely cut leaves.

Rosa 'Blush Noisette'
SOIL: Any, except sand and pure chalk.
CONDITIONS: Sun.
COLOUR: Blush pink or pale lilac pink.
FLOWERING: Produces sprays of semi-double flowers almost continuously from mid-spring onwards.
FEEDING: Spring, and again in mid-summer with rose food.
PRUNING: Cut out dead wood, but otherwise restrict pruning to a minimum as it does not respond well to being cut.
GENERAL COMMENTS: A really lovely rose, which is healthy and full of flowers over a long period. Has a delicate scent and no faults. We love it.

A SUNNY BED AGAINST A WALL: MIXED COLOURS

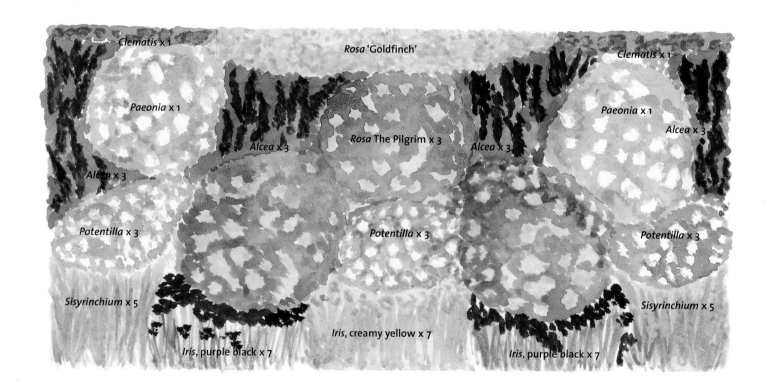

Clematis x 1
Rosa 'Goldfinch'
Clematis x 1
Paeonia x 1
Paeonia x 1
Alcea x 3
Alcea x 3
Rosa The Pilgrim x 3
Alcea x 3
Alcea x 3
Potentilla x 3
Potentilla x 3
Potentilla x 3
Sisyrinchium x 5
Sisyrinchium x 5
Iris, creamy yellow x 7
Iris, purple black x 7
Iris, purple black x 7

	THE PLANTS	QUANTITIES
1	*Rosa* The Pilgrim	3
2	*Clematis* 'Carmencita'	2
3	*Paeonia*, any white variety (e.g. *P. lactiflora* 'White Wings' or *P. suffrutucosa* 'Joseph Rock', also named *P. rockii*)	2
4	*Rosa* 'Goldfinch'	1
5	*Potentilla rupestris*	9
6	*Sisyrinchium striatum*	10
7	*Alcea rosea* 'Nigra'	12
8	*Iris*, any creamy yellow variety with light purple falls (e.g. 'Sally Jane' or 'Pale Shades')	7
9	*Iris*, any purple black variety (e.g. 'Superstition' or 'Deep Black')	14

SIZE AND POSITION

Alcea rosea 'Nigra' grows to 6ft x 18in/1.8m x 45cm. Plant 18in/45cm apart.

Clematis 'Carmencita' grows to 12ft x 36in/3.7m x 90cm.

The creamy yellow irises with light purple falls grow to 36in x 8in/90cm x 20cm. Plant 6in/15cm apart.

The purple black irises grow up to 4ft x 8in/1.2m x 20cm. Plant 6in/15cm apart.

The peonies grow up to 30in x 24in/75cm x 60cm.

Potentilla rupestris leaves grow to 24in x 18in/60cm x 45cm. Plant 12in/30cm apart.

Rosa 'Goldfinch' grows to 15ft x 8ft/4.5m x 2.5m. Plant 12in/30cm away from the wall.

Rosa The Pilgrim grows to 36in x 36in/90cm x 90cm. Plant 24in/60cm apart.

Sisyrinchium striatum grows to 18in x 12in/45cm x 30cm. Plant 12in/30cm apart.

ADDITIONAL PLANTING

SPRING COLOUR

In autumn:
Plant 50 *Tulipa* Bakeri Group 'Lilac Wonder' bulbs towards the front of the bed, and 50 *T.* 'Maja' and 50 'Queen of Night' bulbs in groups of 10 throughout the bed.

In spring:
Plant 20 violas throughout the bed. We suggest any lemon variety or 'Molly Sanderson' (black).

SUMMER COLOUR

In late spring:
Plant white cleomes, dotted through the bed in gaps. They grow up to 4ft/1.2m.

In mid-spring:
Scatter seeds of *Nemophila menziesii* 'Penny Black' and *Limnanthes douglasii* (poached egg plant) throughout the bed.

GENERAL CARE

Wire the wall with vine eyes.
Feed the whole bed in spring.
Keep climbers well tied in with string.
Keep an eye out for diseases and pests on roses – e.g. greenfly, white powdery mildew, black spot – and spray if required.
Take out old bedding in autumn and compost.

PLANT DETAILS

Alcea rosea **'Nigra' (hollyhock)**
SOIL: Any.
CONDITIONS: Sun.
COLOUR: Deep maroon/black.
FLOWERING: Early summer to mid-summer.
FEEDING: Spring.
PRUNING: Cut down old flowering stems in autumn.
GENERAL COMMENTS: Tends to self-seed, so keep an eye out for seedlings and transplant them to another part of the garden. It also tends to get rust: we spray with unpasteurized milk in spring to help combat this.

Clematis **'Carmencita'**
SOIL: Good, rich, with added manure or leaf mould.
CONDITIONS: Sun or partial shade.
COLOUR: Carmine.
FLOWERING: Early summer to mid-autumn.
FEEDING: Spring.
PRUNING: Prune each stem down to 12in/30cm in late winter.
GENERAL COMMENTS: Make sure that you put crocks around the roots to keep them cool. This is another very pretty clematis; you cannot plant too many of these climbers.

*Iris***, pale yellow cream with light purple falls**
SOIL: Light, well drained.
CONDITIONS: Sun.
COLOUR: Straw yellow, cream and light purple.

FLOWERING: Late spring to early summer.
FEEDING: Spring.
PRUNING: In late summer cut the leaves into a fan shape about 9in/23cm high.
GENERAL COMMENTS: Irises are valuable plants for adding structure to the border, and the flowers of 'Sally Jane' or 'Pale Shades' are a lovely combination of colours. They can be divided and replanted in mid-summer. When planting, mound up the soil and place the iris rhizome on top, allowing only the roots to go into the soil. The rhizome likes to be baked by the sun.

Iris, any purple black variety
SOIL: Light, with really sharp drainage.
CONDITIONS: Sun.
COLOUR: Glossy purple black.
FLOWERING: Late spring to early summer.
FEEDING: Spring.
PRUNING: In late summer cut the leaves into a fan shape about 9in/23cm high.
GENERAL COMMENTS: 'Deep Black' is a very stately iris with wonderful flower colouring. When planting, mound up the soil and place the iris rhizome on top, allowing only the roots to go into the soil. The

rhizome likes to be baked by the sun. Can be divided and replanted in mid-summer.

Paeonia, any white variety
SOIL: Good, enriched with manure or leaf mould.
CONDITIONS: Sun.
COLOUR: White.
FLOWERING: Late spring to early summer.
FEEDING: Spring.
PRUNING: Cut off old foliage in autumn.
GENERAL COMMENTS: It will need some support while it is flowering, as the flowers are very heavy.

Potentilla rupestris
SOIL: Any well drained.
CONDITIONS: Sun.
COLOUR: White.
FLOWERING: Early summer to early autumn.
FEEDING: General fertilizer in early spring, then mulch with well-rotted manure in spring.
PRUNING: Cut back to 12in/30cm in autumn.
GENERAL COMMENTS: Water in dry weather, as it does not like to dry right out. This is a pretty plant with strawberry-like grey-green leaves and many flowers on upright stems. They like to grow through other plants, and should be more widely used.

Rosa 'Goldfinch'
SOIL: Any except chalk or sand. It benefits from added manure.
CONDITIONS: Sun.
COLOUR: Creamy buff, with stronger yellow buds.
FLOWERING: Early summer to mid-summer.
FEEDING: General fertilizer in spring and a rose food in mid-summer.
PRUNING: Cut back after flowering, but removing only any spindly, dead or diseased growth.
GENERAL COMMENTS: A healthy rose with a striking colour which looks good planted with anything.

Rosa The Pilgrim
SOIL: Any that is not pure sand or chalk.
CONDITIONS: Full sun.
COLOUR: Yellow.
FLOWERING: Mid-summer, and continues into autumn.
FEEDING: General fertilizer in spring and a rose food in mid-summer.
PRUNING: In winter, when the weather is not too cold. This rose responds well to hard pruning, so cut it back to a good basic shape. Deadheading is very important, and will ensure that it keeps producing more and more flowers.
GENERAL COMMENTS: A very pretty yellow rose

with double flowers, an old-fashioned look and a good smell.

Sisyrinchium striatum
SOIL: Well drained.
CONDITIONS: Sun.
COLOUR: Creamy yellow flowers and blue-grey leaves.
FLOWERING: Early summer to early autumn.
FEEDING: General fertilizer in spring.
PRUNING: Remove old flower heads as they finish. Cut off leaves as they go black.
GENERAL COMMENTS: Keep the base of the plant clear of leaves. If it likes its spot, it will make many seedlings which can be replanted in spring. A very pretty plant which also looks very good planted by itself in gravel.

A SUNNY BED AGAINST A WALL: MIXED PLANTING

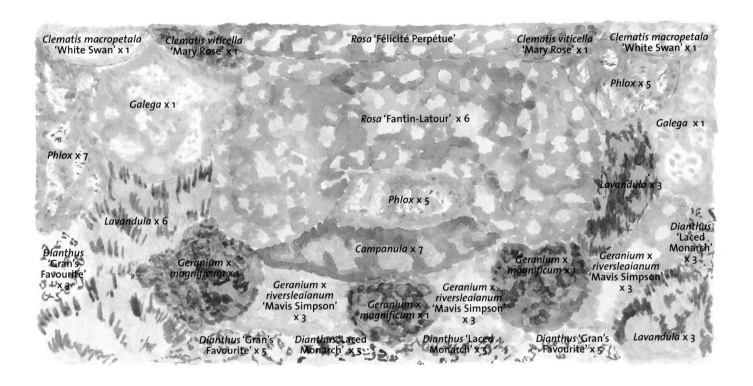

Clematis macropetala 'White Swan' x 1

Clematis viticella 'Mary Rose' x 1

Rosa 'Félicité Perpétue'

Clematis viticella 'Mary Rose' x 1

Clematis macropetala 'White Swan' x 1

Galega x 1

Phlox x 5

Rosa 'Fantin-Latour' x 6

Galega x 1

Phlox x 7

Lavandula x 3

Phlox x 5

Lavandula x 6

Dianthus 'Laced Monarch' x 3

Campanula x 7

Dianthus 'Gran's Favourite' x 3

Geranium x magnificum x 1

Geranium x magnificum x 1

Geranium x riversleaianum 'Mavis Simpson' x 3

Geranium x riversleaianum 'Mavis Simpson' x 3

Geranium x riversleaianum 'Mavis Simpson' x 3

Geranium x magnificum x 1

Dianthus 'Gran's Favourite' x 5

Dianthus 'Laced Monarch' x 5

Dianthus 'Laced Monarch' x 5

Dianthus 'Gran's Favourite' x 5

Lavandula x 3

	THE PLANTS	QUANTITIES
1	Dianthus 'Laced Monarch'	13
2	Galega officinalis	2
3	Phlox maculata 'Omega'	17
4	Clematis macropetala 'White Swan' (or any white variety, e.g. 'Snowbird')	2
5	Dianthus 'Gran's Favourite'	13
6	Geranium x magnificum	3
7	Rosa 'Fantin-Latour'	6
8	Rosa 'Félicité Perpétue'	1
9	Clematis viticella 'Mary Rose' (syn. C.v. 'Flore Pleno')	2
10	Campanula lactiflora 'Loddon Anna'	7
11	Lavandula angustifolia 'Hidcote'	12
12	Geranium x riversleaianum 'Mavis Simpson'	9

SIZE AND POSITION

Campanula lactiflora 'Loddon Anna' grows to 4ft x 24in/1.2m x 60cm. Plant 18in/45cm apart.

Clematis macropetala 'White Swan' grows to 6ft x 36in/1.8m x 90cm.

Clematis viticella 'Mary Rose' grows to 8ft x 36in/2.5m x 90cm.

Dianthus 'Gran's Favourite' grows to 9in x 6in/23cm x 15cm. Plant 6in/15cm apart.

Dianthus 'Laced Monarch' grows to 8in x 8in/20cm x 20cm. Plant 8in/20cm apart.

Galega officinalis grows to 5ft x 36in/1.5m x 90cm.

Geranium x *magnificum* grows to 24in x 18in/60cm x45cm. Plant 12in/30cm apart.

Geranium x *riversleaianum* 'Mavis Simpson' grows to 9in x 12in/23cm x 30cm. Plant 8in/20cm apart.

Lavandula angustifolia 'Hidcote' grows to 15in x 15in/38cm x 38cm. Plant 12in/30cm apart.

Phlox maculata 'Omega' grows to 36in x 18in/90cm x 45cm. Plant 18in/45cm apart.

Rosa 'Fantin-Latour' grows to 5ft x 6ft/1.5m x 1.8m. Plant 30in/75cm apart.

Rosa 'Félicité Perpétue' grows to 18ft x 6ft/5.5m x 1.8m.

ADDITIONAL PLANTING

SPRING COLOUR

In autumn:
Plant 15 of each of the following tulip bulbs, in drifts of the same type, wherever there are spaces: 'Peach Blossom', 'Dreaming Maid' and 'White Triumphator'.

Plant 25 *Camassia leichtlinii* 'Alba' bulbs at each side of the bed.

Plant 50 *Anemone blanda* 'Pink Star' corms at the front and 50 *Narcissus* 'Thalia' bulbs throughout the bed.

SUMMER COLOUR

In autumn:
Plant 25 *Allium caeruleum* and 25 *A. unifolium* bulbs around the shrub roses.

In spring:
Plant *Papaver somniferum* in pink, mauve and deep purple at the back of the bed.

In late spring:
Sow *Consolida* (larkspur) seeds and plant 20 pink cosmos in any gaps towards the back.

GENERAL CARE

Wire the wall with vine eyes.

Cut the 'Mary Rose' clematis down to 18in/45cm in late winter.

Mulch the roses and clematis with leaf mould or well-rotted manure in spring.

Clean over the bed in winter, removing any debris.

Tidy over the *Clematis macropetala* 'Snowbird' after it finishes flowering in late spring.

Keep the roses and clematis well tied in.

Stake the galega if necessary.

Shape up the lavenders in mid-spring.

Deadhead roses and pinks as the flowers fade.

Feed with a general fertilizer in spring, and thoroughly clean around all plants, cutting off any dead leaves.

Cut back the lavender after flowering.

Cut the phlox and campanulas down to the ground in autumn.

Compost dead summer bedding in late autumn.

Feed roses with rose food in mid-summer.

PLANT DETAILS

***Campanula lactiflora* 'Loddon Anna'**
SOIL: Any.
CONDITIONS: Sun or part shade.
COLOUR: Lilac pink.
FLOWERING: Summer.
FEEDING: Spring.
PRUNING: Cut back to 12in/30cm after flowering.
GENERAL COMMENTS: A good and very easy upright plant for the border.

***Clematis macropetala* 'White Swan'**
SOIL: Good, rich.
CONDITIONS: Sun or part shade.
COLOUR: White.
FLOWERING: Late spring to early summer.
FEEDING: Spring.
PRUNING: Prune after flowering if necessary to retain shape.
GENERAL COMMENTS: A very pretty early clematis.

***Clematis viticella* 'Mary Rose'**
SOIL: Well drained, fertile.
CONDITIONS: Sun, with the roots protected and shaded with crocks.
COLOUR: Small flowers of dark purple fading to grey.
FLOWERING: Mid-summer to early autumn.
FEEDING: Spring, and during the summer with a liquid fertilizer every two weeks.
PRUNING: In late winter, cut down to 12in/30cm, cutting each stem above a pair of healthy buds.
GENERAL COMMENTS: This is an unusual and delicate little clematis with small double

flowers and some single flowers on the same plant.

Dianthus 'Gran's Favourite' and Dianthus 'Laced Monarch'

SOIL: Light, free-draining.
CONDITIONS: Sun.
COLOUR: 'Gran's Favourite' white with maroon markings, 'Laced Monarch' maroon double with cream markings.
FLOWERING: Early summer.
FEEDING: Bonemeal in late autumn, and in spring and summer with a high potash fertilizer.
PRUNING: Cut off old flower heads and keep the plant as compact as possible.
GENERAL COMMENTS: These old-fashioned laced pinks, with a wonderful scent, look superb planted in groups. They add a soft romantic feel to any border.

Galega officinalis

SOIL: Dry, poor.
CONDITIONS: Sun or part shade.
COLOUR: Lilac and white.
FLOWERING: Mid-summer to early autumn.
FEEDING: A little general fertilizer in spring.
PRUNING: Cut back to ground level in autumn.
GENERAL COMMENTS: A good reliable plant with a pretty, finely cut leaf.

Geranium x magnificum

SOIL: Good well drained.
CONDITIONS: Full sun.
COLOUR: Purplish blue.
FLOWERING: Late spring to early summer.
FEEDING: Spring.
PRUNING: Cut back the old flowering stems to the leaf clump.
GENERAL COMMENTS: The only bad thing about this geranium is its short flowering time.

Geranium x riversleaianum 'Mavis Simpson'

SOIL: Any.
CONDITIONS: Sun or part shade.
COLOUR: Silver pink.
FLOWERING: Mid-summer to late summer.
FEEDING: Spring.
PRUNING: Cut back after flowering to encourage more flowers and new leaves.
GENERAL COMMENTS: Has pretty grey-green leaves.

Lavandula angustifolia 'Hidcote'

SOIL: Ordinary well drained.
CONDITIONS: Full sun.
COLOUR: Deep purple blue.
FLOWERING: Mid-summer to early autumn.
FEEDING: Spring.
PRUNING: Trim off the old flower heads after flowering, and trim up the whole bush in mid-spring, being careful not to cut back into old wood.
GENERAL COMMENTS: If you want to dry the lavender to have in the house or to make into lavender bags, it is best to cut it just before the flowers are fully open. This is the time when it smells strongest.

Phlox maculata 'Omega'

SOIL: Fertile, which does not dry out.
CONDITIONS: Sun or part shade.
COLOUR: White with a pink eye.
FLOWERING: Mid-summer to early autumn.
FEEDING: Spring and after the first flush of flowers.
PRUNING: Cut back the old flower stems to encourage new ones.
GENERAL COMMENTS: Invaluable plants in any border, or planted amongst shrubs. They have a wonderful scent. They benefit from a mulch of manure in spring; this should not touch the stems.

Rosa 'Fantin-Latour'

SOIL: Any.
CONDITIONS: Sun.
COLOUR: Soft pale pink.
FLOWERING: Early summer to mid-summer.
FEEDING: Spring with a general fertilizer and again in mid-summer with rose food.
PRUNING: Prune lightly after flowering to maintain a good shape.
GENERAL COMMENTS: One of the very best old-fashioned roses.

Rosa 'Félicité Perpétue'

SOIL: Any well drained.
CONDITIONS: Sun.
COLOUR: Creamy white.
FLOWERING: Mid-summer.
FEEDING: Spring with a general fertilizer and in mid-summer with rose food.
PRUNING: After flowering, cut any weak stems right back to the ground. Otherwise just shape.
GENERAL COMMENTS: A lovely rose which is healthy and full of flowers.

A SHADY BED AGAINST A WALL: LEAF SHAPES

THE PLANTS	QUANTITIES
1 *Choisya ternata*	2
2 *Clematis montana alba*	1
3 *Daphne odora*	3
4 *Epimedium perralderianum*	10
5 *Acanthus spinosus*	2
6 *Hosta* 'Krossa Regal'	3
7 *Milium effusum* 'Aureum'	3
8 *Ophiopogon planiscapus* 'Nigrescens'	14
9 *Vitis coignetiae*	1
10 *Helleborus argutifolius*	10
11 *Acer palmatum* var. *dissectum* 'Garnet'	2
12 *Mahonia* x *media* 'Charity'	3
13 *Viburnum davidii*	3

SIZE AND POSITION

Acanthus spinosus grows to 36in x 36in/90cm x 90cm. Plant 24in/60cm apart.

Acer palmatum var. *dissectum* 'Garnet' grows to 36in x 36in/90cm x 90cm.

Choisya ternata grows to 5ft x 5ft/1.5m x 1.5m.

Clematis montana alba grows to 20ft x 10ft/6m x 3m.

Daphne odora grows to 3½ft x 36in/ 1.1m x 90cm. Plant 18in/45cm apart.

Epimedium perralderianum grows to 12in x 8in/30cm x 20cm. Plant 6in/15cm apart.

Helleborus argutifolius grows to 30in x 24in/75cm x 60cm. Plant 15in/38cm apart.

Hosta 'Krossa Regal' grows to 36in x 18in/90cm x 45cm. Plant 12in/30cm apart.

Mahonia x *media* 'Charity' grows to 8ft x 4ft/2.5m x 1.2m. Plant 30in/75cm apart.

Milium effusum 'Aureum' grows to 36in x 24in/90cm x 60cm. Plant 18in/45cm apart.

Ophiopogon planiscapus 'Nigrescens' grows to 8in x 8in/20cm x 20cm. Plant 8in/20cm apart.

Viburnum davidii grows to 36in x 36in/90cm x 90cm or larger. Plant 24in/60cm apart.

Vitis coignetiae grows to at least 20ft/6m and spreads as far as you let it.

ADDITIONAL PLANTING

SPRING COLOUR

In autumn:
Plant 20 *Primula vulgaris* (common primroses) alongside the black grass.

Plant 40 *Muscari azureum* 'Album' (white grape hyacinth) bulbs across the front of the bed.

Plant 10 *Erythronium* 'Citronella' bulbs, 5 under each acer.

SUMMER COLOUR

In spring:
Plant 40 violas in mixed colours throughout the bed.

In late spring:
Plant 20 *Impatiens* (busy Lizzies) in pale pink in any gaps.

Plant 12 *Nicotiana sylvestris* (tobacco plants) throughout the bed. (You may have to badger local nurseries to grow these, or grow them from seed yourself.)

GENERAL CARE

Wire the walls with vine eyes.

Keep an eye out for slugs. They love the hostas and the nicotiana, so put pellets down as soon as the hosta spikes appear and keep up the protection through the season.

Feed with a general fertilizer in spring.

Keep the climbers tied in during their first season. After this they will take care of themselves, and you will have to restrain them to the size you want.

The acanthus is a rampant self-seeder and you need to keep one step ahead to make sure that it does not take over.

In autumn tidy through the bed and mulch. Clear away the old, soggy leaves of the hostas and acanthus.

PLANT DETAILS

Acanthus spinosus
SOIL: Well drained.
CONDITIONS: Shade or partial shade.
COLOUR: White and purple.
FLOWERING: Mid-summer to late summer.
FEEDING: Spring.
PRUNING: Cut flower spikes down to the ground after flowering.
GENERAL COMMENTS:
A handsome glossy-leaved plant, but it tends to spread and has very deep roots to dig out.

Acer palmatum var. *dissectum* 'Garnet'
SOIL: Any well drained.
CONDITIONS: Part shade or shade.
COLOUR: Deep, rich, purple-red leaves.
FLOWERING: None.
FEEDING: Spring.
PRUNING: Simply remove any dead or broken wood.
GENERAL COMMENTS: Needs to be protected from cold scorching winds, and from any direct sunlight. It has wonderful autumn colouring.

Choisya ternata
SOIL: Any.
CONDITIONS: Sun, part shade or shade.
COLOUR: White.
FLOWERING: Mid-spring to early summer and a few flowers in autumn.
FEEDING: Spring.
PRUNING: Prune after flowering to keep to a good shape. It will withstand quite severe pruning.
GENERAL COMMENTS:
One of the most versatile shrubs: it goes with anything. It has shiny

leaves, which are aromatic when touched. It looks very good when picked.

Clematis montana alba
SOIL: Good, well drained.
CONDITIONS: Sun, or part shade. Needs some shade at the roots.
COLOUR: White.
FLOWERING: Mid-spring to early summer.
FEEDING: Spring.
PRUNING: Prune after flowering.
GENERAL COMMENTS: A good plant for quick cover. You will need to keep it tied in to establish some shape, and you really will need to cut it back to stop it romping away in every direction. We prefer this white variety, but there are others in varying shades of pink.

Daphne odora
SOIL: Good, moist but well drained.
CONDITIONS: Sun, part shade or shade.
COLOUR: Pinkish white.
FLOWERING: Late winter to mid-spring.
FEEDING: Spring.
PRUNING: None.
GENERAL COMMENTS: Has a magnificent strong scent. A very good flower to pick: it will last for ages.

Epimedium perralderianum
SOIL: Good, moist.
CONDITIONS: Shade or partial shade.

COLOUR: Strong yellow.
FLOWERING: Mid-spring to late spring.
FEEDING: Spring.
PRUNING: Pull off any straggly or brown leaves, and just tidy up as necessary.
GENERAL COMMENTS: A delicate little plant.

Helleborus argutifolius
SOIL: Moisture-retentive, but not boggy.
CONDITIONS: Semi shade.
COLOUR: Pale green.
FLOWERING: Mid-winter to early summer.
FEEDING: Bonemeal in late autumn, and general fertilizer in spring.
PRUNING: Remove the flowers when they look unattractive and take the same action with any leaves that are past their prime.
GENERAL COMMENTS: A sculptural plant with striking green flowers and coarse spiny leaves. It is a handsome addition to the border.

Hosta 'Krossa Regal'
SOIL: Well drained, moisture-retentive, enriched with some leaf mould or manure.
CONDITIONS: Partial shade or shade.
COLOUR: Lilac flowers above blue-grey leaves.
FLOWERING: Mid-summer to late summer.
FEEDING: Spring.
PRUNING: Cut off the old flower spikes as they finish.

GENERAL COMMENTS: A tall shapely hosta with grey-green leaves. Protect from slugs and snails as soon as you see the first hint of the leaf spikes in early spring.

Mahonia x media 'Charity'
SOIL: Any.
CONDITIONS: Shade or partial shade.
COLOUR: Yellow.
FLOWERING: Winter.
FEEDING: Spring.
PRUNING: After flowering, to keep the shape shorten any branches that are too long.
GENERAL COMMENTS: The flowers have a wonderful scent of lily-of-the-valley.

Milium effusum 'Aureum'
SOIL: Any.
CONDITIONS: Shade.
COLOUR: Bright gold.
FLOWERING: Greenish yellow drooping spikes in summer.
FEEDING: Spring.
PRUNING: Pull off any leaves that are not in their prime.
GENERAL COMMENTS: A really bright golden grass which makes its mark in any planting.

Ophiopogon planiscapus 'Nigrescens'
SOIL: Rich, well drained.
CONDITIONS: Part shade.
COLOUR: Attractive small bronzy flowers, but the black leaf is the point.
FLOWERING: Mid-summer to late summer.

FEEDING: Spring.
PRUNING: None.
GENERAL COMMENTS: A very striking small black grass-like plant which acts as a foil to other planting. It looks wonderful planted with primroses.

Viburnum davidii
SOIL: Good, moist.
CONDITIONS: Any, but needs shelter from cold winds.
COLOUR: White flowers, followed by blackish berries with a turquoise bloom.
FLOWERING: Late spring to early summer.
FEEDING: Spring.
PRUNING: Cut out any dead or damaged wood in May.
GENERAL COMMENTS: A dense shrub with tough, long and deeply veined leaves. It is easy to grow and evergreen. You will need to grow male and female varieties for berries.

Vitis coignetiae
SOIL: Moist, loamy.
CONDITIONS: Sun or shade.
COLOUR: Fantastic autumn leaf colour: orange, red, copper and purple.
FEEDING: Spring.
PRUNING: Cut at any time to keep in shape and under control.
GENERAL COMMENTS: Has huge leaves and is well worth planting where you have space. It is useful for covering ugly buildings.

A SHADY BED AGAINST A WALL: MIXED PLANTING

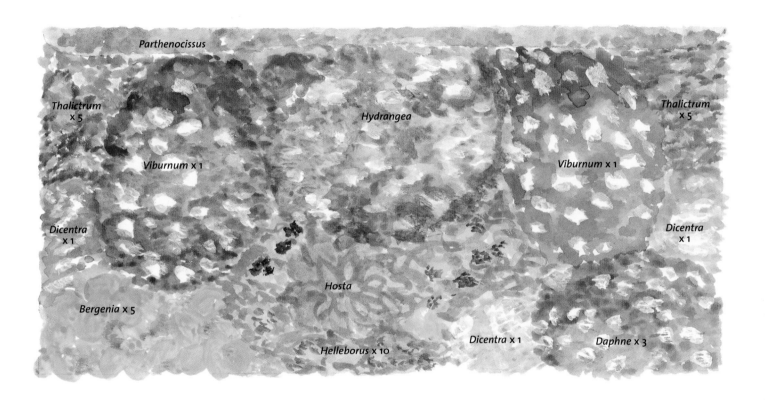

Parthenocissus

Thalictrum x 5

Hydrangea

Thalictrum x 5

Viburnum x 1

Viburnum x 1

Dicentra x 1

Dicentra x 1

Bergenia x 5

Hosta

Dicentra x 1

Daphne x 3

Helleborus x 10

	THE PLANTS	QUANTITIES
1	*Dicentra spectabilis* 'Alba'	3
2	*Bergenia*, any pink variety (e.g. *B.* 'Sunningdale' or *B. cordifolia*)	5
3	*Thalictrum delavayi*	10
4	*Helleborus orientalis* (also named *Helleborus* x *hybridus*)	10
5	*Viburnum* x *burkwoodii*	2
6	*Daphne tangutica*	3
7	*Parthenocissus henryana*	1
8	*Hydrangea villosa* (also named *Hydrangea aspera* Villosa Group)	1
9	*Hosta* 'Hadspen Blue'	1

SIZE AND POSITION

Bergenias grow to 18in x 12in/45cm x 30cm. Plant 12in/30cm apart.

Daphne tangutica grows to 36in x 24in/90cm x 60cm. Plant 12in/30cm apart.

Dicentra spectabilis 'Alba' grows to 36in x 24in/90cm x 60cm.

Helleborus orientalis grows to 24in x 18in/60cm x 45cm. Plant 12in/30cm apart.

Hosta 'Hadspen Blue' grows to 12in x 12in/30cm x 30cm.

Hydrangea villosa grows to 5ft x 5ft/1.5m x 1.5m.

Parthenocissus henryana grows! You will need to restrict its size.

Thalictrum delavayi grows to 4ft x 18in/1.2m x 45cm. Plant 12in/30cm apart.

Viburnum x burkwoodii grows 5ft x 4½ft/1.5m x 1.4m.

ADDITIONAL PLANTING

SPRING COLOUR

In autumn:
Plant white tulip bulbs around the shrubs, e.g. 50 'Purissima' and 50 'White Triumphator'.

SUMMER COLOUR

In spring:
Plant lavender-coloured violas at the front of the bed to take over from the dicentra as it finishes flowering.

Plant pale lilac *Impatiens* (busy Lizzies) in any gaps in front of the shrubs.

In late spring:
Plant *Nicotiana sylvestris* and *N. affinis* (tobacco plants) – the *N. sylvestris* at the back of the bed and the *N. affinis* in front of the shrubs.

GENERAL CARE

Put down slug pellets in early spring, especially around the hosta (before the leaves show) and bergenias.

Feed with a general fertilizer in spring.

In autumn clear the bed of old leaves and feed the whole bed with bonemeal.

Mulch the bed in winter.

Make sure that the new shrubs are kept well watered.

PLANT DETAILS

Bergenia, any pink variety

SOIL: Well drained.
CONDITIONS: Sun, partial shade or shade.
COLOUR: Pink.
FLOWERING: Early spring.
FEEDING: Spring.
PRUNING: Cut off the old flower stalks when they look ugly, and pull off any brown leaves.
GENERAL COMMENTS: Wonderful ground-cover plant with large thick rounded leaves and strong stems that hold the flower heads, which last for weeks. Keep an eye out for slugs and snails. Bergenias make new plants which can be easily pulled off the main plant and replanted elsewhere.

Daphne tangutica

SOIL: Loamy, moist and well drained.
CONDITIONS: Half shade to shade.
COLOUR: White flushed rose purple.
FLOWERING: Early spring to mid-spring.
FEEDING: Spring.
PRUNING: None.
GENERAL COMMENTS: When it is happy and planted in the right conditions this daphne produces wonderfully scented flowers. It is good for picking, and one sprig will fill the room with scent.

Dicentra spectabilis 'Alba' (white bleeding heart)

SOIL: Rich and fertile.
CONDITIONS: Sun, partial shade or shade.

COLOUR: White.
FLOWERING: Mid-spring until early summer.
FEEDING: Spring.
PRUNING: None.
GENERAL COMMENTS: Beautiful ferny foliage with heart-shaped flowers. It is a very easy plant which grows happily in woods or in the border. It can be divided in early spring.

Helleborus orientalis

SOIL: Moist, which does not dry out.
CONDITIONS: Does best in half shade.
COLOUR: White, pink, greeny pinks, purple.
FLOWERING: Late winter to mid-spring.
FEEDING: With bonemeal in autumn, and with a general fertilizer in spring.
PRUNING: Pull off any old leaves before the flowers appear. Cut back the old flower stems when they die. From time to time cut off any tired growth.
GENERAL COMMENTS: A beautiful plant if it is happy in its position, and it will make many seedlings. The subtly coloured flowers can be picked, but tend to flop. We find that the best thing is to float their flower heads in water. It is very easy to become an admirer of this hellebore: it is magical.

Hosta 'Hadspen Blue'

SOIL: Well drained, moisture-retentive, enriched with leaf mould or manure.
CONDITIONS: Sun or partial shade.
COLOUR: Blue-grey leaves with white spiky flowers held above the leaves.
FLOWERING: Mid-summer to late summer.
FEEDING: Spring.
PRUNING: None.
GENERAL COMMENTS: The really important thing to remember is slug pellets: put these down as soon as you see the first sign of a leaf coming through the soil in spring. Otherwise this hosta is an easy plant and can be left undisturbed for years.

Hydrangea villosa

SOIL: Any fertile, which does not dry out.
CONDITIONS: Half shade.
COLOUR: Lilac blue to purple.
FLOWERING: Late summer.
FEEDING: Spring.
PRUNING: It dislikes being pruned, so leave it alone as much as possible and leave old flowers on over winter.
GENERAL COMMENTS: An eyecatching shrub which is easy to grow.

Parthenocissus henryana

SOIL: Any.
CONDITIONS: Sun or shade.
COLOUR: Grown for its leaf colour: pink, white and dark green, turning to reds and golds in autumn.
FLOWERING: Has insignificant greenish flowers in summer.
FEEDING: Spring.
PRUNING: Cut it in the autumn if it is growing too big.
GENERAL COMMENTS: A very pretty self-clinging – and really rampant – climber, which is useful for quick cover, but remember that it is not evergreen.

Thalictrum delavayi

SOIL: Any.
CONDITIONS: Light shade or sun.
COLOUR: Sprays of single purple stars with cream stamens.
FLOWERING: Early summer to late summer.
FEEDING: Spring.
PRUNING: Cut old flower stalks down to 12in/30cm in late autumn.
GENERAL COMMENTS: A pretty flower with attractive ferny foliage, which creates a light and airy feel.

Viburnum x burkwoodii

SOIL: Any fertile.
CONDITIONS: Tolerant of sun or shade.
COLOUR: Pink buds with white flowers.
FLOWERING: Mid-winter to late spring.
FEEDING: Spring.
PRUNING: None, unless to remove damaged growth or restrict size, which can be done after flowering.
GENERAL COMMENTS: A very easy plant with highly scented flowers which are good for picking in winter.

A SHADY BED AGAINST A WALL: MIXED PLANTING

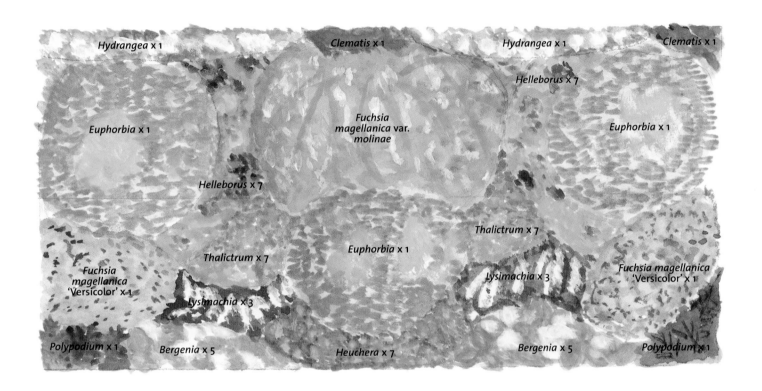

Hydrangea x 1   *Clematis* x 1   *Hydrangea* x 1   *Clematis* x 1

Helleborus x 7

Euphorbia x 1   *Fuchsia magellanica* var. *molinae*   *Euphorbia* x 1

Helleborus x 7

Thalictrum x 7

Thalictrum x 7   *Euphorbia* x 1

Fuchsia magellanica 'Versicolor' x 1   *Lysimachia* x 3   *Fuchsia magellanica* 'Versicolor' x 1

Lysimachia x 3

Polypodium x 1   *Bergenia* x 5   *Heuchera* x 7   *Bergenia* x 5   *Polypodium* x 1

	THE PLANTS	QUANTITIES
1	*Euphorbia characias* subsp. *wulfenii*	3
2	*Fuchsia magellanica* var. *molinae* (also known as F.m. 'Alba')	1
3	*Clematis* 'Blue Bird'	2
4	*Lysimachia ephemerum*	6
5	*Heuchera cylindrica* 'Greenfinch'	7
6	*Helleborus orientalis* 'Sirius' (also named *Helleborus* x *hybridus*)	14
7	*Bergenia* 'Bressingham White'	10
8	*Thalictrum aquilegiifolium* 'Thundercloud'	14
9	*Polypodium vulgare*	2
10	*Fuchsia magellanica* 'Versicolor'	2
11	*Hydrangea anomala* subsp. *petiolaris*	2

SIZE AND POSITION

Bergenia 'Bressingham White' grows to 12in x 12in/30cm x 30cm. Plant 12in/30cm apart.

Clematis 'Blue Bird' grows to 6ft x 4ft/1.8m x 1.2m.

Euphorbia characias subsp. *wulfenii* grows to 4ft x 4ft/1.2m x 1.2m.

Fuchsia magellanica var. *molinae* grows to 6ft x 5ft/1.5m x 1.2m.

Fuchsia magellanica 'Versicolor' grows to 36in x 36in/90cm x 90cm.

Helleborus orientalis 'Sirius' grows to 15in x 12in/38cm x 30cm. Plant 12in/30cm apart.

Heuchera cylindrica 'Greenfinch' grows to 12in x 9in/30cm x 23cm. Plant 12in/30cm apart.

Hydrangea anomala subsp. *petiolaris* grows to 15ft x 4ft/4.5m x 1.2m.

Lysimachia ephemerum grows to 4ft x 12in/1.2m x 30cm. Plant 12in/30cm apart.

Polypodium vulgare grows to 10in x 12in/25cm x 30cm.

Thalictrum aquilegiifolium 'Thundercloud' grows to 4ft x 18in/1.2m x 45cm. Plant 18in/45cm apart.

ADDITIONAL PLANTING

SPRING COLOUR

In autumn:
Plant 50 *Narcissus* 'Hawera' bulbs all over the bed.

Plant 20 white and pale pink polyanthus all over the bed.

Plant 20 *Ornithogalum arabicum* bulbs in groups of 5.

Plant 50 *Hyacinthoides non-scripta* (bluebells) bulbs all over the bed.

Plant 20 *Erythronium dens-canis* bulbs in groups of 5 towards the front of the bed.

SUMMER COLOUR

In spring:
Plant 50 pink, white and blue violas in any gaps towards the front of the bed.

Plant 25 white *Impatiens* (busy Lizzies) in any spaces throughout the bed.

GENERAL CARE

Wire the wall with vine eyes.

Feed the whole bed with a general fertilizer in spring.

Cut back the fuchsias as hard as you like in mid-spring.

Keep the climbers well tied in during the first year. After that the hydrangea will look after itself but the clematis may still need tying in to control the direction of growth.

Once the euphorbia flower bracts start to look messy, cut them down towards the base, making sure that you do not get the sap on your skin as it is a strong irritant.

Cut the thalictrum and lysimachia down to 12in/30cm in the autumn.

Clear through the rest of the bed at the same time leaving bed free of debris. Mulch with well-rotted manure in winter.

Put gravel under the hellebores through the winter months, so that the rain does not splash the flowers with soil.

PLANT DETAILS

Bergenia 'Bressingham White'
SOIL: Well drained.
CONDITIONS: Sun, half shade or shade.
COLOUR: White.
FLOWERING: Early spring.
FEEDING: Spring.
PRUNING: None. Just cut off the old flower stalks as they die, and pull off any leaves that turn brown.
GENERAL COMMENTS: Wonderful ground-cover plant with large, thick, rounded leaves and sturdy stems which hold the flower heads above. They need protection from slugs and snails.

Clematis 'Blue Bird'
SOIL: Rich, fertile, with added leaf mould or manure.
CONDITIONS: Tolerant of sun or shade.
COLOUR: Lavender-blue flowers with a greenish white centre.
FLOWERING: Mid-spring to late spring.
FEEDING: Spring.
PRUNING: None, but you can tidy up the plant after flowering.
GENERAL COMMENTS: Large, nodding flowers of a lovely soft blue.

Euphorbia characias subsp. *wulfenii*
SOIL: Ordinary, well drained.
CONDITIONS: Sun, light shade or shade.
COLOUR: Greenish yellow bracts on glaucous green foliage.
FLOWERING: Late spring to mid-summer.
FEEDING: Spring.

PRUNING: Cut the faded stems towards the base.
GENERAL COMMENTS: A stately and impressive plant. The stems produce grey-green leaves in the first year, which are followed in spring with yellow-green flower bracts. Beware: wear gloves when you prune this plant. It has highly irritant sap and can give a nasty burn.

Fuchsia magellanica var. molinae
SOIL: Any.
CONDITIONS: Sun, part shade or shade.
COLOUR: Very pale pink, fading to white.
FLOWERING: Early summer to mid-autumn.
FEEDING: Spring.
PRUNING: Cut back as hard as you like in spring.
GENERAL COMMENTS: Looks good anywhere, with other shrubs, in the wild garden or in a herbaceous border. It is a wonderful shrub tolerant of most conditions. The bark peels on the stem as it gets older, giving it yet another attribute.

Fuchsia magellanica 'Versicolor'
SOIL: Any.
CONDITIONS: Part shade or shade.
COLOUR: Red.
FLOWERING: Early summer

to early autumn.
FEEDING: Spring.
PRUNING: Cut back to ground level in spring.
GENERAL COMMENTS: A very pretty fuchsia with an arching habit and foliage of pink, green and cream.

Helleborus orientalis 'Sirius'
SOIL: Damp, which does not dry out.
CONDITIONS: Half shade.
COLOUR: White, pink, greenish pink and purple.
FLOWERING: Late winter to mid-spring.
FEEDING: With bonemeal in autumn, and again with general fertilizer in spring.
PRUNING: Cut off dead leaves as the new flowers appear. When the flowers are finished cut back the old stems.
GENERAL COMMENTS: These are really beautiful hellebores, and it is very easy to become a fanatical admirer of their grace and unusual colours. They wilt if they are picked, and we have found that the best way of showing them off indoors is to float the flower heads in a bowl of water.

Heuchera cylindrica 'Greenfinch'
SOIL: Tolerant of dry or wet, but not waterlogged.
CONDITIONS: Partial shade.
COLOUR: Pale green.

FLOWERING: Late spring to mid-summer.
FEEDING: Spring.
PRUNING: Cut off the dead flower stalks when they have finished.
GENERAL COMMENTS: The leaves are a little more untidy than those of other heucheras, but the unusual creamy green flowers held up like drumsticks make this well worth a space in the border.

Hydrangea anomala subsp. petiolaris
SOIL: Any.
CONDITIONS: Part shade.
COLOUR: White.
FLOWERING: Late spring to late summer.
FEEDING: Spring.
PRUNING: Only prune to shape. This might include pruning to restrict its growth.
GENERAL COMMENTS: A graceful self-clinging climber. It takes time to get established but once it gets going is well worth the wait.

Lysimachia ephemerum
SOIL: Any, but it does not like to dry out.
CONDITIONS: Tolerant of sun or shade.
COLOUR: White.
FLOWERING: Mid-summer to early autumn.
FEEDING: Spring.
PRUNING: Cut old flower stems down to 12in/30cm

as they finish.
GENERAL COMMENTS: A proud and upright plant which needs no staking. An excellent companion for a shady border. It should be used more often.

Polypodium vulgare
SOIL: Any well drained, which does not dry out.
CONDITIONS: Shade.
COLOUR: Good strong green leaves.
FLOWERING: None.
FEEDING: Spring.
PRUNING: None.
GENERAL COMMENTS: A fern with narrow divided leaves in a herringbone pattern. A pretty and structural plant.

Thalictrum aquilegiifolium 'Thundercloud'
SOIL: Any.
CONDITIONS: Sun or shade.
COLOUR: White flowers with purple stamens and grey-green leaves.
FLOWERING: Late spring to early summer.
FEEDING: Spring.
PRUNING: Cut down to 12in/30cm in late autumn.
GENERAL COMMENTS: A graceful plant with lovely grey-green leaves like a maidenhair fern. It is very pretty and versatile.

A SHADY BED AGAINST A WALL:
BLUE AND WHITE

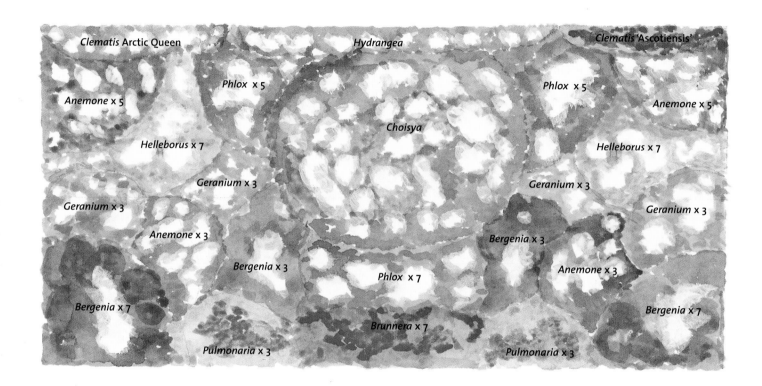

Clematis Arctic Queen   *Hydrangea*   *Clematis* 'Ascotiensis'

Phlox x 5   *Phlox* x 5

Anemone x 5   *Anemone* x 5

Choisya

Helleborus x 7   *Helleborus* x 7

Geranium x 3   *Geranium* x 3

Geranium x 3   *Geranium* x 3

Anemone x 3   *Bergenia* x 3

Anemone x 3

Bergenia x 3

Phlox x 7   *Bergenia* x 7

Bergenia x 7

Brunnera x 7

Pulmonaria x 3   *Pulmonaria* x 3

THE PLANTS	QUANTITIES
1 *Clematis* 'Ascotiensis'	1
2 *Clematis* Arctic Queen (or any pure white double early, e.g. 'Duchess of Edinburgh')	1
3 *Hydrangea anomala* subsp. *petiolaris*	1
4 *Helleborus niger*	14
5 *Phlox paniculata* var. *alba*	17
6 *Brunnera macrophylla*	7
7 *Bergenia* 'Bressingham White'	20
8 *Anemone* x *hybrida* 'Honorine Jobert'	16
9 *Choisya ternata*	1
10 *Geranium phaeum* 'Album'	12
11 *Pulmonaria* 'Blue Ensign'	6

SIZE AND POSITION

Anemone x *hybrida* 'Honorine Jobert' grows to 36in x 24in/90cm x 60cm. Plant 12in/30cm apart.

Bergenia 'Bressingham White' grows to 12in x 12in/30cm x 30cm. Plant 12in/30cm apart.

Brunnera macrophylla grows to 18in x 18in/45cm x 45cm. Plant 12in/30cm apart.

Choisya ternata grows to 5ft x 5ft/1.5m x 1.5m.

Clematis 'Ascotiensis' grows to 12ft x 4ft/3.6m x 1.2m.

Clematis Arctic Queen grows to 12ft x 36in/3.6m x 90cm.

Geranium phaeum 'Album' grows to 18in x 12in/45cm x 30cm. Plant 12in/30cm apart.

Helleborus niger grows to 8in x 8in/ 20cm x 20cm. Plant 8in/20cm apart.

Hydrangea anomala subsp. *petiolaris* grows to 15ft x 4ft/4.5m x 1.2m.

Phlox paniculata var. *alba* grows to 3½ft x 18in/1.1m x 45cm. Plant 12in/30cm apart.

Pulmonaria 'Blue Ensign' grows to 12in x 12in/30cm x 30cm. Plant 12in/30cm apart.

ADDITIONAL PLANTING

SPRING COLOUR

In autumn:
Plant 50 *Narcissus* 'Minnow' bulbs in groups of 10 towards the front.

Plant 50 *Muscari armeniacum* 'Blue Spike' (grape hyacinths) bulbs all over the bed.

In spring:
Plant 50 *Galanthus nivalis* (snowdrops) in groups of 10. These are best planted after flowering.

Plant 20 blue crocus corms singly all over the bed.

Plant 10 *Corydalis flexuosa* 'Père David' in two groups of 5.

SUMMER COLOUR

In spring plant 30 *Nicotiana sylvestris* (large tobacco plants) towards the back of the bed.

Plant white *Impatiens* (busy Lizzies) in any gaps.

Plant 50 violas in blue and white towards the front of the bed.

GENERAL CARE

Wire the wall with vine eyes.

Tidy through the bed in early spring.

Mulch the whole bed in spring with leaf mould or compost.

Scatter slug pellets over the bed in early spring, and keep an eye out for slug damage, especially in spring.

Leave the narcissus leaves on until they yellow, then cut them off and feed.

Feed the bed with a general fertilizer in spring.

Keep the clematis well tied in, helping them to start on the wire with a bamboo cane.

If you want to shape up the choisya cut it back after its first flowering.

Tidy over the bed in early autumn.

PLANT DETAILS

Anemone x *hybrida* **'Honorine Jobert'**

SOIL: Fertile, which will not dry out.

CONDITIONS: Partial shade.

COLOUR: White with a yellow centre.

FLOWERING: Late summer to mid-autumn.

FEEDING: Spring.

PRUNING: Cut down flower spikes after flowering.

GENERAL COMMENTS: A good plant for late summer, especially when planted with shrubs. Once planted it does not like to be moved, but when established it will spread quickly and you will probably need to pull some out.

Bergenia **'Bressingham White'**

SOIL: Well drained.

CONDITIONS: Sun, half shade or shade.

COLOUR: White.

FLOWERING: Early spring.

FEEDING: Spring.

PRUNING: Cut back old flower stalks as they die. Pull off any leaves that go brown.

GENERAL COMMENTS: Very useful ground-cover plant with glossy round dark green leaves. It is easy and tolerant, but you need to protect it against slugs and snails.

Brunnera macrophylla

SOIL: Any.

CONDITIONS: Sun, part shade or shade.

COLOUR: Bright blue.

FLOWERING: Early spring to late spring.

FEEDING: Spring.
PRUNING: Cut back old flower stems once they look messy.
GENERAL COMMENTS: Reliable and easy, it makes good spring ground cover with pretty sprays of blue flowers.

Choisya ternata
SOIL: Any.
CONDITIONS: Sun, part shade or shade.
COLOUR: White.
FLOWERING: Mid-spring to early summer and a few flowers in the autumn.
FEEDING: Spring.
PRUNING: Can be pruned as much or as little as you want after flowering.
GENERAL COMMENTS: A really versatile shrub which has many merits. It has highly aromatic leaves when touched. It is very good for cutting and lasts very well inside.

Clematis 'Ascotiensis'
SOIL: Good, rich, with added manure or leaf mould.
CONDITIONS: Sun or partial shade.
COLOUR: Deep blue purple.
FLOWERING: Mid-summer to early autumn.
FEEDING: Spring, and with a liquid feed every two weeks during the summer.
PRUNING: In late winter, cut each stem down to 12in/30cm, cutting above a

pair of healthy buds.
GENERAL COMMENTS: Produces a mass of flowers which are a good strong colour, useful for this time of year.

Clematis **Arctic Queen (or any pure white early clematis)**
SOIL: Good, rich, with added leaf mould or manure.
CONDITIONS: Sun or partial shade.
COLOUR: White double flowers.
FLOWERING: Late spring to early summer and again in late summer.
FEEDING: Spring.
PRUNING: Cut back in February to 18in/45cm.
GENERAL COMMENTS: A pretty clematis with double white flowers and green and white tepals just underneath. It can be difficult to establish, but is worth the effort.

Geranium phaeum 'Album'
SOIL: Any.
CONDITIONS: Shade or partial shade.
COLOUR: White.
FLOWERING: Late spring to mid-summer.
FEEDING: Spring.
PRUNING: Cut back the flower spikes to the leaf clump after flowering.
GENERAL COMMENTS: An excellent ground-cover plant for deep shade.

Helleborus niger **(Christmas rose)**
SOIL: Fertile, moist.
CONDITIONS: Shade or partial shade.
COLOUR: White.
FLOWERING: Mid-winter to mid-spring.
FEEDING: With bonemeal in late autumn, and with general spring fertilizer after flowering.
PRUNING: None. Cut off any old leaves just before the plant starts to flower. Cut off dead flower stems.
GENERAL COMMENTS: One of the earliest flowers, a lovely pure white which is a harbinger of spring.

Hydrangea anomala **subsp.** *petiolaris*
SOIL: Any.
CONDITIONS: Shade or part shade.
COLOUR: White.
FLOWERING: Late spring to late summer.
FEEDING: Spring.
PRUNING: None needed unless you want to shape it or restrict its size.
GENERAL COMMENTS: A really useful self-clinging climber which takes a little time to get going, but is well worth the wait.

Phlox paniculata **var.** *alba*
SOIL: Fertile, moisture-retentive but well drained.
CONDITIONS: Sun or partial shade.

COLOUR: White.
FLOWERING: Mid-summer to early autumn.
FEEDING: Spring.
PRUNING: Cut back to 12in/30cm after flowering.
GENERAL COMMENTS: A stately phlox with a lovely smell. When the clump gets too large you can divide it with a spade in autumn or spring.

Pulmonaria 'Blue Ensign'
SOIL: Any.
CONDITIONS: Tolerant of sun or shade.
COLOUR: A strong bright blue.
FLOWERING: Late winter to early spring.
FEEDING: Spring.
PRUNING: Shear the whole plant to the ground after flowering to get a second flush of healthier foliage and to eliminate seeding.
GENERAL COMMENTS: Provides a lovely strong blue in spring, with the flower sprays appearing before the leaves are fully open. The leaves are a good dark green.

A SHADY BED AGAINST A WALL: YELLOW AND WHITE

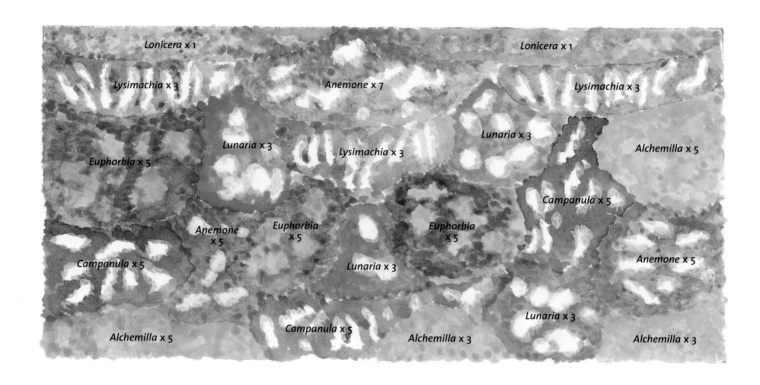

Lonicera x 1
Lonicera x 1
Lysimachia x 3
Anemone x 7
Lysimachia x 3
Lunaria x 3
Lunaria x 3
Alchemilla x 5
Lysimachia x 3
Euphorbia x 5
Campanula x 5
Anemone x 5
Euphorbia x 5
Euphorbia x 5
Campanula x 5
Lunaria x 3
Anemone x 5
Lunaria x 3
Campanula x 5
Alchemilla x 5
Campanula x 5
Alchemilla x 3
Alchemilla x 3

THE PLANTS	QUANTITIES
1 *Euphorbia amygdaloides* var. *robbiae*	15
2 *Anemone* x *hybrida* 'Honorine Jobert'	17
3 *Lonicera tragophylla*	2
4 *Lysimachia ephemerum*	9
5 *Campanula persicifolia* var. *alba*	15
6 *Alchemilla mollis*	16
7 *Lunaria annua* var. *albiflora*	12

SIZE AND POSITION

Alchemilla mollis grows to 12in x 12in/30cm x 30cm. Plant 12in/30cm apart.

Anemone x *hybrida* 'Honorine Jobert' grows 36in–4ft x 24in/90cm–1.2m x 60cm. Plant 12in/30cm apart.

Campanula persicifolia var. *alba* grows to 30in x 12in/75cm x 30cm. Plant 8in/20cm apart.

Euphorbia amygdaloides var. *robbiae* grows to 12in x 12in/30cm x 30cm. Plant 12in/30cm apart.

Lonicera tragophylla grows to 20ft x 6ft/6m x 1.8m.

Lunaria annua var. *albiflora* grows to 24in x 12in/60cm x 30cm. Plant 12in/30cm apart.

Lysimachia ephemerum grows to 4ft x 12in/1.2m x 30cm.

ADDITIONAL PLANTING

SPRING COLOUR

In autumn:
Plant 25 *Primula vulgaris* (primroses) scattered throughout the bed.

Plant 20 *Leucojum aestivum* throughout the bed.

Plant 50 *Muscari armeniacum* 'Blue Spike' (grape hyacinth) bulbs interplanted with 50 *Narcissus* 'Hawera' bulbs towards the front of the bed.

Plant 40 white *Narcissus* 'Cheerfulness' bulbs at the back of the bed.

Plant 20 *Tulipa* 'Bellona' bulbs and 20 *T.* 'Purissima' bulbs all over the bed.

SUMMER COLOUR

In spring:
Plant 15 *Digitalis purpurea* f. *albiflora* (white foxgloves) in spaces throughout the bed.

In autumn plant 20 *Ornithogalum arabicum* bulbs and 20 *Camassia quamash* bulbs throughout the bed.

In late spring plant white *Impatiens* (busy Lizzies) in any gaps in the summer.

GENERAL CARE

Wire the wall with vine eyes.

Feed in spring with a general fertilizer.

Watch out for blackfly infestation on the honeysuckle early in the year, and spray or pinch and wash off.

Cut off old flower spikes as they fade.

Cut off tulips as the leaves yellow, and feed.

Keep the lonicera tied in, as it grows very quickly.

Pull out the busy Lizzies after the first frost.

PLANT DETAILS

Alchemilla mollis **(lady's mantle)**
SOIL: Any, except boggy.
CONDITIONS: Sun or shade.
COLOUR: Greenish yellow.
FLOWERING: Early summer to mid-summer.
FEEDING: Spring.
PRUNING: Cut to the ground after flowering to encourage fresh foliage and eliminate seeding.
GENERAL COMMENTS: A truly versatile plant with sprays of tiny flowers held above pretty leaves which look lovely when wet. It can be dried. It is very good for picking, especially with roses.

Anemone x *hybrida* **'Honorine Jobert'**
SOIL: Fertile, which does not dry out.
CONDITIONS: Part shade.
COLOUR: Single white flowers with a yellow centre.
FLOWERING: Late summer to mid-autumn.
FEEDING: Spring.
PRUNING: Cut down old flower stems after flowering.
GENERAL COMMENTS: An extremely valuable plant for late summer. It does not like to be moved, but spreads once it has settled down, so you will need to restrict the size of the clump.

Campanula persicifolia **var.** *alba*
SOIL: Any.
CONDITIONS: Sun or shade.
COLOUR: White.
FLOWERING: Early summer to late summer.

FEEDING: Spring.
PRUNING: Cut the old flower stems down to 12in/30cm in late autumn.
GENERAL COMMENTS: Produces a neat mat of leaves from which grow tall spikes of white bell-like flowers.

Euphorbia amygdaloides var. robbiae
SOIL: Ordinary, well drained.
CONDITIONS: Sun, part shade or shade.
COLOUR: Greeny yellow.
FLOWERING: Early spring to late spring.
FEEDING: Spring.
PRUNING: When the flowers go brown cut them off either to the leaves or right to the ground.
GENERAL COMMENTS: A very useful plant, which will spread once it is established. Be careful when you cut it, as the milky sap is a bad skin irritant.

Lonicera tragophylla
SOIL: Any.
CONDITIONS: Will grow in deep shade.
COLOUR: Golden yellow.
FLOWERING: Early summer to mid-summer.
FEEDING: Spring.
PRUNING: Prune after flowering to keep to the height you want.
GENERAL COMMENTS: A very showy plant with red berries in the autumn. You need to keep an eye out for blackfly early in the year and clean them off manually. It also looks good grown up into a tree.

Lunaria annua var. albiflora (honesty)
SOIL: Any.
CONDITIONS: Sun or shade.
COLOUR: White.
FLOWERING: Spring.
FEEDING: Spring.
PRUNING: None.
GENERAL COMMENTS: This white-flowered honesty is a wonderful plant, but if you don't want too many leave the pretty seed pods on the plant and pull it up in the autumn and throw away the old plant.

Lysimachia ephemerum
SOIL: Any, but it does not like to dry out.
CONDITIONS: Tolerant of sun or shade.
COLOUR: White.
FLOWERING: Mid-summer to early autumn.
FEEDING: Spring.
PRUNING: Cut old flower stems down to 12in/30cm as they finish.
GENERAL COMMENTS: A proud and upright plant which needs no staking. An excellent companion for a shady border. It should be used more often.

A SHADY BED AGAINST A WALL: GREEN, PURPLE AND WHITE

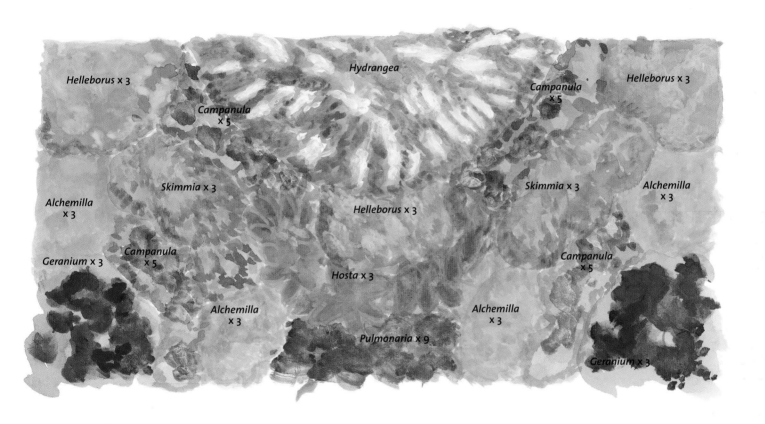

Helleborus x 3

Hydrangea

Campanula x 5

Helleborus x 3

Campanula x 5

Skimmia x 3

Alchemilla x 3

Alchemilla x 3

Skimmia x 3

Helleborus x 3

Geranium x 3

Campanula x 5

Campanula x 5

Hosta x 3

Alchemilla x 3

Alchemilla x 3

Pulmonaria x 9

Geranium x 3

	THE PLANTS	QUANTITIES
1	*Hosta* 'Frances Williams'	3
2	*Helleborus argutifolius*	9
3	*Pulmonaria* 'Lewis Palmer'	9
4	*Hydrangea paniculata* 'Grandiflora'	1
5	*Skimmia* x *confusa* 'Kew Green'	6
6	*Alchemilla mollis*	12
7	*Geranium* 'Johnson's Blue'	6
8	*Campanula persicifolia*	20

SIZE AND POSITION

Alchemilla mollis grows to 12in x 12in/30cm x 30cm. Plant 12in/30cm apart.

Campanula persicifolia grows to 24in x 12in/60cm x 30cm. Plant 12in/30cm apart.

Geranium 'Johnson's Blue' grows to 12in x 18in/30cm x 45cm. Plant 12in/30cm apart.

Helleborus argutifolius grows to 30in x 24in/75cm x 60cm. Plant 15in/38cm apart.

Hosta 'Frances Williams' grows to 30in x 24in/75cm x 60cm. Plant 18in/45cm apart.

Hydrangea paniculata 'Grandiflora' grows to 6ft x 6ft/1.8m x 1.8m.

Pulmonaria 'Lewis Palmer' grows to 18in x 12in/45cm x 30cm. Plant every 9in/23cm.

Skimmia x *confusa* 'Kew Green' grows to 24in x 24in/60cm x 60cm. Plant 18in/45cm apart.

ADDITIONAL PLANTING

SPRING COLOUR

In autumn:
Plant 50 *Anemone blanda* corms in mixed colours throughout the bed.

Plant 5 *Fritillaria imperialis* 'Lutea' (crown imperials) bulbs in front of the hydrangea.

Plant 20 *Cyclamen coum* corms all over the bed.

Plant 50 *Puschkinia scilloides* var. *libanotica* all over the bed.

Plant 20 dwarf *Narcissus* 'Minnow' bulbs and 50 *Muscari azureum* 'Album' (grape hyacinths) bulbs in drifts throughout the bed.

SUMMER COLOUR

In autumn:
Plant 20 bulbs of *Hyacinthoides hispanica* 'Alba' (white bluebells) and 20 *Ornithogalum arabicum* bulbs in drifts between the plants towards the front.

Plant pale yellow *Viola* 'Moonlight' around the pulmonarias – as many as are needed to fill any gaps.

GENERAL CARE

This bed needs remarkably little care.

In spring tidy through the whole bed, pulling off any dead leaves, and feed with a general fertilizer.

Keep the hostas well protected from slugs before the leaves appear.

Make sure that the plants do not dry out.

PLANT DETAILS

Alchemilla mollis (lady's mantle)
SOIL: Any, except boggy.
CONDITIONS: Sun or shade.
COLOUR: Greenish yellow.
FLOWERING: Early summer to mid-summer.
FEEDING: Spring.
PRUNING: Cut back to the ground after flowering.
GENERAL COMMENTS: A truly versatile plant with delicate sprays of tiny flowers held above very pretty leaves. The leaves look wonderful with raindrops sitting on them.

Campanula persicifolia
SOIL: Any.
CONDITIONS: Sun or shade.
COLOUR: Purple blue.
FLOWERING: Early summer to late summer.
FEEDING: Spring.
PRUNING: Cut the old flower stems down to 12in/30cm in autumn.
GENERAL COMMENTS: Has pretty purple-blue bells on upright stems, which grow from a neat mat of mid-green leaves.

Geranium 'Johnson's Blue'
SOIL: Good, but not too wet.
CONDITIONS: Sun or shade.
COLOUR: Lavender blue.
FLOWERING: Late spring to late summer.
FEEDING: Spring, and when the first flowering is over.
PRUNING: Cut back and tidy up when first flowering is finished.

GENERAL COMMENTS:
A lovely strong blue geranium, easy to grow and easy to obtain. It also looks good planted in long grass.

Helleborus argutifolius
SOIL: Moisture-retentive but not boggy.
CONDITIONS: Semi shade.
COLOUR: Pale apple green.
FLOWERING: Mid-winter to early summer.
FEEDING: With bonemeal in autumn and general fertilizer in spring.
PRUNING: Remove old flower branches and old leaves when they start to look unattractive.
GENERAL COMMENTS:
A sculptural plant with striking early green flowers and coarse, spiny, deeply divided leaves.

Hosta **'Frances Williams'**
SOIL: Well drained but moisture-retentive, enriched with leaf mould or manure.
CONDITIONS: Best in shade or partial shade, to ensure that the variegation on the leaves remains at its best.
COLOUR: Lavender flower spikes.
FLOWERING: Mid-summer to late summer.
FEEDING: Spring.
PRUNING: Cut off old flower spikes.

GENERAL COMMENTS:
Hostas are wonderful eyecatching plants, and 'Frances Williams' has lovely dark green leaves with yellow green margins. It needs protection from slugs and snails from the moment it starts to poke through the earth in spring.

Hydrangea paniculata **'Grandiflora'**
SOIL: Damp, rich.
CONDITIONS: Shade.
COLOUR: Greeny white in bud, cream when in full flower and fading to pink.
FLOWERING: Mid-summer to mid-autumn.
FEEDING: Mulch in winter and feed with a general fertilizer in spring.
PRUNING: Only prune to keep to the required shape.
GENERAL COMMENTS:
A very handsome shrub, which is easy to grow.

Pulmonaria **'Lewis Palmer'**
SOIL: Any.
CONDITIONS: Tolerant of sun or shade.
COLOUR: Rich purple blue.
FLOWERING: Late winter to mid-spring.
FEEDING: Spring.
PRUNING: Shear the whole plant to the ground after flowering to get a second flush of healthier foliage and to eliminate seeding.

GENERAL COMMENTS: The flower sprays are at their best before the leaves are fully open, but once the leaves open out they are a good dark green with silver spots.

Skimmia x *confusa* **'Kew Green'**
SOIL: Rich, fertile, which does not dry out.
CONDITIONS: Prefers shade.
COLOUR: White.
FLOWERING: Mid-spring to late spring.
FEEDING: Spring.
PRUNING: None.
GENERAL COMMENTS:
A reliable and handsome small evergreen shrub. It has good green glossy leaves, which are a wonderful foil for other plants, and pretty, fragrant flowers.

A SUNNY BED AT WATER'S EDGE

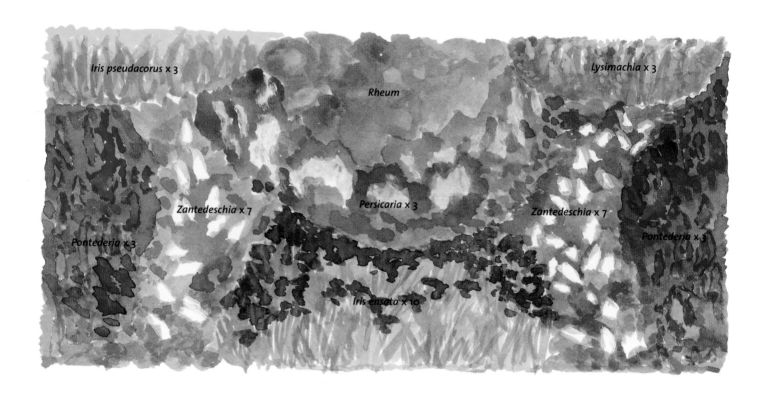

THE PLANTS	QUANTITIES
1 *Lysimachia vulgaris*	3
2 *Persicaria campanulata*	3
3 *Iris pseudacorus*	3
4 *Pontederia cordata*	6
5 *Rheum* 'Ace of Hearts'	1
6 *Iris ensata*	10
7 *Zantedeschia aethiopica*	14

SIZE AND POSITION

Iris ensata grows to 24–36in/60–90cm and spreads. Plant 18in/45cm apart.

Iris pseudacorus grows up to 6ft/1.8m and spreads. Plant 30in/75cm apart.

Lysimachia vulgaris grows to 4ft x 4ft/1.2m x 1.2m and spreads. Plant 30in/75cm apart.

Persicaria campanulata grows to 24in–4ft x 24in/60cm–1.2m x 60cm and spreads. Plant 36in/90cm apart.

Pontederia cordata grows to 4ft/1.2m and spreads. Plant 30in/75cm apart.

Rheum 'Ace of Hearts' grows to 4ft x 4ft/1.2m x 1.2m.

Zantedeschia aethiopica grows to 18–36in x 24in/45–90cm x 60cm. Plant 18in/45cm apart.

ADDITIONAL PLANTING

SPRING COLOUR

In autumn:
Plant 25 *Cyclamen coum* and 25 *C. c.* f. *pallidum* 'Album' corms in any gaps at the front and sides of the bed.

SUMMER COLOUR

This bed will spread to fill its position in a year and will not need any extra planting. Rather the reverse: you will need to pull things out to keep them in check.

GENERAL CARE

Pull off any dead leaves and clean out the bed in early spring.

Keep an eye on how things are growing and restrict the clumps to the sizes required.

Cut off the iris flowers as they brown off and tidy over the clumps if necessary at any time.

Protect the crown of the rheum in winter.

PLANT DETAILS

Iris ensata (**Japanese flag**)
SOIL: Wet.
CONDITIONS: Sun or partial shade.
COLOUR: Purple with a yellow blaze on the falls.
FLOWERING: Late spring to mid-summer.
FEEDING: Spring.
PRUNING: Thin out if the clump gets too big.
GENERAL COMMENTS: Has a prominent mid-rib to the leaves. A pretty plant, but it likes to spread.

Iris pseudacorus (**yellow flag**)
SOIL: Wet.
CONDITIONS: Sun.
COLOUR: Yellow.
FLOWERING: Mid-spring to early summer.
FEEDING: Spring.
PRUNING: Pull out any parts you do not want, as it will start to creep from its allotted area.
GENERAL COMMENTS: A reliable native plant which is very pretty.

Lysimachia vulgaris
SOIL: Wet.
CONDITIONS: Sun or partial shade.
COLOUR: Yellow.
FLOWERING: Late spring to mid-summer.
FEEDING: Spring.
PRUNING: Cut back the old

flowering stems in autumn.
GENERAL COMMENTS: A reliable and rewarding plant which carries its yellow spikes on strong upright stems.

Persicaria campanulata

SOIL: Wet.
CONDITIONS: Any situation except completely sun-baked.
COLOUR: Pale pink and white.
FLOWERING: Late spring to early autumn.
FEEDING: Spring.
PRUNING: None.
GENERAL COMMENTS: A pretty plant for a damp position. It will start to wander sideways, so just pull out any that you do not need.

Pontederia cordata

SOIL: Moist, by water.
CONDITIONS: Sun or partial shade.
COLOUR: Blue.
FLOWERING: Early summer to late autumn.
FEEDING: Spring.
PRUNING: Pull out as it spreads beyond its allotted area.
GENERAL COMMENTS: Has good blue drumsticks held over pretty leaves. Can be invasive.

Rheum 'Ace of Hearts'

SOIL: Deep, rich and moist.
CONDITIONS: Sun or shade.
COLOUR: White.
FLOWERING: Late spring to early summer.
FEEDING: Spring.
PRUNING: None.
GENERAL COMMENTS: A very striking plant with huge rhubarb-like leaves. Add manure each year in winter to protect the crowns.

Zantedeschia aethiopica (arum lily)

SOIL: Wet.
CONDITIONS: Sun.
COLOUR: White.
FLOWERING: Mid-summer to late autumn.
FEEDING: Spring.
PRUNING: None.
GENERAL COMMENTS: A stately plant, which has clean green leaves and pure white furled flowers. Cover with bracken or straw in the winter to protect it from hard frosts.

A SHADY ISLAND BED NEAR WATER; MIXED PLANTING

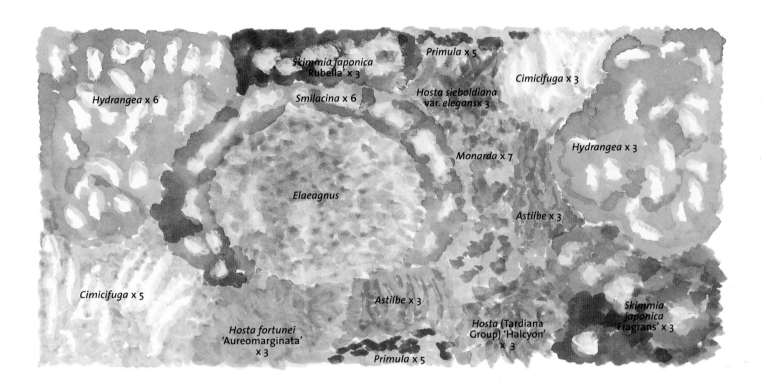

Hydrangea x 6

Skimmia japonica 'Rubella' x 3

Smilacina x 6

Primula x 5

Hosta sieboldiana var. elegans x 3

Cimicifuga x 3

Hydrangea x 3

Monarda x 7

Elaeagnus

Astilbe x 3

Cimicifuga x 5

Astilbe x 3

Hosta fortunei 'Aureomarginata' x 3

Primula x 5

Hosta (Tardiana Group) 'Halcyon' x 3

Skimmia japonica 'Fragrans' x 3

	THE PLANTS	QUANTITIES
1	*Astilbe* var. *taquetti* 'Visions' (or any purple/pink variety)	6
2	*Hydrangea quercifolia*	9
3	*Cimicifuga simplex* 'White Pearl' (recently renamed *Actaea matsumurae* 'White Pearl')	8
4	*Skimmia japonica* 'Fragrans'	3
5	*Smilacina racemosa*	6
6	*Primula pulverulenta*	10
7	*Hosta fortunei* 'Aureomarginata'	3
8	*Hosta* (Tardiana Group) 'Halcyon'	3
9	*Elaeagnus angustifolia*	1
10	*Monarda* 'Cambridge Scarlet'	7
11	*Hosta sieboldiana* var. *elegans*	3
12	*Skimmia japonica* 'Rubella'	3

SIZE AND POSITION

Astilbe var. *taquetti* 'Visions' grows to 36in x 12in/90cm x 30cm. Plant 12in/30cm apart.

Cimicifuga simplex 'White Pearl' grows to 36in x 18in/90cm x 45cm. Plant 18in/45cm apart.

Elaeagnus angustifolia grows to 8ft x 5ft/2.5m x 1.5m.

Hosta fortunei 'Aureomarginata' grows to 24in x 18in/60cm x 45cm. Plant 12in/30cm apart.

Hosta (Tardiana Group) 'Halcyon' grows to 18in x 18in/45cm x 45cm. Plant 12in/30cm apart.

Hosta sieboldiana var. *elegans* grows to 36in x 24in/90cm x 60cm. Plant 18in/45cm apart.

Hydrangea quercifolia grows to 4ft x 36in/1.2m x 90cm. Plant 24in/60cm apart.

Monarda 'Cambridge Scarlet' grows to 36in x 12in/90cm x 30cm. Plant 18in/45cm apart.

Primula pulverulenta grows to 18in x 12in/45cm x 30cm. Plant 8in/20cm apart.

Skimmia japonica 'Fragrans' grows to 30in x 24in/75cm x 60cm. Plant 18in/45cm apart.

Skimmia japonica 'Rubella' grows to 30in x 24in/75cm x 60cm. Plant 18in/45cm apart.

Smilacina racemosa grows to 36in x 24in/90cm x 60cm. Plant 15in/38cm apart.

ADDITIONAL PLANTING

SPRING COLOUR

In autumn:
Plant 30 *Erythronium revolutum* 'White Beauty' bulbs in any gaps towards the front.

Plant 23 *Iris* 'George' at the front of the bed.

SUMMER COLOUR

In spring:
Plant dark purple and pale pink violas in spaces at the edges of the bed.

In early summer:
Plant white *Impatiens* (busy Lizzies) in any spaces throughout the bed.

GENERAL CARE

Tidy over the cimicifugas, astilbes, monarda and smilacina as they die back in late autumn.

Feed in spring with a general fertilizer.

Protect the hostas with slug pellets as soon as the first spikes appear in early spring.

Tidy through the bed in spring, clearing away any debris.

PLANT DETAILS

Astilbe var. *taquetti* 'Visions'
SOIL: Wet or boggy, which does not dry out.
CONDITIONS: Tolerates full sun or partial shade.
COLOUR: Purple or pink.
FLOWERING: Late spring to late summer.
FEEDING: Spring.
PRUNING: Leave the old flower heads on over winter as they look pretty, especially if covered in frost. Cut back in the spring.
GENERAL COMMENTS: Has good plumes of colour.

Cimicifuga simplex 'White Pearl'
SOIL: Cool, moist.
CONDITIONS: Sun or part shade.
COLOUR: White.
FLOWERING: Early autumn to late autumn.
FEEDING: Spring.
PRUNING: None.
GENERAL COMMENTS:
A wonderful plant for late impact, guaranteed to prompt a response to its stately and showy display of tall branched flower spikes with many elegant white plumes. Once you have planted it do not disturb it.

Elaeagnus angustifolia
SOIL: Fertile, rich, not chalk.
CONDITIONS: Sun or part shade.
COLOUR: White.
FLOWERING: Early summer.
FEEDING: Spring.
PRUNING: After flowering if you need to restrict the height.
GENERAL COMMENTS: A good tough shrub with silver willow-

like leaves. It is very fragrant.

Hosta fortunei 'Aureomarginata'
SOIL: Well drained but moisture-retentive, enriched with leaf mould or manure.
CONDITIONS: Best in shade or partial shade.
COLOUR: Green leaves edged with gold, lavender flowers.
FLOWERING: Mid-summer to late summer.
FEEDING: Spring.
PRUNING: Cut off old flower spikes.
GENERAL COMMENTS: A pretty hosta with green leaves edged with gold. It keeps its variegation best in shade. Beware of slugs and snails and protect as soon as the plant starts to appear.

Hosta (Tardiana Group) 'Halcyon'
SOIL: Well drained but moisture-retentive.
CONDITIONS: Sun, partial shade, shade.
COLOUR: Blue-grey leaves and large lavender flowers.
FLOWERING: Mid-summer to late summer.
FEEDING: With a general fertilizer in spring.
PRUNING: Cut off old flower spikes once they have finished.
GENERAL COMMENTS: This

is a lovely hosta with strongly coloured leaves. Remember to put down slug and snail protection as soon as you see the first spike of a leaf in early spring and carry on protecting it throughout the year.

Hosta sieboldiana var. elegans
SOIL: Well drained, moisture-retentive.
CONDITIONS: Sun or shade.
COLOUR: Grey leaves and pale lilac flowers.
FLOWERING: Mid-summer to late summer.
FEEDING: General fertilizer in spring.
PRUNING: Cut off the old flower spikes as they finish.
GENERAL COMMENTS: A stately hosta with lovely deeply veined grey-green leaves.

Hydrangea quercifolia
SOIL: Moist and well drained; dislikes dryness at its roots.
CONDITIONS: Best in partial shade or shade.
COLOUR: Creamy white.
FLOWERING: Mid-summer to early autumn.
FEEDING: With a general fertilizer in spring. Sometimes benefits from an additional summer feed.
PRUNING: Cut out any weak stems in spring.
GENERAL COMMENTS: The

oak-leaved hydrangea. As well as having beautiful panicles of white flowers, its leaves colour beautifully in autumn, making it a very attractive shrub. Its only drawback is that it can be slow to establish.

Monarda 'Cambridge Scarlet' (bergamot)
SOIL: Any that does not dry out.
CONDITIONS: Sun, part shade or shade.
COLOUR: Deep scarlet.
FLOWERING: Early summer to late summer.
FEEDING: Spring.
PRUNING: Cut back old flower stems in autumn.
GENERAL COMMENTS: Has unusual hooded flowers all the way up a straight stem over a dense clump of aromatic leaves.

Primula pulverulenta
SOIL: Fertile, which does not dry out.
CONDITIONS: Full sun or partial shade.
COLOUR: Crimson.
FLOWERING: Early summer to mid-summer.
FEEDING: Spring, and again after flowering.
PRUNING: Cut back old flower stems to the base as they die.
GENERAL COMMENTS: The bright flowers are carried on strong upright stems in several tiers. They originate

from a neat rosette of mid-green leaves.

Skimmia japonica 'Fragrans' and S.j. 'Rubella'
SOIL: Any.
CONDITIONS: Part shade or shade.
COLOUR: White.
FLOWERING: Early spring to late spring.
FEEDING: Spring.
PRUNING: Not much required, but can be cut after flowering to improve their shape.
GENERAL COMMENTS: Tough, shiny leaves make this a good solid handsome plant. 'Fragrans' has deliciously fragrant flowers. 'Rubella' has distinctive red buds which last on the plant all winter before they break into white flowers.

Smilacina racemosa
SOIL: Moisture-retentive, with plenty of leaf mould.
CONDITIONS: A natural woodland plant, it prefers shade.
COLOUR: Creamy white.
FLOWERING: Late spring to mid-summer.
FEEDING: Spring.
PRUNING: Cut back old flower stems in autumn unless you particularly want the red berries.
GENERAL COMMENTS: The pretty, fluffy flowers have a lovely scent.

A SEASIDE ISLAND BED IN SUN: MIXED PLANTING

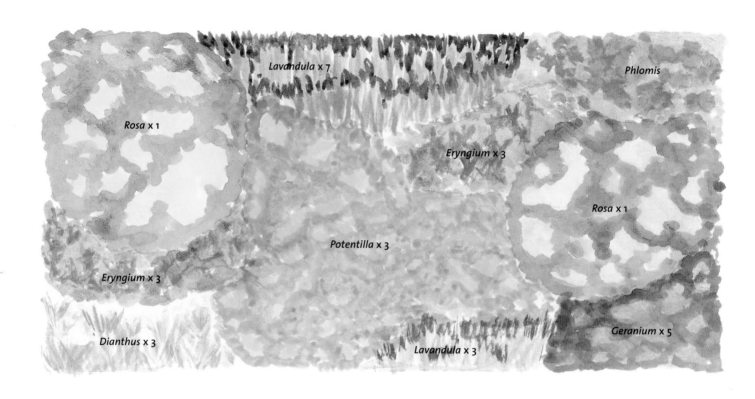

THE PLANTS	QUANTITIES
1 *Phlomis fruticosa*	1
2 *Dianthus* 'Haytor White'	13
3 *Lavandula* x *intermedia* 'Grosso'	10
4 *Eryngium bourgatii*	6
5 *Potentilla fruticosa* 'Moonlight' (also known as P.f. 'Maanelys')	3
6 *Geranium maculatum* 'Chatto'	5
7 *Rosa* 'Agnes'	2

SIZE AND POSITION

Dianthus 'Haytor White' grows to 9in x 9in/23cm x 23cm. Plant 6in/15cm apart.

Eryngium bourgatii grows to 3½ft x 24in/1.1m x 60cm. Plant 12in/30cm apart.

Geranium maculatum 'Chatto' grows to 18in x 18in/45cm x 45cm. Plant 12in/30cm apart.

Lavandula x intermedia 'Grosso' grows to 18in x 18in/45cm x 45cm. Plant 12in/30cm apart.

Phlomis fruticosa grows to 36in–4ft x 24in/90cm–1.2m x 60cm.

Potentilla fruticosa 'Maanelys' grows to 4ft x 5ft/1.2m x 1.5m. Plant 18in/45cm apart.

Rosa 'Agnes' grows 6ft x 5ft/1.8m x 1.5m.

ADDITIONAL PLANTING

SPRING COLOUR

In autumn:
Plant 50 *Scilla siberica* bulbs all over the bed.

Plant 20 *Narcissus poeticus* var. *recurvus* (old pheasant's eye) bulbs in groups of 5.

In autumn plant 20 chionodoxa bulbs all over the bed.

Plant 25 crocus corms in blue and yellow all over the bed.

In spring:
Plant 30 *Bellis* (white carpet plants) towards the front.

SUMMER COLOUR

In autumn:
Plant 25 Dutch *Iris* 'White Bridge' or 'Hildegarde' in groups of 5 all over the bed.

In spring:
Scatter seed of pink linaria over the bed, and thin them out as they grow.

In late spring:
Sow seeds of *Mentzelia lindleyi* (also known as *Bartonia aurea*) in any gaps. They have strongly scented yellow flowers from early summer until autumn.

GENERAL CARE

Clean the bed of any old leaves in either autumn or spring.

Feed the whole bed in spring with a general fertilizer.

Clip the lavender in early spring and cut back again when the flowers fade.

Keep the roses and dianthus deadheaded.

Feed the roses again in mid-summer.

Clip over the phlomis in late summer to stop it from getting too big and straggly.

Prune the roses in winter.

Put some grit under the dianthus and convolvulus in the autumn.

Cut off the eryngium flower stalks in late autumn.

PLANT DETAILS

Dianthus **'Haytor White'**
SOIL: Well drained, light.
CONDITIONS: Sun.
COLOUR: Pure white.
FLOWERING: Late spring to late summer.
FEEDING: Bonemeal in autumn, and a summer feed after it has finished flowering.
PRUNING: Cut back old flower stalks after flowering and trim the plant to a neat mound.
GENERAL COMMENTS: A pretty plant with a neat habit and tidy scented flowers.

Eryngium bourgatii
SOIL: Dry, well drained.
CONDITIONS: Sun.
COLOUR: Steely blue.
FLOWERING: Mid-summer to early autumn.
FEEDING: Spring.
PRUNING: Cut off old flower heads in spring.
GENERAL COMMENTS: Has neat tufts of divided blue-grey foliage from which the lovely thistle-like flowers stand on strong branched stems.

Geranium maculatum **'Chatto'**
SOIL: Good, fertile.
CONDITIONS: Sun or part shade.
COLOUR: Pale pink.
FLOWERING: Early summer and mid-summer.
FEEDING: Spring.
PRUNING: Cut off the old flowering stems and dead leaves once they are finished.
GENERAL COMMENTS: One of the best geraniums: very pretty.

Lavandula x intermedia 'Grosso'

SOIL: Light.
CONDITIONS: Full sun.
COLOUR: Purple blue.
FLOWERING: Early summer to late summer.
FEEDING: Spring.
PRUNING: Trim off the flowers once they have finished, and shape up the bush to stop it getting too sprawly. Trim over the whole plant again in mid-spring, but avoid cutting back into old wood.
GENERAL COMMENTS: This is one of the most scented lavenders, widely used for its oil. If you want to save and dry it, cut the flower stalks before the flowers are fully open to maximize the scent.

Phlomis fruticosa

SOIL: Light, free-draining.
CONDITIONS: Sun.
COLOUR: Yellow.
FLOWERING: Early summer to mid-summer.
FEEDING: Spring.
PRUNING: Shape up in early autumn if required.
GENERAL COMMENTS: A native Mediterranean, this has lovely grey-green felted leaves from which grow long stalks of whorled yellow flowers.

Potentilla fruticosa 'Maanelys'

SOIL: Well drained.
CONDITIONS: Sun or part shade.
COLOUR: Soft pale yellow.
FLOWERING: Late spring to mid-autumn.
FEEDING: Spring.
PRUNING: If necessary trim to shape in spring. Do not cut too hard.
GENERAL COMMENTS: Their long flowering time and tough nature make potentillas invaluable. This one has a slightly upright habit and green leaves, and is smothered by pale yellow flowers.

Rosa 'Agnes'

SOIL: Any that is not pure chalk or sun.
CONDITIONS: Sun or part shade.
COLOUR: Pale yellow.
FLOWERING: Spring, and sporadically in late summer.
FEEDING: Spring, and again in mid-summer. It will also appreciate a mulch with manure in winter.
PRUNING: In winter when it is not frosty, cut out any dead, crossing, weak or diseased wood and reduce the rose if necessary by about a third.
GENERAL COMMENTS: A wonderful soft yellow rose, with pretty green leaves with distinctive veins. It can also be grown as a climber.

A COLD EXPOSED SITE: A WINDBREAK

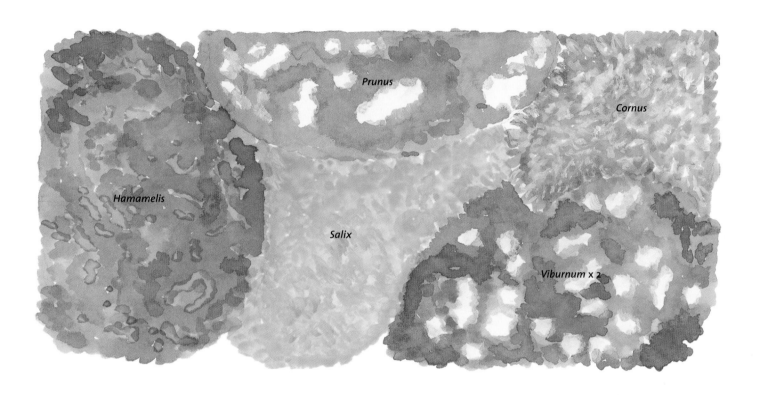

THE PLANTS	QUANTITIES
1 *Cornus alba* 'Elegantissima'	1
2 *Hamamelis* x *intermedia* 'Hiltingbury'	1
3 *Viburnum opulus*	2
4 *Salix alba* 'Chermesina' (also known as *S.a.* subsp.
5 *vitellina* 'Britensis')	1
Prunus spinosa	1

This planting is designed to cope with a place where very little else will grow and is not so much a bed as a windbreak. The blackthorn will also be an excellent security defence. All the plants can be kept smaller than their full size.

SIZE AND POSITION

Cornus alba 'Elegantissima' grows to 6ft x 5ft/1.8m x 1.5m.

Hamamelis x *intermedia* 'Hiltingbury' grows to 10ft x 8ft/3m x 2.5m.

Prunus spinosa grows to 10ft x 10ft/3m x 3m and larger, but can and must be kept in check.

Salix alba 'Chermesina' grows to 10ft x 5ft/3m x 1.5m.

Viburnum opulus grows to 6ft x 6ft/1.8m x 1.8m. Plant 36in/90cm apart.

ADDITIONAL PLANTING

SPRING COLOUR

In autumn:
Plant 100 *Anemone nemorosa* (wood anemones) all over the bed in any gaps.

Plant 50 *Ornithogalum umbellatum* (star of Bethlehem) to give some colour in mid-spring.

In spring:
Plant 50 *Cyclamen coum* and *C. hederifolium* (autumn flowering) corms, dotted throughout the bed.

Plant 50 *Galanthus nivalis* (snowdrops) for early winter colour, after flowering.

SUMMER COLOUR

We do not recommend planting any additional annuals for the summer. The shrubs in this planting are big and will quickly dry out the soil and swamp any annuals.

GENERAL CARE

Make sure that the plants are well mulched on planting. Do not let them dry out during the growing season.

Add a general fertilizer in the first spring to get them going.

After this these plants are tough enough to take care of themselves. The only work needed is to cut out any dead wood and to restrict the size of the plants as required. The *Cornus alba* can be pruned hard in early spring to encourage new growth, which will produce the strongest red stems in winter.

PLANT DETAILS

***Cornus alba* 'Elegantissima'**
SOIL: Any.
CONDITIONS: Sun or part shade.
COLOUR: Small white flowers. Bright red stems in winter.
FLOWERING: Late spring to early summer.
FEEDING: Spring.
PRUNING: Prune hard in mid-spring to encourage new bright red stems for good colour in winter.
GENERAL COMMENTS: They have lovely variegated leaves, and the bright stems in winter are very attractive.

***Hamamelis* x *intermedia* 'Hiltingbury' (witch hazel)**
SOIL: Any.
CONDITIONS: Tolerant of many extremes.
COLOUR: Coppery coloured spider-like flowers.
FLOWERING: Early winter to early spring.
FEEDING: Spring.
PRUNING: Shape up if required after flowering.
GENERAL COMMENTS: An extremely tough and hardy plant with hazel-like leaves. The flowers are beautifully scented – a bonus during the winter months.

Prunus spinosa **(blackthorn)**
SOIL: Any.
CONDITIONS: Tolerant of extreme conditions.
COLOUR: White.
FLOWERING: Early spring to mid-spring.
FEEDING: Spring.
PRUNING: After flowering.
GENERAL COMMENTS:
A dense thorny shrub which forms a very good windbreak. The small black fruits in autumn are sloes which can be used to flavour gin or vodka. Be careful of its really sharp thorns.

Salix alba **'Chermesina'**
SOIL: Any.
CONDITIONS: Very tolerant of extreme conditions.
COLOUR: Grown for the brilliant red of its stems in winter.
FLOWERING: Pretty catkins appear in spring.
FEEDING: Spring.
PRUNING: Cut back really hard every other year and the brilliance of its winter stems will increase.
GENERAL COMMENTS:
It looks at its best in the winter when the brilliance of its scarlet stems is at its height.

Viburnum opulus
(guelder rose)
SOIL: Any.
CONDITIONS: Sun or shade.
COLOUR: White.
FLOWERING: Early summer to mid-summer.
FEEDING: Spring.
PRUNING: Cut out any diseased or dead wood in autumn. Prune to shape if necessary.
GENERAL COMMENTS: Has lovely autumn colouring, and pretty red berries in autumn and winter which make it very popular with birds.

A WINDY, COLD AND EXPOSED BED:
SHRUBS ONLY

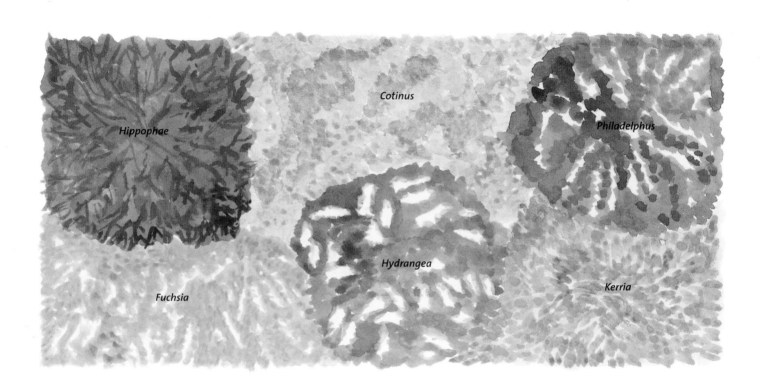

THE PLANTS	QUANTITIES
1 *Hippophae rhamnoides*	1
2 *Philadelphus* 'Virginal'	1
3 *Hydrangea paniculata* 'Grandiflora'	1
4 *Fuchsia magellanica* 'Alba' (also known as *F.m.* var *molinae*)	1
5 *Cotinus coggygria*	1
6 *Kerria japonica* 'Picta'	1

SIZE AND POSITION

Cotinus coggygria grows to 8ft x 8ft/2.5m x 2.5m.

Fuchsia magellanica 'Alba' grows to 6ft x 5ft/1.8m x 1.5m, if restricted.

Hippophae rhamnoides grows to 10ft x 6ft/3m x 1.8m.

Hydrangea paniculata 'Grandiflora' grows to 6ft x 6ft/1.8m x 1.8m.

Kerria japonica 'Picta' grows to 4ft x 4ft/1.2m x 1.2m.

Philadelphus 'Virginal' grows to 9ft x 4½ft/2.75m x 1.4m.

ADDITIONAL PLANTING

SPRING COLOUR

In spring:
Plant *Myosotis* (forget-me-nots) throughout the bed.

Plant *Galium odoratum* (sweet woodruff) throughout the bed as permanent ground cover, which will spread where it wants to.

In autumn:
Plant 50 *Narcissus* 'Hawera' bulbs and 50 *N.* 'Thalia' bulbs throughout the bed.

SUMMER COLOUR

Plant violas throughout the bed.

In spring:
Plant *Tropaeolum peregrinum* (canary creeper) to wander through the shrubs. It grows up to 6ft/1.8m and is pale yellow with frilled flowers. It is tolerant of sun or shade and is an annual that will not be swamped by the large shrubs once it has got going.

GENERAL CARE

Clean the bed up in the early spring.

Feed with a general fertilizer in the spring.

Mulch with well-rotted manure in late winter.

Plant the tropaeolum after the danger of frost has passed, and take it out when it loses its vigour in autumn. Keep it well watered throughout the growing season and feed with tomato fertilizer every two weeks.

Keep an eye on the size of the shrubs and prune to restrict their growth or improve their shapes as necessary.

PLANT DETAILS

Cotinus coggygria
SOIL: Well drained.
CONDITIONS: Sun or partial shade.
COLOUR: Fluffy fawn-coloured flowers.
FLOWERING: Early summer to mid-summer.
FEEDING: Spring.
PRUNING: Not necessary, but can be pruned in autumn if required.
GENERAL COMMENTS: Often known as the smoke bush because of its clouds of fluffy flowers. It has wonderful autumn colouring, but do not let it come into contact with manure or else it will not colour up.

Fuchsia magellanica 'Alba'
SOIL: Any.
CONDITIONS: Sun, part shade or shade.
COLOUR: Very pale pink fading to white.
FLOWERING: Early summer to mid-autumn.
FEEDING: Spring.
PRUNING: Cut back as much as you like in early spring.
GENERAL COMMENTS: A very pretty and hardy fuchsia which is covered with pale single flowers like raindrops. It has lovely peeling papery bark as it gets older.

Hippophae rhamnoides
SOIL: Well drained, ordinary.
CONDITIONS: Sun or part shade.
COLOUR: Yellow.
FLOWERING: Mid-spring.

FEEDING: Spring.
PRUNING: Shape up in mid-summer to late summer, cutting off any long growth.
GENERAL COMMENTS:
A tough plant. It may have the added bonus of orange berries (which are untouched by birds) in winter if there are others planted near by.

Hydrangea paniculata 'Grandiflora'
SOIL: Damp, rich.
CONDITIONS: Shade.
COLOUR: Creamy white flowers which fade to pinky white.
FLOWERING: Mid-summer to mid-autumn.
FEEDING: Mulch in winter and feed in spring.
PRUNING: Just trim in spring to keep in shape.
GENERAL COMMENTS:
A very handsome hydrangea.

Kerria japonica 'Picta'
SOIL: Ordinary.
CONDITIONS: Sun or part shade.
COLOUR: Rich golden yellow flowers with green and white variegated leaves.
FLOWERING: Mid-spring to late spring.
FEEDING: Spring.
PRUNING: Very little – just tidy up after flowering, if necessary.

GENERAL COMMENTS:
Should be more widely grown, if only for its pretty foliage.

Philadelphus 'Virginal'
SOIL: Any, including chalk.
CONDITIONS: Tolerant of difficult conditions in sun or part shade.
COLOUR: White.
FLOWERING: Early summer to mid-summer.
FEEDING: Spring.
PRUNING: Thin out and cut back old wood after flowering. Take some stems right back to the base and leave the new shoots to ripen for next year's flowers.
GENERAL COMMENTS:
A wonderfully scented upright-growing philadelphus.

A DROUGHT-RESISTANT ISLAND BED WITH THIN DRY SOIL

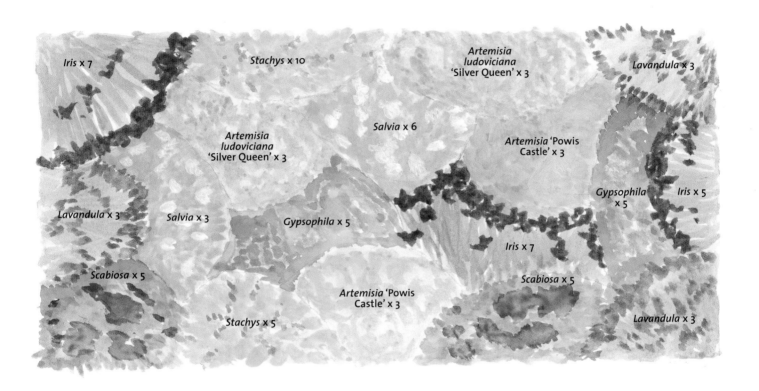

Iris x 7

Stachys x 10

Artemisia
ludoviciana
'Silver Queen' x 3

Lavandula x 3

Artemisia
ludoviciana
'Silver Queen' x 3

Salvia x 6

Artemisia 'Powis
Castle' x 3

Lavandula x 3

Salvia x 3

Gypsophila x 5

Gypsophila
x 5

Iris x 5

Iris x 7

Scabiosa x 5

Artemisia 'Powis
Castle' x 3

Scabiosa x 5

Stachys x 5

Lavandula x 3

	THE PLANTS	QUANTITIES
1	*Iris* 'Ever After' (or any deep wine red variety, e.g. 'Winemaster')	19
2	*Gypsophila* 'Rosenschleier'	10
3	*Scabiosa caucasica* 'Crimson Cushion'	10
4	*Lavandula stoechas* (e.g. 'Papillon')	9
5	*Stachys byzantina* 'Big Ears'	15
6	*Artemisia ludoviciana* 'Silver Queen'	6
7	*Salvia argentea*	9
8	*Artemisia* 'Powis Castle'	6

SIZE AND POSITION

Artemisia ludoviciana 'Silver Queen' grows to 36in x 24in/90cm x 60cm. Plant 15in/38cm apart.

Artemisia 'Powis Castle' grows to 24in x 12in/60cm x 30cm. Plant 12in/30cm apart.

Gypsophila 'Rosenschleier' grows to 3½ft x 12in/1.1m x 30cm. Plant 8in/20cm apart.

Iris 'Ever After' grows to 30in x 8in/75cm x 20cm. Plant 6in/15cm apart.

Lavandula stoechas grows to 15in x 15in/38cm x 38cm. Plant 12in/30cm apart.

Salvia argentea grows to 36in x 12in/90cm x 30cm. Plant 12in/30cm apart.

Scabiosa caucasica 'Crimson Cushion' grows to 12in x 8in/30cm x 20cm. Plant 12in/30cm apart.

Stachys byzantina 'Big Ears' grows to 18in x 12in/45cm x 30cm. Plant 12in/30cm apart.

ADDITIONAL PLANTING

SPRING COLOUR

In autumn:
Plant 40 *Narcissus* 'Geranium' bulbs in groups of 10 all over the bed.

Plant 20 bulbs of each of the following tulips in groups of 5 all over the bed: 'Marilyn', 'Bellflower', 'White Triumphator' and 'Angélique'.

SUMMER COLOUR

In autumn:
Plant 15 Dutch *Iris* 'Purple Sensation' in a group among the *Artemisia* 'Powis Castle' at the front of the bed.

Plant 30 *Allium unifolium* and 30 *A. neapolitanum* bulbs singly all over the bed.

In spring:
Plant 10 pink cosmos in any gaps.

Plant 15 pale pink dahlias in any gaps.

GENERAL CARE

In autumn clear the bed of any debris. Mulch with leaf mould.

Feed with a general fertilizer in spring.

Trim over the lavenders in mid-spring, but do not cut into old wood. Shape up the artemisias in spring, cutting back to new growth.

Cut or pull off the old narcissus leaves after they have died back.

Cut the tulip leaves off once they have gone yellow and feed.

Shape up the artemisias again in July to keep to shape.

Shape up lavenders as they finish flowering, cutting off all old flower stems.

Deadhead scabious to encourage them to keep flowering.

PLANT DETAILS

***Artemisia ludoviciana* 'Silver Queen'**
SOIL: Well drained.
CONDITIONS: Sun.
COLOUR: Grown for its silver leaves.
FLOWERING: Do not allow it to flower.
FEEDING: Spring.
PRUNING: Cut back to new growth in spring, and cut off the flowers before they form in early summer.
GENERAL COMMENTS: Grown for its silver feathery foliage.

***Artemisia* 'Powis Castle'**
SOIL: Well drained.
CONDITIONS: Sun.
COLOUR: Grown for its silvery white foliage.
FLOWERING: Do not let it flower.
FEEDING: Spring.
PRUNING: Cut back in spring to new growth to keep a good shape to the plant and cut off the flowers before they form.
GENERAL COMMENTS: One of the best silver plants. It makes an excellent companion to other silver-leaved plants.

***Gypsophila* 'Rosenschleier'**
SOIL: Well drained.
CONDITIONS: Sun.
COLOUR: Pale pinky white.
FLOWERING: Early summer to late summer.
FEEDING: Spring.
PRUNING: Cut off old flowering stems in autumn.
GENERAL COMMENTS: A pretty delicate plant with clouds of tiny

flowers. It likes to sprawl into other plants.

Iris 'Ever After'
SOIL: Well drained.
CONDITIONS: Sun.
COLOUR: Deep wine red.
FLOWERING: Late spring to early summer.
FEEDING: Spring.
PRUNING: Cut the leaves back to a fan shape about 9in/23cm high in summer after flowering has finished.
GENERAL COMMENTS: A beautifully coloured iris which gives good structure to the bed.

Lavandula stoechas
SOIL: Well drained.
CONDITIONS: Sun.
COLOUR: Dark purple.
FLOWERING: Late spring to mid-summer.
FEEDING: Spring.
PRUNING: Cut off old flower stems as soon as flowering is finished. Trim over the whole plant again in mid-spring, being careful not to cut into old wood.
GENERAL COMMENTS: A pretty French lavender with rounded flowers and showy ears.

Salvia argentea
SOIL: Dry.
CONDITIONS: Sun.
COLOUR: White.
FLOWERING: Mid-summer to late summer.
FEEDING: Spring.

PRUNING: Cut back to new growth in spring.
GENERAL COMMENTS: A lovely plant with leaves covered with silver hairs. It can be rather short-lived, but is well worth growing.

Scabiosa caucasica 'Crimson Cushion'
SOIL: Light, well drained.
CONDITIONS: Sun.
COLOUR: Crimson.
FLOWERING: Mid-summer to early autumn.
FEEDING: Spring.
PRUNING: Cut down old flower stems once they have finished.
GENERAL COMMENTS: A lovely free-flowering scabious which is very good towards the front of the border.

Stachys byzantina 'Big Ears'
SOIL: Well drained.
CONDITIONS: Sun or partial shade.
COLOUR: Puce.
FLOWERING: Mid-summer to late summer.
FEEDING: Spring.
PRUNING: Pull off the leaves if they go brown or if the plant gets too big.
GENERAL COMMENTS: Famous for its large felty silver leaves.

A BED WITH ACID SOIL:
MIXED PLANTING

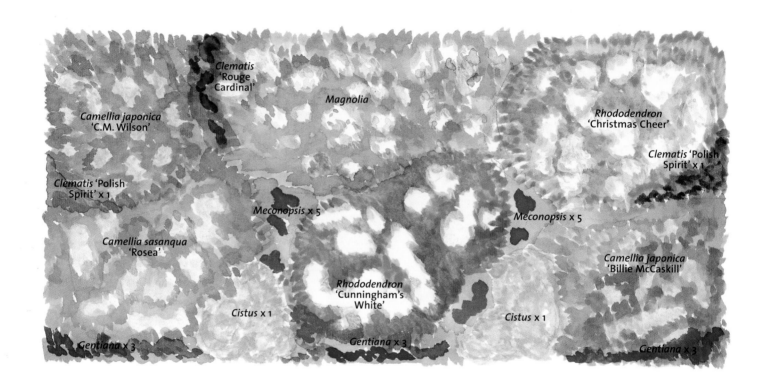

Clematis 'Rouge Cardinal'

Magnolia

Rhododendron 'Christmas Cheer'

Camellia japonica 'C.M. Wilson'

Clematis 'Polish Spirit' x 1

Clematis 'Polish Spirit' x 1

Meconopsis x 5

Meconopsis x 5

Camellia sasanqua 'Rosea'

Camellia japonica 'Billie McCaskill'

Rhododendron 'Cunningham's White'

Cistus x 1

Cistus x 1

Gentiana x 3

Gentiana x 3

Gentiana x 3

THE PLANTS	QUANTITIES
1 *Camellia japonica* 'Billie McCaskill' (or any pale pink single variety)	1
2 *Clematis* 'Polish Spirit'	2
3 *Meconopsis betonicifolia*	10
4 *Gentiana sino-ornata*	9
5 *Camellia sasanqua* 'Rosea' (or any pale pink variety)	1
6 *Magnolia* x *soulangeana* 'Lennei'	1
7 *Cistus* x *argenteus* 'Silver Pink'	2
8 *Clematis* 'Rouge Cardinal'	1
9 *Rhododendron* 'Cunningham's White'	1
10 *Rhododendron* 'Christmas Cheer' (or any large white flushed pale pink, e.g. *R. decorum*)	1
11 *Camellia japonica* 'C.M. Wilson' (or any pale pink double variety)	1

SIZE AND POSITION

Camellia japonica 'Billie McCaskill' and 'C.M. Wilson' grow to approximately 6ft x 3½ft/1.8m x 1.1m.

Camellia sasanqua 'Rosea' grows to 6ft x 4ft/1.8m x 1.2m.

Cistus x *argenteus* 'Silver Pink' grows to 24in x 24in/60cm x 60cm. Plant 18in/45cm apart.

Clematis 'Rouge Cardinal' grows to 12ft x 36in/3.7m x 90cm.

Clematis 'Polish Spirit' grows to 12ft x 36in/3.7m x 90cm.

Gentiana sino-ornata grows to 5in x 5in/13cm x 13cm.

Magnolia x *soulangeana* 'Lennei' grows to 15ft x 6ft/4.5m x 1.8m.

Meconopsis betonicifolia grows to 36in x 12in/90cm x 30cm. Plant 12in/30cm apart.

Rhododendron 'Cunningham's White' grows to 6ft x 4ft/1.8m x 1.2m.

Rhododendron decorum grows to 10ft x 5ft/3m x 1.5m.

ADDITIONAL PLANTING

SPRING COLOUR

In autumn:
Plant hyacinth bulbs in pink and white singly throughout the bed, 15 of each colour.

Plant 50 *Tulipa* Bakeri Group 'Lilac Wonder' bulbs in and out of the gentians at the front of the bed.

SUMMER COLOUR

In autumn:
Plant 10 *Cardiocrinum giganteum*: 5 on each side of the bed at the edge of the shrubs.

Plant 15 *Lilium* Pink Perfection Group bulbs in front of the *Rhododendron* 'Cunningham's White'.

Plant 14 *Lilium martagon* var. *album* bulbs around the two clumps of cistus.

In spring:
Plant white *Impatiens* (busy Lizzies) where there are spaces.

GENERAL CARE

Cut back the clematis in late winter.

Feed the bed in spring with a fertilizer for acid soil.

Feed the camellias and rhododendrons once more after they have finished flowering.

Take care that the new planting does not dry out.

Help the clematis into their host plants with bamboo canes, keeping them tied in until they start to scramble.

Prune to tidy up growth only.

Mulch with leaf mould in winter.

PLANT DETAILS

Camellia japonica
SOIL: Acid, moist but free-draining.
CONDITIONS: Semi shade, protected from morning sun.
COLOUR: Pale pink.
FLOWERING: Late winter to late spring.
FEEDING: Feed with an ericaceous plant food in spring.
PRUNING: Very little required, but any misplaced branches can be shaped up after flowering.
GENERAL COMMENTS: A beautiful plant that is easy to grow and good for picking. It is best to buy from a specialist camellia nursery.

Camellia sasanqua 'Rosea'
SOIL: Acid, moist but free-draining.
CONDITIONS: Semi shade, protected from early sun and protected from wind.
COLOUR: Soft pale pink single flowers.
FLOWERING: Autumn and winter.
FEEDING: Feed with an ericaceous food after flowering in spring.
PRUNING: Shape up in spring if necessary.
GENERAL COMMENTS: Has lovely scented flowers which are an unusual colour for autumn and winter.

Cistus x *argenteus* 'Silver Pink'
SOIL: Any well drained.
CONDITIONS: Sun.
COLOUR: Pale silvery pink.
FLOWERING: Late spring to mid-summer.

FEEDING: Spring.
PRUNING: Just trim after flowering if necessary.
GENERAL COMMENTS: A lovely soft pink form with silvery green leaves.

Clematis 'Polish Spirit'
SOIL: Good, rich, enriched with manure or leaf mould.
CONDITIONS: Shade at the roots and sun at the flowers.
COLOUR: Purple blue with slate on the reverse.
FLOWERING: Mid-summer to early autumn
FEEDING: Spring.
PRUNING: In late winter cut each stem down to 12in/30cm above a pair of sprouting buds.
GENERAL COMMENTS: Another lovely clematis. It is a greedy feeder, so give it a mulch with manure during the winter.

Clematis 'Rouge Cardinal'
SOIL: Deep, rich.
CONDITIONS: Sun, but protect at the base of the plant with crocks to keep the roots cool.
COLOUR: Rich velvet maroon.
FLOWERING: Mid-summer to early autumn.
FEEDING: Spring, and every two weeks during summer with a liquid feed.
PRUNING: Late winter. Cut each stem down to

12in/30cm above a pair of healthy buds.
GENERAL COMMENTS: A beautifully coloured clematis which really looks like velvet. As it grows, guide it into the magnolia and tie it into the branches.

Gentiana sino-ornata
SOIL: Acid, free-draining.
CONDITIONS: Sun or part shade.
COLOUR: Bright blue.
FLOWERING: Early autumn to mid-autumn.
FEEDING: Spring with ericaceous fertilizer.
GENERAL COMMENTS: Lovely bright leaves and beautiful flowers in autumn. It hates being dripped on, so plant it at the edge of the bed.

Magnolia x soulangeana 'Lennei'
SOIL: Rich, heavy, with good drainage.
CONDITIONS: Shade or semi shade.
COLOUR: Rose purple outside and creamy white inside.
FLOWERING: Early spring to late spring.
FEEDING: Mulch well with leaf mould in winter and feed with an ericaceous plant food in spring.
PRUNING: If necessary to shape up, prune after flowering.

GENERAL COMMENTS: No good for shallow soils. It can be slow to get going.

Meconopsis betonicifolia
SOIL: Acid, peaty.
CONDITIONS: Cool and shady.
COLOUR: Bright blue with clear yellow stamens.
FLOWERING: Early summer to late summer.
FEEDING: With an ericaceous plant food in spring.
PRUNING: None.
GENERAL COMMENTS: Unusual delicate flowers carried on straight stems. Well worth growing in the right conditions.

Rhododendron 'Cunningham's White'
SOIL: Good, sandy loam, well drained and enriched with leaf mould.
CONDITIONS: Semi shade, sheltered from strong wind. Must not dry out.
COLOUR: Mauve, ageing to pure white.
FLOWERING: Mid-spring to early summer.
FEEDING: Ericaceous plant food after flowering.
PRUNING: Shape up after flowering and cut out any damaged branches.
GENERAL COMMENTS: A reliable and handsome white rhododendron.

Rhododendron 'Christmas Cheer'
SOIL: Well-drained sandy loam, enriched with leaf mould.
CONDITIONS: Sheltered, semi shade. It does not like to dry out.
COLOUR: White, suffused with shell pink.
FLOWERING: Mid-spring to early summer.
FEEDING: Feed with ericaceous fertilizer in spring.
PRUNING: Deadhead when the flowers have faded. If it outgrows its position it is better to move it than to hard prune. It can be trimmed to shape after flowering, when any damaged branches should be cut out.
GENERAL COMMENTS: A very pretty and reliable plant.

AN ISLAND BED WITH ACID SOIL: MIXED PLANTING

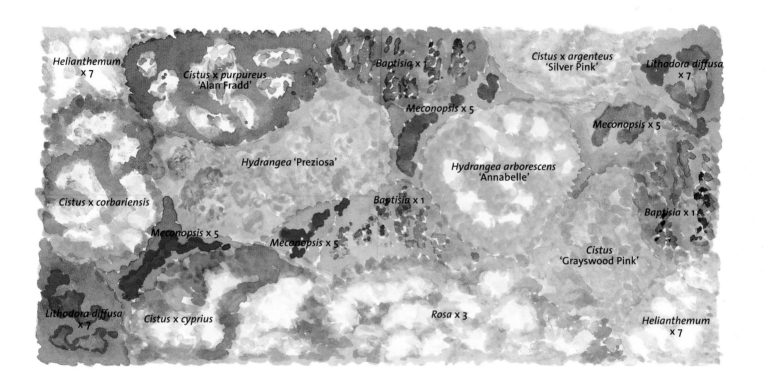

Helianthemum x 7

Cistus x purpureus 'Alan Fradd'

Baptisia x 1

Cistus x argenteus 'Silver Pink'

Lithodora diffusa x 7

Meconopsis x 5

Meconopsis x 5

Hydrangea 'Preziosa'

Hydrangea arborescens 'Annabelle'

Cistus x corbariensis

Baptisia x 1

Baptisia x 1

Meconopsis x 5

Meconopsis x 5

Cistus 'Grayswood Pink'

Lithodora diffusa x 7

Cistus x cyprius

Rosa x 3

Helianthemum x 7

	THE PLANTS	QUANTITIES
1	*Meconopsis grandis*	20
2	*Baptisia australis*	3
3	*Cistus* x *corbariensis* (syn. *Cistus* x *hybridus*)	1
4	*Cistus* x *cyprius*	1
5	*Cistus* x *purpureus* 'Alan Fradd'	1
6	*Hydrangea arborescens* 'Annabelle'	1
7	*Hydrangea* 'Preziosa'	1
8	*Lithodora diffusa* (syn. *Lithospermum diffusum*)	14
9	*Helianthemum* 'The Bride' (or any pale colour, e.g. 'Wisley Primrose')	14
10	*Cistus* 'Grayswood Pink'	1
11	*Rosa pimpinellifolia*	3
12	*Cistus* x *argenteus* 'Silver Pink'	1

SIZE AND POSITION

Baptisia australis grows to 3½ft x 24in/1.1m x 60cm.

Cistus x *argenteus* 'Silver Pink' grows 24in x 24in/60cm x 60cm.

Cistus x *corbariensis* grows to 36in x 36in/90cm x 90cm.

Cistus x *cyprius* grows to 6ft x 36in/1.8m x 90cm.

Cistus 'Grayswood Pink' grows to 36in x 36in/90cm x 90cm.

Cistus x *purpureus* 'Alan Fradd' grows to 36in x 36in/90cm x 90cm.

Helianthemum 'The Bride' grows to 8in x 8in/20cm x 20cm. Plant 6in/15cm apart.

Hydrangea arborescens 'Annabelle' grows 36in x 36in/90cm x 90cm.

Hydrangea 'Preziosa' grows to 36in x 36in/90cm x 90cm.

Lithodora diffusa grows to 8in x 8in/20cm x 20cm. Plant 6in/15cm apart.

Meconopsis grandis grows to 36in x 12in/90cm x 30cm. Plant 8in/20cm apart.

Rosa pimpinellifolia grows to 36in x 36in/90cm x 90cm. Plant 30in/75cm apart

ADDITIONAL PLANTING

SPRING COLOUR

In autumn:
Plant tulip bulbs throughout the bed: 20 'Oratorio' (early spring flowering); 20 'Purissima' in groups of 5; 10 'Peach Blossom' in groups of 5; 10 'Angélique' in groups of 5. Also plant 10 'Carnaval de Nice' singly in any gaps.

SUMMER COLOUR

In late spring:
Plant 20 pink cosmos in any gaps throughout the bed.

Plant 20 *Lupinus texensis* near the front of the bed.

GENERAL CARE

Mulch with leaf mould in early spring.

Feed the bed with an ericaceous fertilizer in spring. Feed the roses again with rose food in mid-summer.

Stake the baptisia if necessary.

Cut the tulip stems down to the ground as they yellow and feed with a general fertilizer.

Clear the bed of any old leaves and debris in late autumn.

PLANT DETAILS

Baptisia australis
SOIL: Good, well drained.
CONDITIONS: Sun or part shade.
COLOUR: Indigo blue.
FLOWERING: Early summer to late summer.
FEEDING: Spring.
PRUNING: Cut back to 12in/30cm in late autumn.
GENERAL COMMENTS: A stately plant, with tall stems of blue-grey leaves and flowers like a lupin.

Cistus x *argenteus* 'Silver Pink'
SOIL: Any well drained.
CONDITIONS: Sun.
COLOUR: Pale silvery pink.
FLOWERING: Late spring to mid-summer.
FEEDING: Spring.
PRUNING: Just trim lightly after flowering if necessary.
GENERAL COMMENTS: A lovely soft pink form with silvery green leaves.

Cistus x *corbariensis*
SOIL: Any well drained.
CONDITIONS: Sun.
COLOUR: White with a yellow middle.
FLOWERING: Late spring to mid-summer.
FEEDING: Spring.
PRUNING: If necessary, tidy up after flowering.
GENERAL COMMENTS:
A good dense shrub with masses of white flowers against green leaves. A very effective variety.

Cistus x cyprius
SOIL: Any well drained.
CONDITIONS: Sun.
COLOUR: White petals with a red blotch at the base and a yellow middle.
FLOWERING: Late spring to mid-summer.
FEEDING: Spring.
PRUNING: If necessary, prune after flowering. It does not like being cut back into old wood.
GENERAL COMMENTS: A large bushy cistus with many flowers. These last only a day, but appear in rapid succession in early summer.

Cistus 'Grayswood Pink'
SOIL: Any free-draining.
CONDITIONS: Sun.
COLOUR: Pale pink.
FLOWERING: Late spring to mid-summer.
FEEDING: Spring.
PRUNING: Cut back after flowering if necessary, but do not cut into old wood.
GENERAL COMMENTS: A tidy pink variety. All cistus have aromatic leaves which smell when touched.

Cistus x purpureus 'Alan Fradd'
SOIL: Any well drained.
CONDITIONS: Sun or part shade.
COLOUR: White with a dark central blotch.
FLOWERING: Late spring to mid-summer.

FEEDING: Spring.
PRUNING: After flowering if necessary to tidy the shape.
GENERAL COMMENTS: This pretty cistus has large white flowers with a brownish blotch in the centre.

Helianthemum 'The Bride'
SOIL: Fast-draining, light.
CONDITIONS: Sun.
COLOUR: White.
FLOWERING: Late spring to mid-summer.
FEEDING: Lightly in spring.
PRUNING: Trim over whole plant after flowering, making a neat mound.
GENERAL COMMENTS: The rock roses are delicate plants that have lovely little flowers and neat foliage.

Hydrangea arborescens 'Annabelle'
SOIL: Moist, enriched with leaf mould, which does not dry out.
CONDITIONS: Sun, or partial shade.
COLOUR: Greenish white in bud opening to creamy white.
FLOWERING: Mid-summer to mid-autumn.
FEEDING: Feed with ericaceous fertilizer in spring.
PRUNING: Prune as little as possible. Leave old flower heads on over winter and cut off above a pair of sprouting buds in mid-spring.

GENERAL COMMENTS: A striking hydrangea which looks lovely when picked.

Hydrangea 'Preziosa'
SOIL: Moist, enriched with leaf mould. It does not like to dry out.
CONDITIONS: Sun or part shade.
COLOUR: Pink flowers changing to deep crimson.
FLOWERING: Mid-summer to mid-autumn.
FEEDING: Feed with ericaceous fertilizer in spring.
PRUNING: Cut out any weak or untidy growth in spring.
GENERAL COMMENTS: A lovely hydrangea. The flowers grow stronger in colour throughout the summer.

Lithodora diffusa
SOIL: Any acid, which is moist but well drained.
CONDITIONS: Sun.
COLOUR: Vibrant blue.
FLOWERING: Late spring to early summer.
FEEDING: Spring.
PRUNING: Trim over lightly after flowering if necessary.
GENERAL COMMENTS: A pretty plant with a mass of funnel-shaped flowers at the end of trailing stems with dark green leaves. It hates to be moved, but likes to be trimmed back after flowering.

Meconopsis grandis
SOIL: Acid, peaty.
CONDITIONS: Cool, dappled shade.
COLOUR: Bright blue.
FLOWERING: Early summer to late summer.
FEEDING: Feed with a general fertilizer in spring and mulch with leaf mould.
PRUNING: None.
GENERAL COMMENTS: The unusual delicate poppy flowers are a wonderful colour, carried on straight stems.

Rosa pimpinellifolia (burnet rose)
SOIL: Any that is not pure sand or chalk.
CONDITIONS: Sun.
COLOUR: Single white flowers with yellow stamens.
FLOWERING: Late spring to early summer.
FEEDING: Mulch with manure in winter. Feed with a general fertilizer in spring. Feed with rose fertilizer in mid-summer.
PRUNING: If necessary lightly prune after flowering, but it produces hips so do not be heavy handed.
GENERAL COMMENTS: A very pretty and healthy rose with delicate ferny bright green foliage.

A CHALK BED AGAINST A WALL: SUN OR PART SHADE

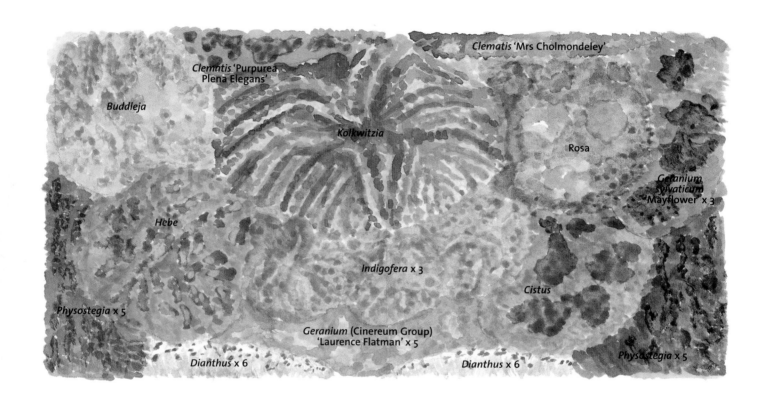

Clematis 'Mrs Cholmondeley'

Clematis 'Purpurea Plena Elegans'

Buddleja

Kolkwitzia

Rosa

Geranium sylvaticum 'Mayflower' x 3

Hebe

Indigofera x 3

Cistus

Physostegia x 5

Geranium (Cinereum Group) 'Laurence Flatman' x 5

Dianthus x 6

Dianthus x 6

Physostegia x 5

THE PLANTS	QUANTITIES
1 Rosa glauca	1
2 Indigofera heterantha	3
3 Hebe 'Great Orme'	1
4 Buddleja 'Pink Pearl'	1
5 Dianthus 'Gran's Favourite'	12
6 Cistus x purpureus	1
7 Clematis 'Purpurea Plena Elegans'	1
8 Kolkwitzia amabilis (e.g. 'Pink Cloud')	1
9 Physostegia virginiana	10
10 Geranium (Cinereum Group) 'Laurence Flatman'	5
11 Clematis 'Mrs Cholmondeley'	1
12 Geranium sylvaticum 'Mayflower'	3

SIZE AND POSITION

Buddleja 'Pink Pearl' grows to 10ft x 5ft/3m x 1.5m.

Cistus x *purpureus* grows to 36in x 36in/90cm x 90cm.

Clematis 'Mrs Cholmondeley' grows to 12ft x 4ft/3.6m x 1.2m.

Clematis 'Purpurea Plena Elegans' grows to 15ft x 36in/4.5m x 90cm.

Dianthus 'Gran's Favourite' grows to 9in x 6in/23cm x 15cm. Plant 8in/20cm apart.

Geranium (Cinereum Group) 'Laurence Flatman' grows to 9in x 6in/23cm x 15cm. Plant 6in/15cm apart.

Geranium sylvaticum 'Mayflower' grows to 36in x 18in/90cm x 45cm. Plant 12in/30cm apart.

Hebe 'Great Orme' grows to 4ft x 3½ft/1.2m x 1.1m.

Indigofera heterantha grows to 4ft x 24in/1.2m x 60cm. Plant 18in/45cm apart.

Kolkwitzia amabilis grows to 6ft x 6ft/1.8m x 1.8m.

Physostegia virginiana grows to 36in x 24in/90cm x 60cm. Plant 12in/30cm apart.

Rosa glauca grows to 5ft x 5ft/1.5m x 1.5m.

ADDITIONAL PLANTING

SPRING COLOUR

In autumn or spring:
Plant 20 pink primulas (primroses) throughout the bed.

In autumn:
Plant tulip bulbs: 25 'Spring Green' towards the back of the bed; 30 'Peach Blossom' near the primulas; and 30 *T.* Bakeri Group 'Lilac Wonder' at the front of the bed.

SUMMER COLOUR

In summer:
Plant *Verbena bonariensis* in gaps all over the bed. These are best treated as annuals and pulled out at the end of the summer, as they are not reliable.

In mid-spring:
Sprinkle seeds of any pale pink poppies (*Papaver*) in any spaces.

In autumn:
Plant 10 *Allium hollandicum* 'Purple Sensation' bulbs singly all over the bed.

GENERAL CARE

Wire the wall with vine eyes.

Cut back the clematis to 18in/45cm at the end of late winter.

Mulch the bed well with organic compost in spring.

Feed the bed with a general fertilizer in spring.

Keep the clematis well tied in.

Cut the buddleja back to about 24in/60cm in early spring.

Cut the indigofera in mid-spring to keep in a good shape.

Shape up the hebe in late spring.

Cut the geraniums back after flowering.

Feed the clematis every two weeks with tomato fertilizer from late spring to early autumn.

Feed the rose with rose food in mid-summer.

Shape up the kolkwitzia after flowering.

Prune the rose to keep it in shape in the winter.

Tidy through the whole bed in winter and remove any debris.

PLANT DETAILS

Buddleja **'Pink Pearl'**
SOIL: Fertile, well drained.
CONDITIONS: Sun or part shade.
COLOUR: Pink.
FLOWERING: Mid-summer to mid-autumn.
FEEDING: Spring.
PRUNING: Prune back to 36in–4ft/90cm–1.2m all over in late winter or early spring.
GENERAL COMMENTS: A lovely shrub in any planting combination. It is very attractive to butterflies.

Cistus **x** *purpureus*
SOIL: Any free-draining.
CONDITIONS: Sun.
COLOUR: Deep purple pink with a red blotch at the base of each petal.
FLOWERING: Late spring to mid-summer.
FEEDING: Spring.
PRUNING: If necessary cut back after flowering, but do not cut into old wood.
GENERAL COMMENTS: An attractive cistus with pretty grey-green leaves contrasting well with the strong-coloured flowers.

Clematis **'Mrs Cholmondeley'**
SOIL: Any well drained, fertile.
CONDITIONS: Sun or part shade.
COLOUR: Lavender blue.
FLOWERING: Late spring to early summer and again in early autumn.
FEEDING: Spring.
PRUNING: In late winter to early spring cut each stem back to 24in/60cm from ground level.

GENERAL COMMENTS: This is a large-flowered clematis in a beautiful blue.

Clematis 'Purpurea Plena Elegans'

SOIL: Good, with good drainage.
CONDITIONS: Sun or part shade.
COLOUR: Soft reddish purple.
FLOWERING: Early summer to mid-autumn.
FEEDING: A hungry feeder: it likes a winter mulch of manure and a spring feed with a general fertilizer.
PRUNING: In late winter cut each stem back to 12in/30cm from the base.
GENERAL COMMENTS: A very pretty clematis which has masses of small double flowers. An unusual colour, and trouble-free.

Dianthus 'Gran's Favourite'

SOIL: Light, with good drainage.
CONDITIONS: Sun.
COLOUR: White with maroon lacing.
FLOWERING: Early summer.
FEEDING: Feed with bonemeal in late autumn and a high-potash feed in spring and again after flowering.
PRUNING: Cut off the old flower heads and trim over the plant after flowering.

GENERAL COMMENTS: Has a wonderful scent. Make sure you keep autumn leaves away from it, as it hates the damp.

Geranium (Cinereum Group) 'Laurence Flatman'

SOIL: Any good.
CONDITIONS: Sun.
COLOUR: Soft pink with a darker centre and maroon veining.
FLOWERING: Late spring to early autumn.
FEEDING: In spring feed with a general fertilizer.
PRUNING: Neaten up the clump after flowering.
GENERAL COMMENTS: A neat geranium with attractive marking, which flowers over a long period.

Geranium sylvaticum 'Mayflower'

SOIL: Any well drained.
CONDITIONS: Sun or partial shade.
COLOUR: Deep violet blue with a white eye.
FLOWERING: Late spring to early summer.
FEEDING: In spring with a general fertilizer.
PRUNING: Cut the old flower heads off after flowering to encourage more flowers later.
GENERAL COMMENTS: A lovely early-flowering geranium, which makes

good ground cover, and is excellent with roses or in a herbaceous border.

Hebe 'Great Orme'

SOIL: Any well drained.
CONDITIONS: Full sun.
COLOUR: Deep pink flowers fading to white.
FLOWERING: Early summer to early autumn.
FEEDING: General fertilizer in spring.
PRUNING: Does not need much, but should be cut to shape after flowering.
GENERAL COMMENTS: Hebes are hardy, useful evergreens, but do not plant in an exposed spot or in soil that is too wet.

Indigofera heterantha

SOIL: Fertile, well drained.
CONDITIONS: Full sun.
COLOUR: Pink or white.
FLOWERING: Early summer to early autumn.
FEEDING: General fertilizer in spring.
PRUNING: Cut back to new growth in the spring.
GENERAL COMMENTS: A graceful arching shrub with a delicate appearance.

Kolkwitzia amabilis

SOIL: Any.
CONDITIONS: Full sun.
COLOUR: Dark pink.
FLOWERING: Late spring to early summer.

FEEDING: Spring.
PRUNING: Cut out any weak or badly placed stems after flowering.
GENERAL COMMENTS: A really lovely shrub which should be planted more often.

Physostegia virginiana

SOIL: Any that does not dry out.
CONDITIONS: Sun.
COLOUR: Several colours of white, pink and lilac.
FLOWERING: Mid-summer to early autumn.
FEEDING: General fertilizer in spring.
PRUNING: None.
GENERAL COMMENTS: A very useful and lovely late-flowering plant, which adds much needed late colour to the border.

Rosa glauca

SOIL: Any good.
CONDITIONS: Sun or part shade.
COLOUR: Pink with a yellow centre.
FLOWERING: Late spring to early summer.
FEEDING: Spring.
PRUNING: Keep to a neat shape by pruning in winter.
GENERAL COMMENTS: Has beautiful plum-grey leaves, which are unique, and attractive hips in autumn. Very good for cutting.

A CHALK ISLAND BED:
SUN OR PART SHADE

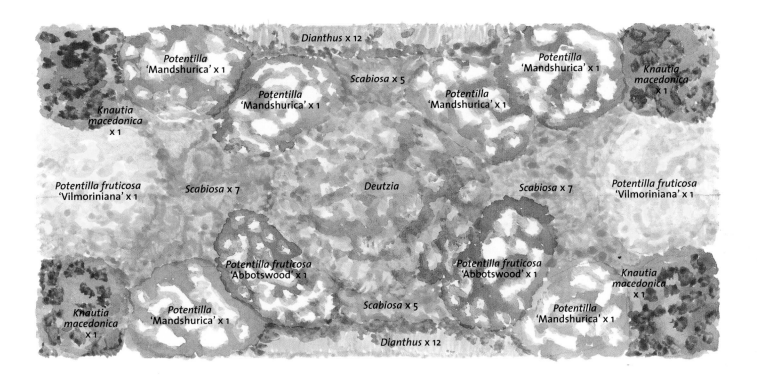

Dianthus x 12

Potentilla 'Mandshurica' x 1

Scabiosa x 5

Potentilla 'Mandshurica' x 1

Knautia macedonica x 1

Potentilla 'Mandshurica' x 1

Potentilla 'Mandshurica' x 1

Knautia macedonica x 1

Potentilla fruticosa 'Vilmoriniana' x 1

Scabiosa x 7

Deutzia

Scabiosa x 7

Potentilla fruticosa 'Vilmoriniana' x 1

Potentilla fruticosa 'Abbotswood' x 1

Potentilla fruticosa 'Abbotswood' x 1

Knautia macedonica x 1

Knautia macedonica x 1

Potentilla 'Mandshurica' x 1

Scabiosa x 5

Potentilla 'Mandshurica' x 1

Dianthus x 12

	THE PLANTS	QUANTITIES
1	*Potentilla fruticosa* 'Abbotswood'	2
2	*Dianthus* 'Laced Monarch'	24
3	*Potentilla* 'Mandshurica' (syn. *P. fruticosa* 'Manchu')	6
4	*Potentilla fruticosa* 'Vilmoriniana'	2
5	*Knautia macedonica*	4
6	*Deutzia* x *hybrida* 'Mont Rose'	1
7	*Scabiosa caucasica* 'Clive Greaves'	24

SIZE AND POSITION

Deutzia x *hybrida* 'Mont Rose' grows to 6ft x 4ft/1.8m x 1.2m.

Dianthus 'Laced Monarch' grows to 8in x 8in/20cm x 20cm. Plant 6in/15cm apart.

Knautia macedonica grows to 18in x 18in/45cm x 45cm.

Potentilla fruticosa 'Abbotswood' grows to 36in x 36in/90cm x 90cm.

Potentilla fruticosa 'Vilmoriniana' grows to 4ft x 36in/1.2m x 90cm.

Potentilla 'Mandshurica' grows to 12in x 30in/30cm x 75cm. Plant 24in/60cm apart.

Scabiosa caucasica 'Clive Greaves' grows to 24in x 8in/60cm x 20cm. Plant 8in/20cm apart.

ADDITIONAL PLANTING

SPRING COLOUR

In autumn:
Plant 50 crocus bulbs in lavender, blue or white throughout the bed.

Plant 100 *Muscari armeniacum* 'Blue Spike' (grape hyacinths) bulbs dotted throughout the bed.

Plant 50 *Anemone blanda* corms in mixed colours all over the bed.

Plant 50 *Narcissus* 'Hawera' bulbs all over the bed.

SUMMER COLOUR

In late spring:
Plant white cleomes and white cosmos towards the back of the bed in any gaps.

GENERAL CARE

Feed the whole bed with a general fertilizer in spring.

In mid-spring trim over the potentillas to improve their shape and cut out any dead wood.

Remove narcissi leaves as they brown off.

Shape up the deutzia after flowering if necessary.

Keep the dianthus well deadheaded throughout the summer.

Deadhead the scabious and the knautia as the flowers fade.

Feed the bed with a liquid fertilizer in summer.

Tidy over the bed in winter and pull out any old summer bedding and compost.

Mulch the bed really well with organic compost in late winter.

PLANT DETAILS

***Deutzia* x *hybrida* 'Mont Rose'**
SOIL: Any.
CONDITIONS: Sun.
COLOUR: Rose pink with darker tints.
FLOWERING: Early summer.
FEEDING: General fertilizer in spring.
PRUNING: After flowering prune out flowering stems and cut the shrub to a neat shape.
GENERAL COMMENTS: This is one of the very best early summer shrubs.

***Dianthus* 'Laced Monarch'**
SOIL: Any well drained, light.
CONDITIONS: Full sun.
COLOUR: Deep pink with darker lacing.
FLOWERING: Early summer.
FEEDING: In spring with a general fertilizer and again in mid-summer with a liquid feed.
PRUNING: Trim over the plant once it has finished flowering.
GENERAL COMMENTS: An old-fashioned pink which definitely deserves its place todayís border. It is deliciously scented.

Knautia macedonica
SOIL: Any well drained.
CONDITIONS: Full sun.
COLOUR: *Deep crimson claret.*
FLOWERING: All summer long.
FEEDING: General fertilizer in spring.
PRUNING: None.

GENERAL COMMENTS: An eyecatching plant with richly coloured scabious-like flowers. It uses the neighbouring planting as support as it likes to sprawl.

Potentilla fruticosa 'Abbotswood'
SOIL: Any, except wet.
CONDITIONS: Sun or part shade.
COLOUR: White.
FLOWERING: Early summer to early autumn.
FEEDING: Spring, with a general fertilizer.
PRUNING: Shape up, if required, in early spring.
GENERAL COMMENTS: The profuse white flowers against the bluish green leaves make a clean neat plant, which has the additional benefit of a long flowering season.

Potentilla fruticosa 'Vilmoriniana'
SOIL: Any, except wet.
CONDITIONS: Sun or partial shade.
COLOUR: Pale creamy yellow.
FLOWERING: Early summer to early autumn.
FEEDING: In spring with a general fertilizer.
PRUNING: Shape up in early spring if necessary.
GENERAL COMMENTS:

A very pretty potentilla with upright growth. Its pale yellow flowers are held against very pretty silvery leaves. A wonderful and versatile shrub.

Potentilla 'Mandshurica'
SOIL: Any well drained.
CONDITIONS: Sun or light shade.
COLOUR: White.
FLOWERING: Early summer to late summer.
FEEDING: With a general fertilizer in early spring.
PRUNING: If it is getting too untidy, shape it up in early spring.
GENERAL COMMENTS: A dainty white potentilla with pretty silvery grey leaves.

Scabiosa caucasica 'Clive Greaves'
SOIL: Well drained.
CONDITIONS: Sun.
COLOUR: Soft violet blue with a pincushion centre.
FLOWERING: Mid-summer to early autumn.
FEEDING: Spring.
PRUNING: Cut old flowering stems back to base in autumn.
GENERAL COMMENTS: A traditional clump-forming perennial with gentle graceful flowers held well above lance-shaped leaves.

A HERB BED: PRETTY PLANTING

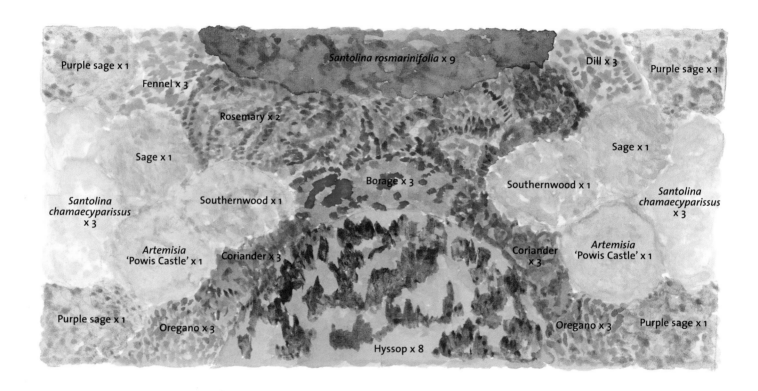

Purple sage x 1

Fennel x 3

Santolina rosmarinifolia x 9

Dill x 3

Purple sage x 1

Rosemary x 2

Sage x 1

Sage x 1

Santolina chamaecyparissus x 3

Southernwood x 1

Borage x 3

Southernwood x 1

Santolina chamaecyparissus x 3

Artemisia 'Powis Castle' x 1

Coriander x 3

Coriander x 3

Artemisia 'Powis Castle' x 1

Purple sage x 1

Oregano x 3

Oregano x 3

Purple sage x 1

Hyssop x 8

THE PLANTS (may be sold by common name)	QUANTITIES
1 *Coriandrum sativum* (coriander)	6
2 *Foeniculum vulgare* (fennel)	3
3 *Salvia officinalis* 'Purpurascens' (purple sage)	4
4 *Salvia officinalis* (sage)	2
5 *Santolina chamaecyparissus* (syn. *S. incana*)	6
6 *Hyssopus officinalis* (hyssop)	8
7 *Anethum graveolens* (dill)	3
8 *Santolina rosmarinifolia* (syn. *S. virens*) (cotton lavender)	9
9 *Artemisia* 'Powis Castle'	2
10 *Borago officinalis* (borage)	3
11 *Artemisia abrotanum* (southernwood)	2
12 *Origanum vulgare* (oregano)	6
13 *Rosmarinus officinalis* 'Miss Jessopp's Upright' (rosemary)	2

SIZE AND POSITION

Dill grows to 36in x 9in/90cm x 23cm. Plant 9in/23cm apart.

Artemisia abrotanum grows to 36in x 24in/90cm x 60cm.

Artemisia 'Powis Castle' grows to 24in x 24in/60cm x 60cm.

Borage grows to 24in x 8in/60cm x 20cm. Plant 8in/20cm apart.

Coriander grows to 18in x 6in/45cm x 15cm. Plant 6in/15cm apart.

Fennel grows to 5ft x 18in/1.5m x 45cm. Plant 12in/30cm apart.

Hyssop grows to 30in x 24in/75cm x 60cm. Plant 12in/30cm apart.

Oregano grows to 12in x 6in/30cm x 15cm. Plant 6in/15cm apart.

Rosemary grows to 36in x 36in/90cm x 90cm. Plant 30in/75cm apart.

Sage grows to 24in x 24in/60cm x 60cm.

Purple sage grows to 24in x 24in/60cm x 60cm.

Santolina chamaecyparissus grows to 18in x 18in/45cm x 45cm. Plant 12in/30cm apart.

Cotton lavender grows to 18in x 24in/45cm x 60cm. Plant 12in/30cm apart.

Add the annual herbs borage, dill and coriander as small plants in mid-spring. You should be able to find these to buy as young plants.

ADDITIONAL PLANTING

SPRING OR SUMMER COLOUR

In autumn or spring:
Violas make a pretty addition to the herb bed in spring or summer in any spaces.

SPRING COLOUR

In autumn:
Plant 50 tall bright tulips such as 'Hamilton', in groups of 5, to make an early splash of colour in any gaps.

GENERAL CARE

Feed the plants requiring feeding in spring with a general fertilizer.

In spring tidy over the plants, cutting the sage, santolinas and artemisias to new growth to shape them up and keep them compact. It is important to keep the herbs under constant watch and to cut them back regularly to stop them from sprawling into each other.

The fennel needs watching and should be cut back if it gets too high.

PLANT DETAILS

Anethum graveolens (dill)
SOIL: Any, but needs to be kept moist.
CONDITIONS: Sun.
COLOUR: Yellow.
FLOWERING: Mid-summer to late summer.
FEEDING: None.
PRUNING: Cut back some stems so that they do not flower and you will be able to keep picking the fine feathery leaves for cooking. Leave some flower heads on the plant so that you can harvest the seeds if you wish.
GENERAL COMMENTS: A useful culinary herb which is slightly milder than fennel. Good in salads, soups and sauces, and with fish or chicken. The seeds are used in pickles; they can also be used ground and soaked in water for tea or a cool drink to soothe indigestion. Grow each year. It is easily available as a young potted plant.

Artemisia abrotanum (southernwood)
SOIL: Well drained, light.
CONDITIONS: Full sun.
COLOUR: Grown for its soft green foliage.
FLOWERING: Do not let it flower.
FEEDING: With a general fertilizer in spring.
PRUNING: Cut back to no more than 12in/30cm in spring. Cut off flower buds as soon as they form in late spring and summer.
GENERAL COMMENTS: Has a very good aromatic leaf which is one of the best natural moth repellents.

Artemisia 'Powis Castle'
SOIL: Well drained.
CONDITIONS: Sun.
COLOUR: Grown for its silver foliage.
FLOWERING: Do not let it flower.

FEEDING: Spring.
PRUNING: Cut back to a good shape in spring, cutting just above new growth. Cut off flower buds as they form.
GENERAL COMMENTS: Delicate divided leaves of bright silver make this a wonderful foil for other plants.

Borago officinalis (borage)
SOIL: Loose, well drained.
CONDITIONS: Sun.
COLOUR: Vibrant blue.
FLOWERING: Early summer to early autumn.
FEEDING: None.
PRUNING: None.
GENERAL COMMENTS: Its bright blue flowers are used in drinks or salads. They can also be used candied or frozen in ice cubes. The young leaves are good in salads. It will self-seed and pop up all round the garden.

Coriandrum sativum (coriander)
SOIL: Light, well drained.
CONDITIONS: Sun.
COLOUR: White.
FLOWERING: Mid-summer to late summer.
FEEDING: None.
PRUNING: None.
GENERAL COMMENTS: The young leaves are widely used in cooking, mainly for curries or salads. The seeds are also used in soups, sauces and stews as well as in some puddings. An annual herb which can be grown from seed planted in mid-spring, or is easily available as a young potted plant.

Foeniculum vulgare (fennel)
SOIL: Well drained, light.

CONDITIONS: Sun.
COLOUR: Yellow flowers on green or bronze foliage.
FLOWERING: Mid-summer to late summer.
FEEDING: None.
PRUNING: A rampant grower. Pinch off the flower heads if you want to use the leaves for cooking. Keep the plant as tidy as you want by cutting back throughout the season. It will always shoot again.
GENERAL COMMENTS: Feathery foliage with a flavour of aniseed. Leaves can be used in sauces and stuffings, particularly with fish, in pickles and chutneys, and sprinkled in salads. A good tea can be made from the leaves or the seeds. It self-seeds vigorously, so you will have a good supply of new plants.

Hyssopus officinalis (hyssop)
SOIL: Well drained, light.
CONDITIONS: Sun.
COLOUR: Intense blue.
FLOWERING: Mid-summer to early autumn.
FEEDING: None.
PRUNING: Shape up in mid-spring and give a good prune in autumn so that it does not get untidy.
GENERAL COMMENTS:
An ancient herb with many uses, though rather too bitter for today's taste. Also used as an aromatic strewing herb. Mainly grown for the intense purplish blue of the flowers, which attract many bees.

Origanum vulgare (oregano)
SOIL: Well drained, but must not dry right out.

CONDITIONS: Sun or part shade.
COLOUR: Mauve.
FLOWERING: Mid-summer to mid-autumn.
FEEDING: None.
PRUNING: At the end of summer clip all flowering stems back to the ground.
GENERAL COMMENTS: Tends to spread, so don't be frightened to use your spade and dig out any you do not need. Many culinary uses as a flavouring herb. Also good in pot pourri, for which the plant should be cut just before the flowers start to open.

Rosmarinus officinalis 'Miss Jessopp's Upright' (rosemary)
SOIL: Ordinary, well drained.
CONDITIONS: Sun.
COLOUR: Pale blue.
FLOWERING: Early summer.
FEEDING: General fertilizer in spring.
PRUNING: Prune to a good shape immediately after flowering. It may need a second more rigorous prune in late summer.
GENERAL COMMENTS:
A widely used herb for flavouring with meats and vegetables. It can also be made into a tea to relieve headaches, or a rinse to condition dark hair.

Salvia officinalis (sage) and S. o. 'Purpurascens' (purple sage)
SOIL: Light, well drained.
CONDITIONS: Sun.
COLOUR: Blue.
FLOWERING: Early summer to mid-summer, but the flowers

are not really the point. It is better to concentrate on keeping the plants neat by constant summer clipping.
FEEDING: Give a light sprinkle of lime in early spring.
PRUNING: Trim lightly to shape up in mid-spring and maintain as a neat mound throughout the summer.
GENERAL COMMENTS: Used in seasonings, stuffings and sauces, especially with pork and chicken. It has many medicinal uses; a soothing tea can be made from the leaves; purple sage makes a good gargle for sore throats. They are pretty plants, although they can be short-lived. The purple sage is a little smaller.

Santolina chamaecyparissus and S. rosmarinifolia (cotton lavender)
SOIL: Well drained.
CONDITIONS: Sun.
COLOUR: The flowers of both are yellow but they are best grown for their foliage. S. chamaecyparissus is silver and S. rosmarinifolia bright green.
FLOWERING: In mid-summer, but if growing for foliage cut them off.
FEEDING: Lightly with a general fertilizer in spring.
PRUNING: Keep them neat. Cut back hard in mid-spring and continue trimming until mid-summer to allow new growth to harden off before winter.
GENERAL COMMENTS: Very pretty plants with aromatic leaves.

A HERB BED: HERBS FOR EATING

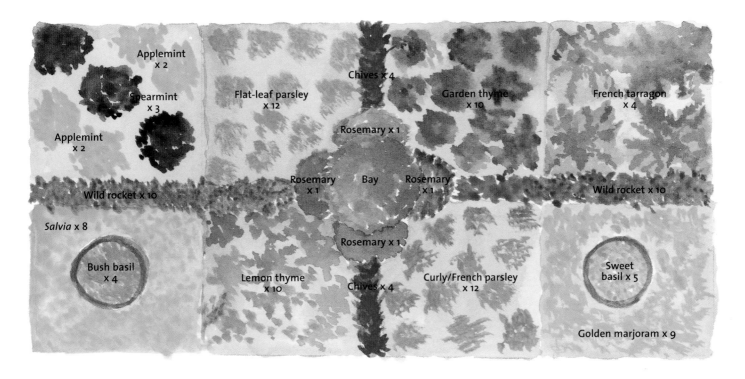

Applemint x 2

Spearmint x 3

Applemint x 2

Flat-leaf parsley x 12

Chives x 4

Garden thyme x 10

French tarragon x 4

Rosemary x 1

Wild rocket x 10

Rosemary x 1   Bay   Rosemary x 1

Wild rocket x 10

Salvia x 8

Rosemary x 1

Bush basil x 4

Lemon thyme x 10

Chives x 4

Curly/French parsley x 12

Sweet basil x 5

Golden marjoram x 9

	THE PLANTS (may be sold by common name)	QUANTITIES
1	*Allium schoenoprasum* (chives)	8
2	*Rosmarinus officinalis* 'Severn Sea' (rosemary)	4
3	*Origanum vulgare* 'Aureum' (golden marjoram)	9
4	*Diplotaxis tenuifolia* (wild rocket)	20
5	*Petroselinum crispum* (flat-leaf parsley)	12
6	*Artemisia dracunculus* 'Sativa' (French tarragon)	4
7	*Thymus vulgaris* (garden thyme)	10
8	*Laurus nobilis* (bay), as a standard tree	1
9	*Ocimum basilicum* (sweet basil)	5
10	*Thymus* x *citriodorus* (lemon thyme)	10
11	*Mentha spicata* (spearmint)	3
12	*Mentha rotundifolia* (syn. *M.* x *villosa*) (applemint)	4
13	*Petroselinum crispum* (curly or French parsley)	12
14	*Salvia officinalis* 'Icterina'	8
15	*Ocimum minimum* 'Golden Globe' (or any other variety) (bush basil)	5

SIZE AND POSITION

Chives grow to 5in x 5in/13cm x 13cm. Plant 5in/13cm apart.

French tarragon grows to 18in x 12in/45cm x 30cm. Plant 12in/30cm apart.

Wild rocket grows to 6in x 9in/15cm x 23cm. Plant 6in/15cm apart.

Bay is grown here as a standard tree. Keep pruned as much as you like; the final size is up to you.

Applemint and spearmint grow to 24in x 12in/60cm x 30cm, and run and spread. Plant in a 14in/35cm pot buried in the ground to restrict the roots.

Bush basil and sweet basil both grow to 6in x 6in/15cm x 15cm. Plant one large pot of each variety close together. For each, use a pot about 18in/45cm in diameter and fill it with first a layer of crocks and then a well-draining compost. Stand the pots in the bed as shown in the plan on page 165, one on the right and one on the left.

Golden marjoram grows to 8in x 8in/20cm x 20cm. Plant 8in/20cm apart.

Parsley grows to 9in x 6in/23cm x 15cm. Plant 6in/15cm apart.

Rosmarinus officinalis 'Severn Sea' grows to 30in x 18in/75cm x 45cm. Plant 36in/90cm apart around the bay tree.

Yellow sage grows to 18in x 12in/45cm x 30cm. Plant 12in/30cm apart.

Green thyme and lemon thyme grow to 6–9in x 12in/15–23cm x 30cm. Plant about 9in/23cm apart.

Plant out curly parsley, flat parsley, bush basil and sweet basil – which are treated as annuals – in mid-spring.

ADDITIONAL PLANTING

There should be no need to add any additional plants throughout the seasons, but if there are any gaps fill them with tall bright tulips in spring (planting the bulbs in autumn) and violas in summer.

GENERAL CARE

Picking and using the herbs will be a great help in keeping them to shape. It is not a good idea to let herbs that are to be eaten run to flower, as flowering tends to make the leaves more coarse and bitter. The exception to this can be the chives, as the flowers are such a pretty part of the plant.

Keep an eye on the mint: even when planted in plastic pots to restrict its growth, it may well try to run across the surface of the soil. Just pull it out if it does.

The *Rosmarinus officinalis* 'Severn Sea' is quite a compact grower, but it will need the occasional shape-up in spring. Feed the bed in spring with a general fertilizer.

Shape up the sage, tarragon and thyme in spring if necessary.

Stake the standard bay until it is established, when the stake can come out.

PLANT DETAILS

***Allium schoenoprasum* (chives)**
SOIL: Medium loamy.
CONDITIONS: Sun or semi shade.
COLOUR: Pink.
FLOWERING: Early summer to mid-summer.
FEEDING: None.
PRUNING: If you do not want the plant to flower, pinch off the flower heads to encourage new leaves. Pull off any leaves that go brown.
GENERAL COMMENTS: Many culinary uses especially in salads, and with vegetables, cheese, soups, omelettes and herb butter.

***Artemisia dracunculus* 'Sativa' (French tarragon)**
SOIL: Light and well drained, but we have also grown it in heavy clay.
CONDITIONS: Sun.
COLOUR: Do not let it flower.
FLOWERING: Do not let it flower.
FEEDING: Lightly in spring with general fertilizer.
PRUNING: Cut back in mid-spring and keep it trimmed back until late summer to stop it from becoming leggy. Cut off the flowers as they form.
GENERAL COMMENTS: One of the very best herbs, widely used in all types of savoury cooking. Delicious with chicken and in soups and sauces.

***Diplotaxis tenuifolia* (wild rocket)**
SOIL: Well drained.
CONDITIONS: Sun or part shade.
COLOUR: Creamy flowers.
FLOWERING: Summer, but do not let it flower.
FEEDING: None.
PRUNING: Younger leaves taste best, so keep cutting it back. Cut off the flowers to improve the leaves' flavour.
GENERAL COMMENTS:
A strongly flavoured plant with

peppery leaves, mostly used in salads or with pasta. The wild variety has a more divided leaf and a more distinct flavour.

Laurus nobilis (bay) as a standard tree
SOIL: Ordinary, well drained.
CONDITIONS: Sun.
COLOUR: Greenish yellow.
FLOWERING: Spring.
FEEDING: In spring with a general fertilizer.
PRUNING: Prune tightly to shape in early summer, and trim to retain the shape thereafter.
GENERAL COMMENTS: Remove any shoots from the stem or base of the tree. Bay has many culinary uses, for flavouring soups and stews and in bouquets garnis. It can sometimes be plagued by insects called bay suckers, so look out for yellowing leaf margins and pick them off as soon as they appear.

Mentha rotundifolia (applemint) and M. spicata (spearmint)
SOIL: Good, enriched with compost.
CONDITIONS: Sun or part shade.
COLOUR: Lilac flowers which should be pinched off. The applemint has lovely soft green leaves.
FLOWERING: Pinch off the flowers as they form.
FEEDING: None.
PRUNING: Mint is so invasive that we recommend planting in a pot about 14in/35cm in diameter and planting the whole pot into the ground. Even then it will try to escape and you will need to pull out any excess.
GENERAL COMMENTS: Applemint grows slightly taller. It is particularly good for sauce, and is delicious added to vegetables, in fruit salad and in iced drinks. Spearmint is best for new potatoes and for making tea.

Ocimum minimum (bush basil) and O. basilicum (sweet basil)
SOIL: Well drained, light.
CONDITIONS: Sun.
COLOUR: White, but do not let it flower.
FLOWERING: Pinch off the flowers to encourage leaves.
FEEDING: None.
GENERAL COMMENTS: Versatile herbs. The bush basil has smaller leaves with a stronger flavour. They are both annuals in England, and you will need to buy new plants each year in mid-spring. Delicious with tomatoes, in salads, pasta, and many other foods.

Origanum vulgare 'Aureum' (golden marjoram)
SOIL: Well drained.
CONDITIONS: Sun or light shade so that the leaves do not go brown at the tips.
COLOUR: Pink, but do not let it flower.
FLOWERING: Summer.
FEEDING: None.
PRUNING: Cut off the flowers and keep the plants trimmed to a good shape.
GENERAL COMMENTS: A useful culinary herb, especially for flavouring pasta, many types of meat and in omelettes. It can be dried for use in pot pourri.

Petroselinum crispum (curly or French parsley or flat-leaf parsley)
SOIL: Well drained, enriched with compost.
CONDITIONS: Sun or part shade.
COLOUR: Grown for its fresh green leaves.
FLOWERING: Summer, but do not let it flower.
FEEDING: Plant in good soil.
PRUNING: Keep trimming to encourage fresh new leaves. Cut off any flowers.
GENERAL COMMENTS: Has many kitchen uses as a flavouring, and is rich in vitamins. It is good to eat after garlic as it neutralizes the smell. Flat parsley (or French parsley) is slightly stronger in taste than curly parsley.

Rosmarinus officinalis 'Severn Sea'
SOIL: Well drained.
CONDITIONS: Full sun.
COLOUR: Bright blue.
FLOWERING: Mid-spring to early summer.
FEEDING: A little general fertilizer in spring.
PRUNING: Shape up after flowering.
GENERAL COMMENTS: Has an attractive growing habit with low arching branches with very aromatic leaves. Delicious cooked with lamb and vegetables, in stews and in bouquets garnis.

Salvia officinalis 'Icterina' (green and yellow sage)
SOIL: Well drained.
CONDITIONS: Sun.
COLOUR: Grown for its golden variegated leaf colour, so do not let it flower.
FLOWERING: Summer, but do not let it flower.
FEEDING: Lightly with a general fertilizer in spring.
PRUNING: Cut to a good shape in spring and keep the leaves for use in cooking. Keep pinching off the flowers as they form. Cut into shape again in late summer.
GENERAL COMMENTS: Delicious cooked with chicken or pork and in stuffings.

Thymus vulgaris (garden thyme) and T. x citriodorus (lemon thyme)
SOIL: Light, which does not retain moisture.
CONDITIONS: Sun.
COLOUR: Dark pink flowers.
FLOWERING: Early summer to late summer.
FEEDING: Likes a light sprinkling of general fertilizer in the early spring.
PRUNING: Cut it back in late spring. It is neater if you do not let it flower.
GENERAL COMMENTS: A wonderful aromatic herb, very good used in stews and as part of a bouquet garni. It is delicious with roast meat or chicken. The young tips can be used in salads.

A WALL BED IN A TOWN:
SUNNY AND SCENTED

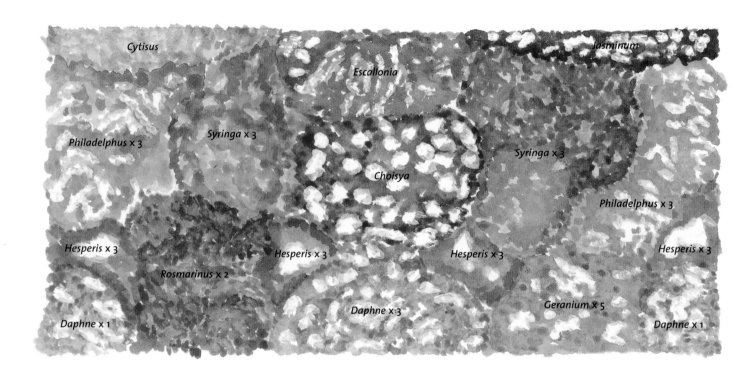

THE PLANTS	QUANTITIES
1 Jasminum officinale	1
2 Syringa meyeri	6
3 Escallonia 'Iveyi'	1
4 Geranium macrorrhizum 'Album'	5
5 Choisya ternata	1
6 Philadelphus 'Manteau d'Hermine'	6
7 Cytisus battandieri	1
8 Daphne bholua 'Jacqueline Postill'	5
9 Hesperis matronalis	12
10 Rosmarinus officinalis 'Severn Sea'	2

SIZE AND POSITION

Choisya ternata grows to 5ft x 5ft/1.5m x 1.5m.

Cytisus battandieri grows to 10ft x 6ft/3m x 1.8m.

Daphne bholua 'Jacqueline Postill' grows to 3½ft x 24in/1.1m x 60cm. Plant 24in/60cm apart.

Escallonia 'Iveyi' grows to 6ft x 4ft/1.8m x 1.2m.

Geranium macrorrhizum 'Album' grows to 12in x 12in/30cm x 30cm. Plant 9in/23cm apart.

Hesperis matronalis grows to 18in x 24in/45cm x 60cm. Plant 12in/30cm apart.

Jasminum officinale grows to 15ft x 20ft/4.5m x 6m but can be kept in check.

Philadelphus 'Manteau d'Hermine' grows to 36in x 24in/90cm x 60cm. Plant 24in/60cm apart.

Rosmarinus officinalis 'Severn Sea' grows to 30in x 18in/75cm x 45cm. Plant 36in/90cm apart.

Syringa meyeri grows to 3½ft x 24in/1.1m x 60cm. Plant 24in/60cm apart.

ADDITIONAL PLANTING

SPRING COLOUR

In autumn:
Plant 40 *Narcissus poeticus* var. *recurvus* bulbs (old pheasant's eye) in groups of 10.

Plant 40 *Narcissus* 'Cheerfulness' bulbs in white in groups of 10.

Plant 15 *Hyacinthus orientalis* 'City of Haarlem' bulbs and 15 *H. o.* 'Amethyst' bulbs singly throughout the bed.

SUMMER COLOUR

In autumn or spring:
Plant 15 *Lilium speciosum* var. *rubrum*

bulbs across the front of the bed, in and out of the shrubs.

Plant 30 pink violas around the daphnes.

In autumn:
Plant 25 *Lilium regale* bulbs in groups of 5.

In late spring:
Plant 15 *Nicotiana affinis* (tobacco plants) in and out of the shrubs at the back of the bed.

Plant 8 scented-leaved geraniums: 5 in and out of the rosemary and 3 behind the geraniums.

GENERAL CARE

Wire the wall with vine eyes, and keep the main stems of the jasmine tied in.

Tie in the trunk of the cytisus, with either old tights or a tree tie, to stop rubbing.

Feed in spring with a general fertilizer.

Leave the daffodils until the leaves have yellowed, pinching off dead flowers, and then cut off, or dig up and leave them to dry in the sun, store and

plant again in the autumn.

Stake the lilies, as necessary.

Cut the escallonia back after first flowering to encourage a second flush.

Cut back all the other shrubs once they have flowered to keep them to a good shape.

Mulch the bed lightly in autumn.

Tidy over the bed in winter.

PLANT DETAILS

Choisya ternata
SOIL: Any.
CONDITIONS: Sun, partial shade or shade.
COLOUR: White.
FLOWERING: Mid-spring to early summer and a little in mid-autumn.
FEEDING: Spring.
PRUNING: Cut to shape after flowering in summer.
GENERAL COMMENTS: It is one of the best shrubs and goes with anything. It is tolerant and hardy, and has lovely shining leaves which are aromatic when touched. It is also very good for picking.

Cytisus battandieri
SOIL: Any well drained.
CONDITIONS: Sun.
COLOUR: Yellow.
FLOWERING: Late spring to early summer.
FEEDING: Early spring.
PRUNING: Prune after flowering to maintain shape if required.
GENERAL COMMENTS: Many cone-shaped flowers which are scented like pineapple and lovely silvery grey leaflets make this a rewarding shrub. Be careful not to plant too close to the wall as the trunk will grow thick in time.

***Daphne bholua* 'Jacqueline Postill'**
SOIL: Cool, moist, with plenty of added humus.
CONDITIONS: Sun or partial shade.
COLOUR: Purplish pink and white.
FLOWERING: Mid-winter to late winter.

FEEDING: Spring.
PRUNING: Should not need much, but can be shaped up in spring after flowering.
GENERAL COMMENTS: A rather upright-growing shrub with glossy evergreen leaves and deliciously scented flowers in winter.

Escallonia 'Iveyi'
SOIL: Any well drained.
CONDITIONS: Sun.
COLOUR: White.
FLOWERING: In spring, and often repeats in early autumn.
FEEDING: Spring.
PRUNING: Trim over the whole plant after first flowering and you will encourage a second flush.
GENERAL COMMENTS: A tough and reliable shrub which is evergreen and has scented flowers.

Geranium macrorrhizum 'Album'
SOIL: Any.
CONDITIONS: Sun, partial shade or shade.
COLOUR: White flowers. The leaves develop a pretty, reddish tinge as they age.
FLOWERING: Mid-spring to early summer.
GENERAL COMMENTS: A useful ground-cover geranium with pretty aromatic leaves.

Hesperis matronalis (sweet rocket)
SOIL: Any well drained, which is not too rich.
CONDITIONS: Sun.
COLOUR: White or violet.
FLOWERING: Late spring to mid-summer, and again in autumn.
FEEDING: Not essential, but a little bonemeal every other winter is a good idea.
PRUNING: Cut down back to new leaves after flowering finishes in autumn.
GENERAL COMMENTS: A true old-fashioned cottage-garden plant with a wonderful full fragrance in the evening.

Jasminum officinale
SOIL: Any.
CONDITIONS: Sun or partial shade.
COLOUR: White.
FLOWERING: Early summer and early autumn and often sporadically in between.
FEEDING: In spring. Once established it will look after itself.
PRUNING: Cut back after flowering to cut out tangled shoots and keep shaped up throughout the growing season.
GENERAL COMMENTS: Has a really delicious scent. Just one flower head indoors will fill a room for days on end. Once it has got going it will need keeping in check, as it loves to romp all over the place.

Philadelphus 'Manteau d'Hermine'
SOIL: Any reasonable, with added humus.
CONDITIONS: Sun or partial shade.
COLOUR: Creamy white.
FLOWERING: Early summer to mid-summer.
FEEDING: Spring.
PRUNING: After flowering tidy up the old flowering stems. Cut one or two old stems right down to the base to encourage new growth.
GENERAL COMMENTS: A good small philadelphus, richly covered with a mass of vanilla-scented flowers in early summer. A great little plant.

Rosmarinus officinalis 'Severn Sea'
SOIL: Any well drained.
CONDITIONS: Full sun.
COLOUR: Bright blue.
FLOWERING: Mid-spring to early summer.
FEEDING: Feed lightly in spring.
PRUNING: Can be cut to maintain a good shape in late spring once flowering has finished.
GENERAL COMMENTS: It has an attractive arching habit, and one of the brightest blue flowers of the rosemaries. It gives off a delicious smell when the leaves are touched.

Syringa meyeri
SOIL: Any.
CONDITIONS: Sun or light shade.
COLOUR: Lavender pink.
FLOWERING: Late spring to early summer.
FEEDING: Benefits from a sprinkling of bonemeal in the autumn.
PRUNING: Remove weak or in-growing shoots after flowering.
GENERAL COMMENTS: A rounded twiggy bush with small round leaves and many panicles of scented flowers in early summer. It is a valuable addition to any garden.

A RAISED BED AGAINST A WALL: SUN OR PART SHADE IN A TOWN

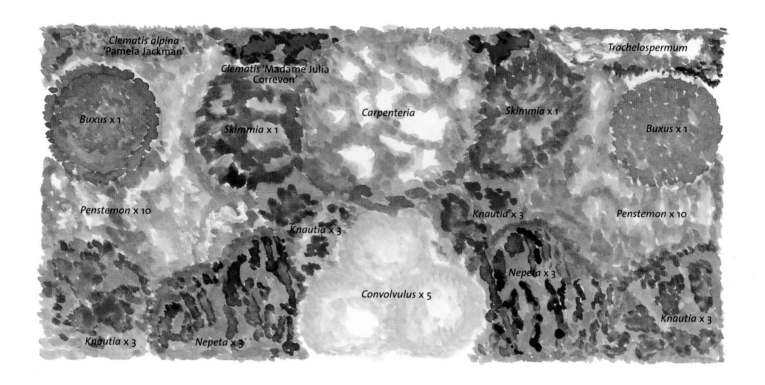

THE PLANTS

	THE PLANTS	QUANTITIES
1	*Carpenteria californica*	1
2	*Buxus sempervirens*	2 balls
3	*Skimmia* x *confusa* 'Kew Green'	2
4	*Clematis* 'Madame Julia Correvon'	1
5	*Penstemon* 'Sour Grapes'	20
6	*Trachelospermum jasminoides*	1
7	*Nepeta* 'Six Hills Giant'	6
8	*Clematis alpina* 'Pamela Jackman'	1
9	*Knautia macedonica*	12
10	*Convolvulus cneorum*	5

SIZE AND POSITION

Buxus sempervirens: keep the balls to 18in x 18in/45cm x 45cm.

Carpenteria californica grows to 5ft x 36in/1.5m x 90cm.

Clematis alpina 'Pamela Jackman' grows to 8ft x 4ft/2.5m x 1.2m.

Clematis 'Madame Julia Correvon' grows to 12ft x 4ft/3.7m x 1.2m.

Convolvulus cneorum grows to 12in x 12in/45cm x 45cm. Plant 12in/30cm apart.

Knautia macedonica grows to 18in x 18in/45cm x 45cm. Plant 18in/45cm apart.

Nepeta 'Six Hills Giant' grows to 30in x 24in/75cm x 60cm. Plant 18in/45cm apart.

Penstemon 'Sour Grapes' grows to 30in x 18in/75cm x 45cm. Plant 12in/30cm apart.

Skimmia x confusa 'Kew Green' grows to 24in x 24in/60cm x 60cm. Plant 18in/45cm apart.

Trachelospermum jasminoides grows to 15ft x 5ft/4.5m x 1.5m.

ADDITIONAL PLANTING

SPRING COLOUR

In autumn:
Plant tulip bulbs all over the bed: 20 *T.* Bakeri Group 'Lilac Wonder', 20 'West Point', 20 'Maja', 20 'Blue Heron' and 20 'Bellflower'.

SUMMER COLOUR

In autumn:
Plant 10 *Allium caeruleum* bulbs and 20 *A. unifolium* bulbs singly throughout the bed.

In spring:
Plant 25 *Nicotiana affinis* (tobacco plants) at the back of the bed in any gaps.

GENERAL CARE

Make sure that the wall is well wired for the climbers with vine eyes and wire. Tie the climbers in as they grow.

In spring feed everything with a general spring fertilizer.

Cut the dead stems of the penstemons in spring down to the new growth.

Trim the nepeta back in the spring.

When the tulips die down, cut off the stems and leaves at ground level and feed.

Put slug pellets down as soon as you plant the nicotianas.

Trim the box balls in early summer to maintain their size and shape.

Tidy up the bed in autumn, pulling out the nicotianas.

PLANT DETAILS

Buxus sempervirens (box)
SOIL: Any that is not waterlogged.
CONDITIONS: Sun or shade.
COLOUR: An evergreen grown for its leaves.
FLOWERING: Insignificant.
FEEDING: Feed with bonemeal in the autumn and a general fertilizer in spring.
PRUNING: Trim to shape in mid-summer and again in early autumn if required to keep to a neat shape.
GENERAL COMMENTS: A reliable tough evergreen to give structure to the garden. If the leaves lose their gloss in early summer, spray with a foliar feed. Buy ready-shaped into a ball.

Carpenteria californica
SOIL: Moist but well drained.
CONDITIONS: Sun.
COLOUR: White flowers with a yellow centre.
FLOWERING: Early summer to mid-summer.
FEEDING: General fertilizer in spring.
PRUNING: Little needed, but trim to shape in mid-spring if required and cut back any excessive growth to keep to a neat shape.
GENERAL COMMENTS: A pretty evergreen shrub with fragrant flowers.

Clematis alpina 'Pamela Jackman'
SOIL: Good, rich and well drained.
CONDITIONS: Sun or part shade.
COLOUR: Dark blue.
FLOWERING: Mid-spring to late spring.

FEEDING: With bonemeal in autumn and a general fertilizer in spring.

PRUNING: If it gets untidy cut back excessive growth after flowering.

GENERAL COMMENTS: Pretty nodding blue flowers and a tough nature make this a useful early-flowering clematis.

Clematis 'Madame Julia Correvon'

SOIL: Rich, well drained.

CONDITIONS: Sun or part shade.

COLOUR: Wine red with pale yellow stamens.

FLOWERING: Mid-summer to early autumn.

FEEDING: With bonemeal in autumn and a general fertilizer in spring.

PRUNING: In late winter cut back to 12in/30cm, cutting each stem above a pair of new buds.

GENERAL COMMENTS: A very free-flowering and healthy clematis.

Convolvulus cneorum

SOIL: Well drained, poor.

CONDITIONS: Full sun.

COLOUR: White flowers, with dark pink on the reverse.

FLOWERING: Late spring to late summer.

FEEDING: Spring.

PRUNING: None.

GENERAL COMMENTS: A very pretty evergreen

with narrow, truly silver leaves. It is rather delicate.

Knautia macedonica

SOIL: Ordinary, well drained.

CONDITIONS: Full sun.

COLOUR: Deep crimson claret.

FLOWERING: Late spring to early autumn – all summer.

FEEDING: Spring.

PRUNING: Cut back in autumn.

GENERAL COMMENTS: A very versatile plant which likes to ramble through its neighbours. It flowers profusely throughout the summer.

Nepeta 'Six Hills Giant'

SOIL: Any well drained.

CONDITIONS: Sun or part shade.

COLOUR: Good strong blue.

FLOWERING: Late spring to late summer.

FEEDING: Spring.

PRUNING: Cut back in late autumn.

GENERAL COMMENTS: Long stems carrying pretty blue flowers which have a valuable place in a soft flowing planting.

Penstemon 'Sour Grapes'

SOIL: Good, well drained.

CONDITIONS: Sun or part shade.

COLOUR: Purple with a smudge of white.

FLOWERING: Mid-summer to early autumn.

FEEDING: Spring.

PRUNING: Leave the old flowering stems on the plant until spring, and then cut back to new shooting growth.

GENERAL COMMENTS: The bell-shaped flowers are pretty and unusually coloured, the colour varying according to soil conditions and situation.

Skimmia x confusa 'Kew Green'

SOIL: Rich, fertile, which does not dry out.

CONDITIONS: Prefers shade.

COLOUR: White.

FLOWERING: Mid-spring to late spring.

FEEDING: Spring.

PRUNING: None.

GENERAL COMMENTS: A reliable and handsome small evergreen shrub with good, green glossy leaves that are a wonderful foil for other plants and pretty, fragrant flowers.

Trachelospermum jasminoides

SOIL: Any well drained.

CONDITIONS: Sun.

COLOUR: Creamy white.

FLOWERING: Summer.

FEEDING: Spring.

PRUNING: Cut out any dead branches in late spring.

GENERAL COMMENTS: Has shiny green leaves and star-shaped creamy flowers with a strong scent. This twining

climber is a sensational plant which deserves a place in any warm sunny bed. It does not grow well in the north of England or Scotland.

A WILDLIFE BED TO ATTRACT
BEES AND BUTTERFLIES

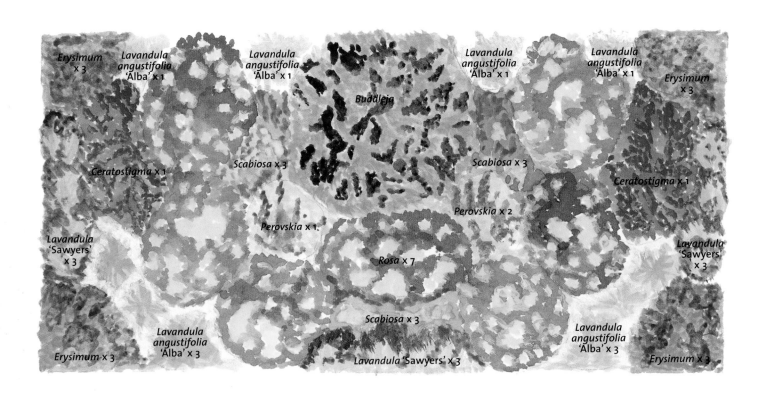

Erysimum x 3   *Lavandula angustifolia* 'Alba' x 1   *Lavandula angustifolia* 'Alba' x 1   *Buddleja*   *Lavandula angustifolia* 'Alba' x 1   *Lavandula angustifolia* 'Alba' x 1   *Erysimum* x 3

Ceratostigma x 1   *Scabiosa* x 3   *Scabiosa* x 3   *Ceratostigma* x 1

Perovskia x 1   *Perovskia* x 2

Lavandula 'Sawyers' x 3   *Rosa* x 7   *Lavandula* 'Sawyers' x 3

Erysimum x 3   *Lavandula angustifolia* 'Alba' x 3   *Scabiosa* x 3   *Lavandula angustifolia* 'Alba' x 3   *Erysimum* x 3

Lavandula 'Sawyers' x 3

	THE PLANTS	QUANTITIES
1	*Buddleja davidii* 'Ile de France'	1
2	*Erysimum* 'Bowles's Mauve'	12
3	*Lavandula* 'Sawyers'	9
4	*Rosa* Charlotte	7
5	*Perovskia* 'Blue Spire'	2
6	*Ceratostigma* 'Autumn Blue' (or *C. griffithii*)	2
7	*Lavandula angustifolia* 'Alba'	10
8	*Scabiosa caucasica* 'Clive Greaves'	9

SIZE AND POSITION

Buddleja davidii 'Ile de France' grows to 8ft x 3½ft/2.5m x 1.1m.

Ceratostigma 'Autumn Blue' grows to 3½ft x 3½ft/1.1m x 1.1m.

Erysimum 'Bowles's Mauve' grows to 18in x 12in/45cm x 30cm. Plant 12in/30cm apart.

Lavandula angustifolia 'Alba' grows to 18in x 15in/45cm x 38cm. Plant 12in/30cm apart.

Lavandula 'Sawyers' grows to 15in x 15in/38cm x 38cm. Plant 12in/30cm apart.

Perovskia 'Blue Spire' grows to 36in x 30in/90cm x 75cm. Plant 12in/30cm apart.

Rosa Charlotte grows to 36in x 30in/90cm x 75cm. Plant 24in/60cm apart.

Scabiosa caucasica 'Clive Greaves' grows to 24in x 8in/60cm x 20cm. Plant 8in/20cm apart.

ADDITIONAL PLANTING

SPRING COLOUR

In spring or autumn:
Plant 40 *Primula vulgaris* (primroses) throughout the bed.

In autumn:
Plant 20 white scilla bulbs throughout the bed.

In spring:
Plant 30 *Myosotis* (forget-me-nots) at the edges of the bed.

SUMMER COLOUR

In autumn or spring:
Plant 25 *Lilium regale* and 25 *L.* Golden Splendor Group around the roses.

In autumn:
Plant *Digitalis purpurea* f. *albiflora* (white foxgloves) in drifts throughout the bed.

GENERAL CARE

Mulch the roses with well-rotted manure after pruning in late winter.

Feed in spring with a general fertilizer.

Tidy through the whole bed in spring, picking up leaves and other debris.

Cut the perovskias back in spring.

Shape up the lavender in mid-spring but do not cut back into old wood.

Feed the roses with rose fertilizer in July.

Cut off the old lavender stalks after flowering.

PLANT DETAILS

Buddleja davidii **'Ile de France'**
SOIL: Any ordinary.
CONDITIONS: Sun or part shade.
COLOUR: Dark purplish blue.
FLOWERING: Mid-summer to early autumn.
FEEDING: Spring.
PRUNING: Cut back hard in early spring down to about 36in/90cm all over.
GENERAL COMMENTS: A pretty deep-coloured buddleja which attracts butterflies and bees throughout its long flowering season.

Ceratostigma **'Autumn Blue'**
SOIL: Good, humus-rich.
CONDITIONS: Sun or part shade.
COLOUR: Bright blue.
FLOWERING: Late summer to mid-autumn.
FEEDING: Spring.
PRUNING: Little, but cut out any dead wood in spring.
GENERAL COMMENTS: A sprawly little shrub which has lovely red-tinted leaves in autumn.

Erysimum **'Bowles's Mauve'**
SOIL: Well drained.
CONDITIONS: Full sun.
COLOUR: Mauve.
FLOWERING: Late spring to mid-autumn.
FEEDING: Spring.
PRUNING: Keep deadheading throughout the flowering season.
GENERAL COMMENTS: A very useful plant which carries its

mauve flowers over blue-green leaves for a very long period. Can be short-lived. It seems to have gone out of fashion but we regard it as one of the very best.

Lavandula angustifolia 'Alba'

SOIL: Any well drained.
CONDITIONS: Sun.
COLOUR: White.
FLOWERING: Mid-summer to early autumn.
FEEDING: Spring.
PRUNING: Cut off the flowering stems after flowering. Trim the whole plant in mid-spring to keep it growing in a good shape, but do not cut back into old wood.
GENERAL COMMENTS: A very pretty white lavender which is at its best planted in a group. It hates the wet, so add grit when planting if you are in any doubt about your soil being free draining. If you want to dry the flower heads to make lavender bags etc. it is important to cut the flowers just before they open when the oil is at its strongest.

Lavandula 'Sawyers'

SOIL: Well drained.
CONDITIONS: Sun.
COLOUR: Deep purple.

FLOWERING: Mid-summer to late summer.
FEEDING: Spring.
PRUNING: Cut off dead flower spikes in autumn. Trim over the whole plant in mid-spring to help maintain a neat shape.
GENERAL COMMENTS: A good dark-flowered lavender with very silver leaves.

Perovskia 'Blue Spire'

SOIL: Well drained.
CONDITIONS: Sun.
COLOUR: Blue purple.
FLOWERING: Late summer to mid-autumn.
FEEDING: Spring.
PRUNING: Cut back hard to about 9in/23cm in late spring.
GENERAL COMMENTS: A mass of bluish purple flowers in spikes over grey-green aromatic leaves make this a very useful small shrub.

Rosa Charlotte

SOIL: Any well drained. except pure chalk or sand.
CONDITIONS: Sun.
COLOUR: Yellow.
FLOWERING: Early summer to late summer.
FEEDING: Mulch with well-rotted manure in autumn. Feed with a general fertilizer in spring and with a rose

fertilizer in mid-summer.
PRUNING: Cut out any weak or crossing growth in winter, and shape the bush to keep it neat.
GENERAL COMMENTS: A very pretty yellow rose with a soft delicate scent.

Scabiosa caucasica 'Clive Greaves'

SOIL: Well drained.
CONDITIONS: Sun.
COLOUR: Soft lavender blue with a pale pincushion centre.
FLOWERING: Mid-summer to early autumn.
FEEDING: Spring.
PRUNING: Cut old flowering stems back to the base after flowering.
GENERAL COMMENTS: A clump-forming perennial with gentle, graceful flowers held well above its lance-shaped leaves.

INDEX

AUTHORS' ACKNOWLEDGMENTS
With many thanks to the editors and staff at Frances Lincoln, especially Anne Fraser, Jo Christian, Anne Askwith, Sue Gladstone and Caroline Clark, who were such a tremendous help to us; and also to Robin Wallis at Chichester Trees, Jacques Amand International, Mr Marshall at North Nibley and Barry Fretwell of Peveril Clematis.

PHOTOGRAPHIC ACKNOWLEDGMENTS
All the photographs in this book are copyright © John Glover, except for those listed below:

a = above, b = below, c = centre, l = left, r = right

© **David Austin Roses Limited**: 177 cl
Richard Bloom/Bloom Pictures: 156 ar
Eric Crichton Photos: 36 al
The Garden Picture Library: 12 cr (Howard Rice), 17 br (J S Sira), 33 al (J S Sira), 41 br (David Askham), 49 ac (David Dixon), 49 br (Clive Nichols), 61 al (Howard Rice), 76 c, 2nd from left (Chris Burrows), 76 bc (Eric Crichton), 80 br (Mark Bolton), 85 b, 2nd from left (David Cavagnaro), 89 bl (Mayer/Le Scanff), 92 al (Clive Nichols), 113 ar (Neil Holmes), 116 br (Marijke Heuff), 121 cr (Eric Crichton), 124 cr (Clive Nichols), 137 ar (Neil Holmes), 145 ac (Andrea Jones), 148 r, 2nd row down, 2nd from right (Neil Holmes), 153 cl (Chris Burrows), 156 3rd row down, right (Jerry Pavia), 161 ar (Jacqui Hurst), 161 3rd row down, left (Jacqui Hurst), 161 3rd row down, centre (Mark Bolton), 164 2nd row down, centre (Christi Carter), 164 c (Jane Legate), 169 ar (Brian Carter), 169 2nd row down, right (Howard Rice)
Marcus Harpur: 85 cl, 97, 2nd row down, centre
Sunniva Harte: 7, 85 al
Andrew Lawson: 33 a, 2nd from right, 36 2nd row down, 3rd from left, 36 br, 56 br, 61 ac, 64 ar, 73 br, 80 b, 2nd from right, 89 c, 92 3rd row down, 2nd from left, 104 c, 109 cr, 129 al, 145 cr, 148 ar, 148 br, 161 al, 164 2nd row down, left, 169 b, 3rd from left, 172 2nd row down, left
Photos Horticultural: 25 cl, 76 ac, 85 bl, 104 bc, 129 cr, 129 br, 148 bl, 161 3rd row down, centre, 161 bc
Visions (www.visions.nl): 129 bl
Steve Wooster: 164 br

PUBLISHER'S ACKNOWLEDGMENTS
Project editor Anne Askwith
Picture editor Sue Gladstone
Picture assistant Milena Michalski
Index by Judith Menes
Production Caterina Favaretto